CEREMONIES OUT OF THE AIR: RALPH LEMON

Edited by Connie Butler, Thomas Lax,
Kari Rittenbach, and Jody Graf

MoMA PS1

Foreword

For the last four decades, Ralph Lemon has been a pillar and
provocateur within both the dance community and the contemporary
art world—at once crucially present and also anathema to performing presence in the manner expected of him. Building from his
time leading the Ralph Lemon Company from 1985 to 1995, he
has shaped the trajectory of postmodern dance with athletic
and virtuosic choreography that weaves together stories spanning
decades and continents. Over the years, his practice has increas-
ingly aspired to a radical formlessness, or, in his words, "no-dance."
It has extended into the interstices of installation, video, drawing,
and the written word and materialized in unexpected corners—in
living rooms and forests as well as on stage and in the gallery.
His first major exhibition in a New York museum, *Ceremonies Out
of the Air* brings together more than forty works made over
the past decade, tracing his multidisciplinary engagement with the
body—and the marks and afterimages left in its wake—as a site
through which to consider questions of memory, race, grief, ecstasy,
and the nature of creativity itself.

Exhibitions typically seek to encapsulate or distill a practice, to find
its edges, if only momentarily. Lemon offers a worthy challenge
to such an endeavor. In a video made after receiving a Heinz Award

in 2018, he noted his effort to make work that reaches "beyond 'this is a performance,' or 'this is something that can go into a museum, or a book' . . . beyond formality, or something being scripted or performed, or held, or framed." Such sidesteps and evasions are core to Lemon's approach, which embraces exhaustion, invisibility, silence, collision, and risk as forms of communication and even grace. As the title suggests, the exhibition and this publication aim to carve out space for the ineffable while simultaneously bringing into focus the myriad objects, sights, and sounds that he has given us—those many small celebrations that Lemon has pulled out of the air.

This publication is not a standard monograph but rather functions as a "devotional" handbook for the exhibition. Wrapping the volume is a dust jacket that unfolds into a poster edition of a recent drawing from Lemon's ongoing series *Untitled (The greatest [Black] art history story ever told. Unfinished)* (2015–), reproduced at nearly actual size. Inside the catalogue, works are illustrated in a loose reverse-chronological order—loose, as the artist's projects are reengaged across the years, and many remain ongoing. The images are interspersed with essays, reflections, lyrics, and sketches, together highlighting key refrains and rhythms in Lemon's practice. The book partakes of the centripetal force at play in Lemon's work: many of the voices in it have danced, thought, and conversed with and alongside him for years. Several of them will also appear in the exhibition at various intervals as performers. I extend my deepest gratitude to Kevin Beasley, Adrienne Edwards, Darrell Jones, Okwui Okpokwasili, Kari Rittenbach, and Kevin Quashie for their contributions, as well as the Estate of Pope.L for graciously allowing us to include a transcript of a talk given by the late (and great) artist. I also applaud Thomas Lax, my cocurator, for their beautiful essay. This book and exhibition would not have been possible without their brilliance and deep ties to Lemon, having first worked with him on a 2012 exhibition at the Studio Museum in Harlem—one that introduced audiences to the artist's long collaboration with Walter Carter, another luminous figure within the constellation of Lemon's world. It has been a privilege and a joy to work with Lax in this endeavor.

I first worked with Lemon as a cocurator of *On Line: Drawing Through the Twentieth Century* at The Museum of Modern Art in 2010–11, for which he performed a duet with Okpokwasili. Soon after, he returned to MoMA as cocurator of *Some sweet day* (2012), a performance series held in the Marron Atrium. As a result of the challenges posed by trying to slot dance into an institution unaccustomed to its presence, he went on to organize *Value Talks* (2013–14), a series of conversations that probed the ways in which art organizations have struggled to understand performance within their existing schematics. In 2016, MoMA published Lemon's first monograph as part of its Modern Dance series, and in 2019 he returned to MoMA to deliver a lecture reflecting on his fraught relationship to the work of Bruce Nauman, for which Pope.L performed a response at Lemon's invitation, the text of which is reprinted in this publication. This is all to say that, for an artist so wary of codification, Lemon has had a surprisingly robust, if at times resistant, relationship with The Museum of Modern Art.

Perhaps more surprising is that *Ceremonies Out of the Air* is Lemon's first presentation at MoMA PS1. While many art institutions only recently began incorporating dance into their purview, movement has been core to PS1 since its founding in 1976. In 1978, we launched a series of multidisciplinary exhibitions highlighting experimental dance, fashion, poetry, and architecture, in addition to media more conventionally encountered in a museum. Since then, PS1 has continued to center the performing arts, from the Spring Dance program of the 1980s to the Summer Dance Warm Up series of the early 2000s and on through the present day. Dance is woven into the DNA of PS1: our very first exhibition, *Rooms* (1976), featured a tongue-in-cheek prom. The "school dance," accompanied by a live band, was held in the large open space that had previously been the gymnasium when the building still housed a public school. It is in this very space where Lemon's exhibition will be held. It seems fitting that his work should occupy the site of the many youthful games, competitions, jumps, shouts, and kicks that came before. With this exhibition, my first as the Director of MoMA PS1, I hope we can channel the energy—uncontained and undaunted— that resides in the bones of this institution.

I am extremely grateful to the Board of MoMA PS1, especially our intrepid Chair Robert Soros and our beloved former Chair Sarah Arison, for their tireless support of artists across all media, including performance. We also thank our municipal partners: Laurie Cumbo and the New York City Department of Cultural Affairs; Donovan Richards, Queens Borough President; Julie Won, New York City Council Member; and the New York City

Council overall. My deepest appreciation goes to Glenn D. Lowry, The David Rockefeller Director of The Museum of Modern Art, for his insight, conversation, and support of this exhibition. *Ceremonies Out of the Air* would not have been possible without major support from Sarah Arison and the Ford Foundation. Additionally, we are grateful for generous support from the Doris Duke Foundation, the Lise M. Stolt-Nielsen Family, and the Wallis Annenberg Director's Fund for Innovation in Contemporary Art. We also extend thanks to A4 Arts Foundation and the Black Arts Council of The Museum of Modern Art for significant support. We thank James Keith (JK) Brown and Eric Diefenbach, Zenas Hutcheson, and an anonymous donor for additional support. Furthermore, MoMA PS1 offers our gratitude for funding from the Harkness Foundation for Dance, Katherine Sachs, and Catharine and Jeffrey Soros. The Mellon Foundation's generous institutional support has been instrumental in making this exhibition a reality.

Finally, and foremost, I would like to thank Ralph Lemon, for his trust and collaboration, for keeping us on our toes, and for sharing with us his devoted and profound attunement to the beauty and complexity hidden in the world around us.

Connie Butler
The Agnes Gund Director, MoMA PS1

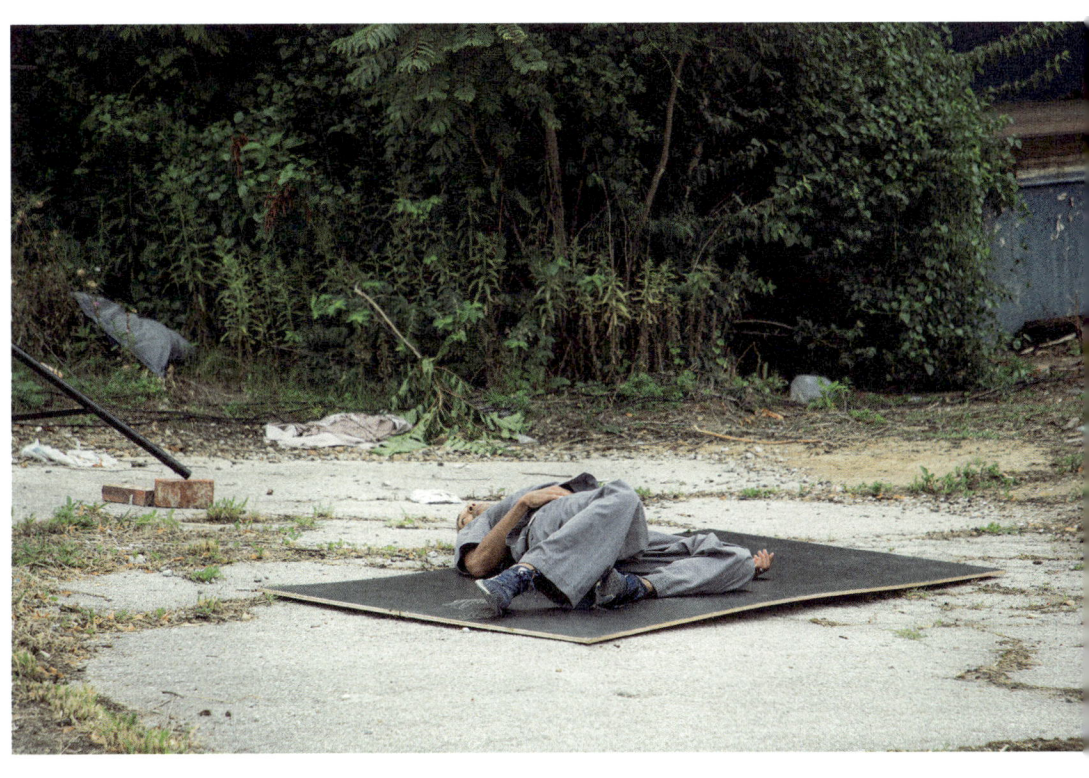

The footers running on image spreads throughout this book refer to the project pictured, starting from Ralph Lemon's most recent works and dating back to circa 2003. Full image captions may be found on pp. 162—64.

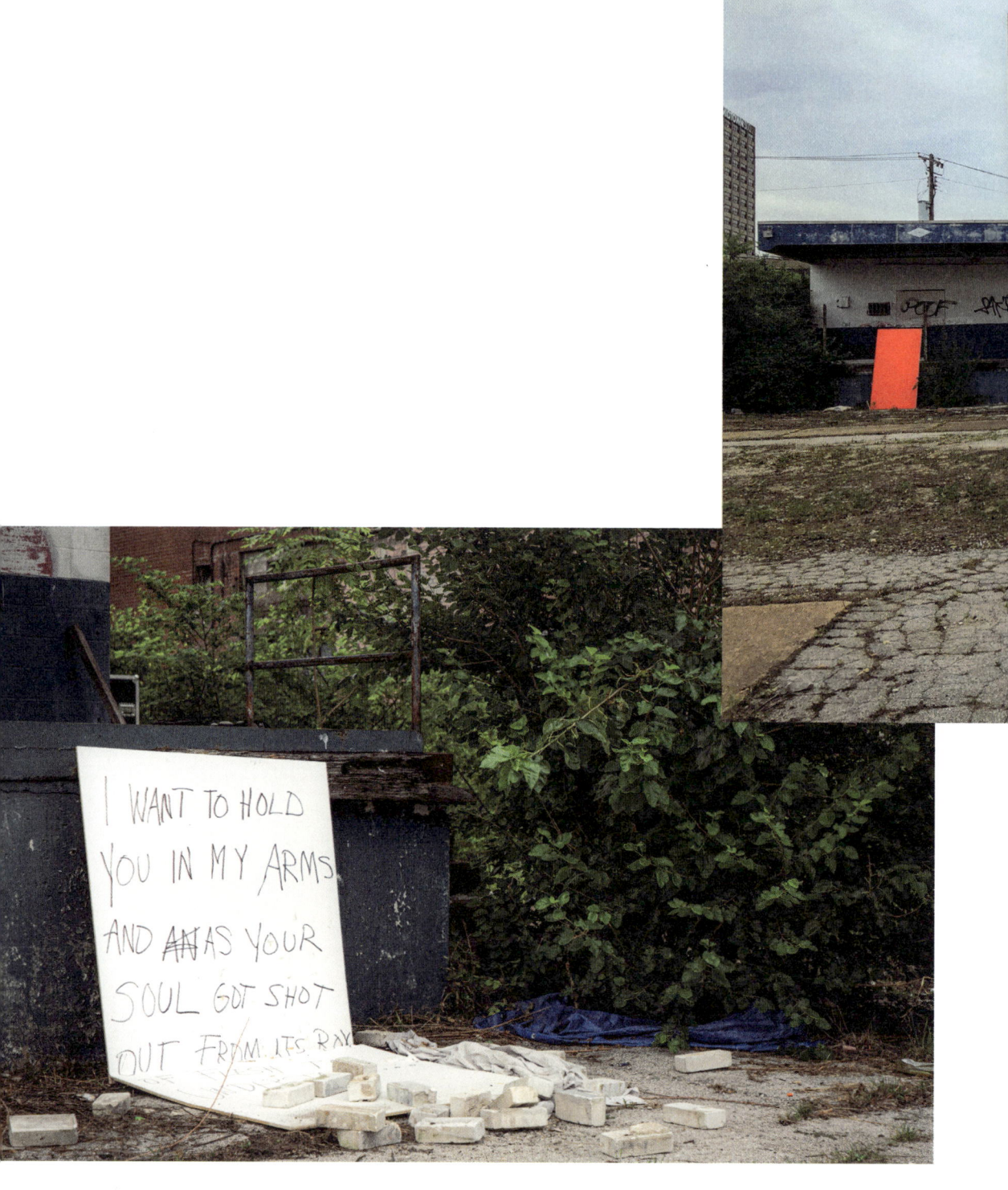

Tell it anyway, 2015—24

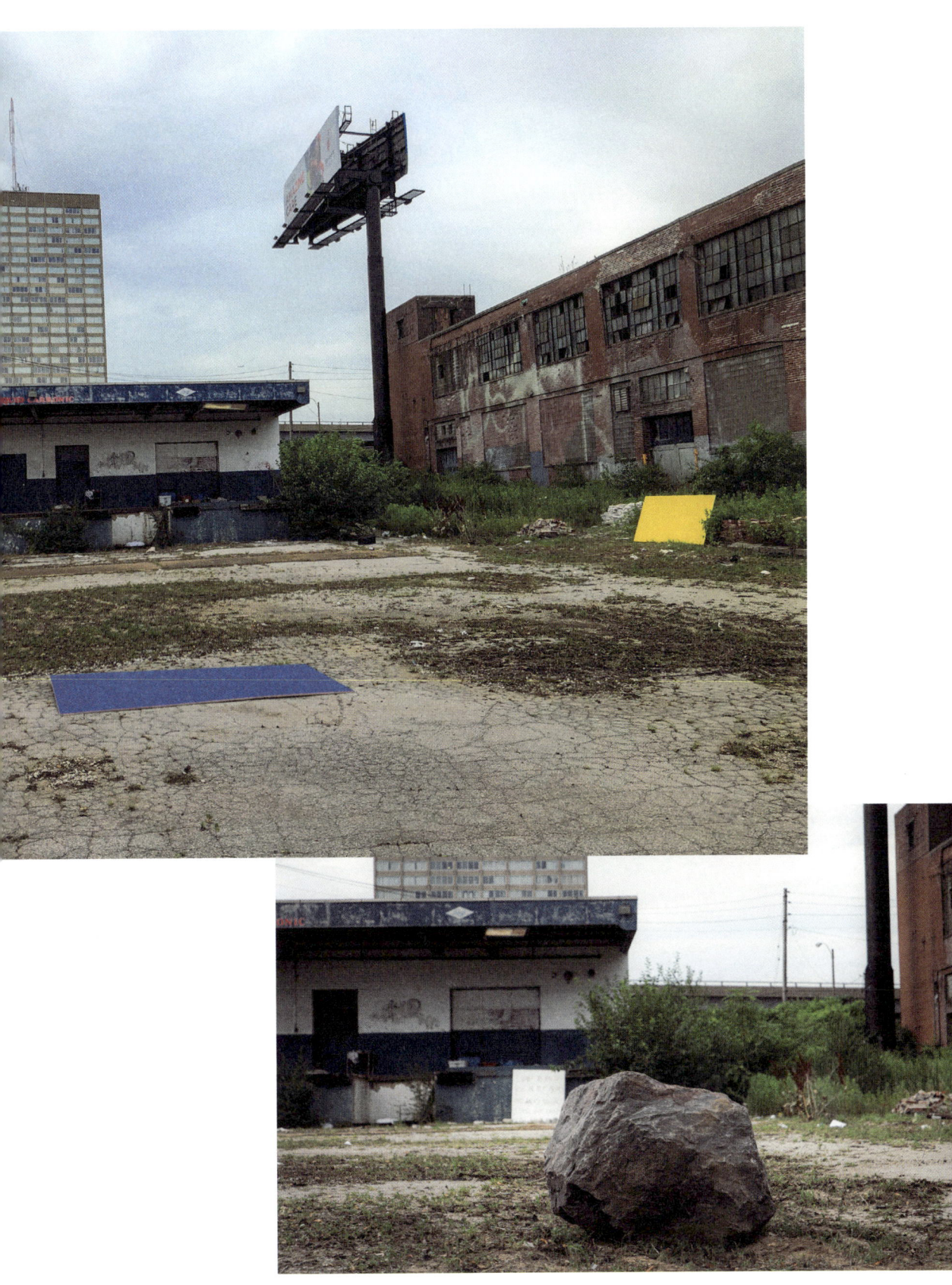

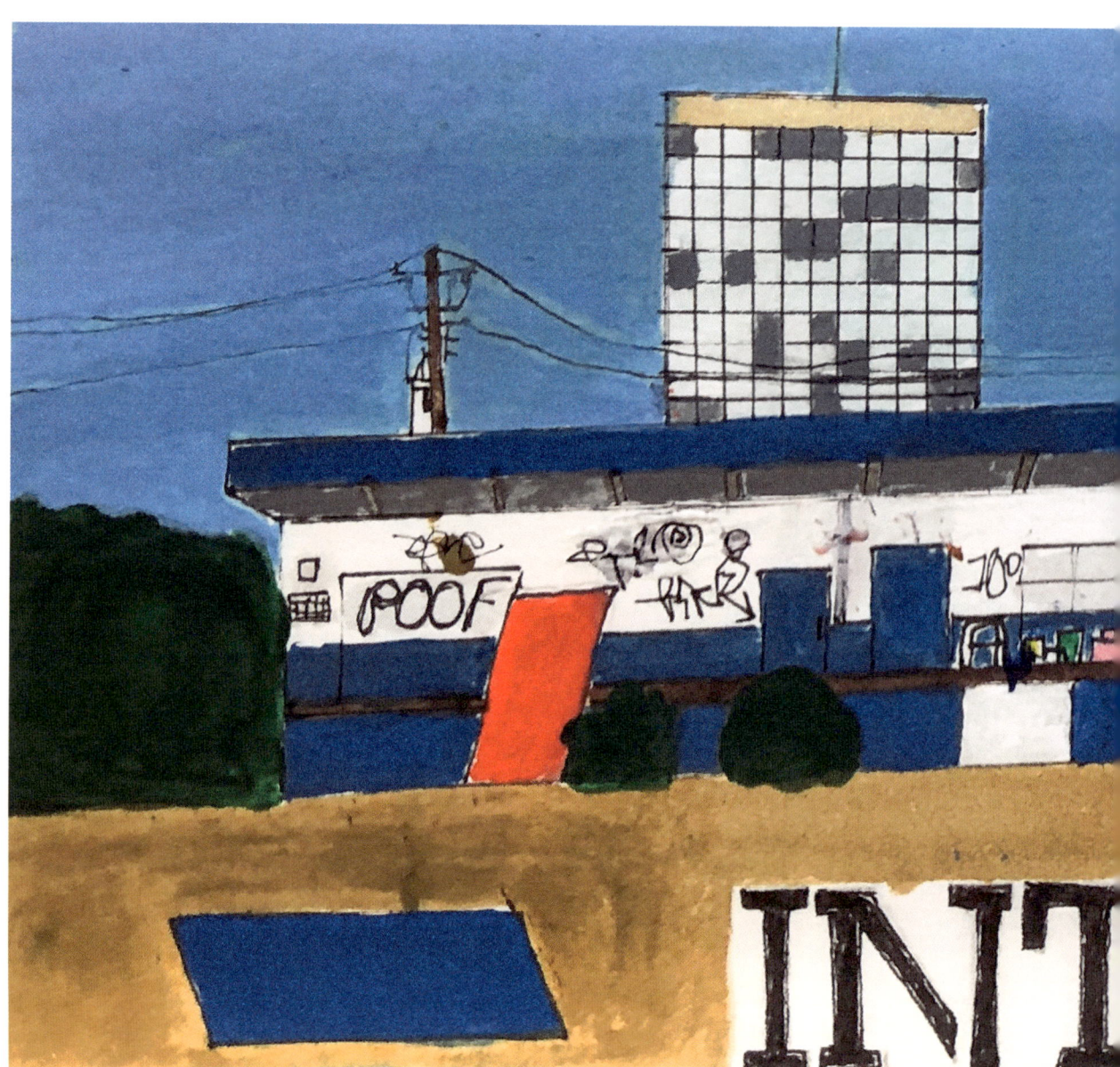

Tell it anyway, 2015—24

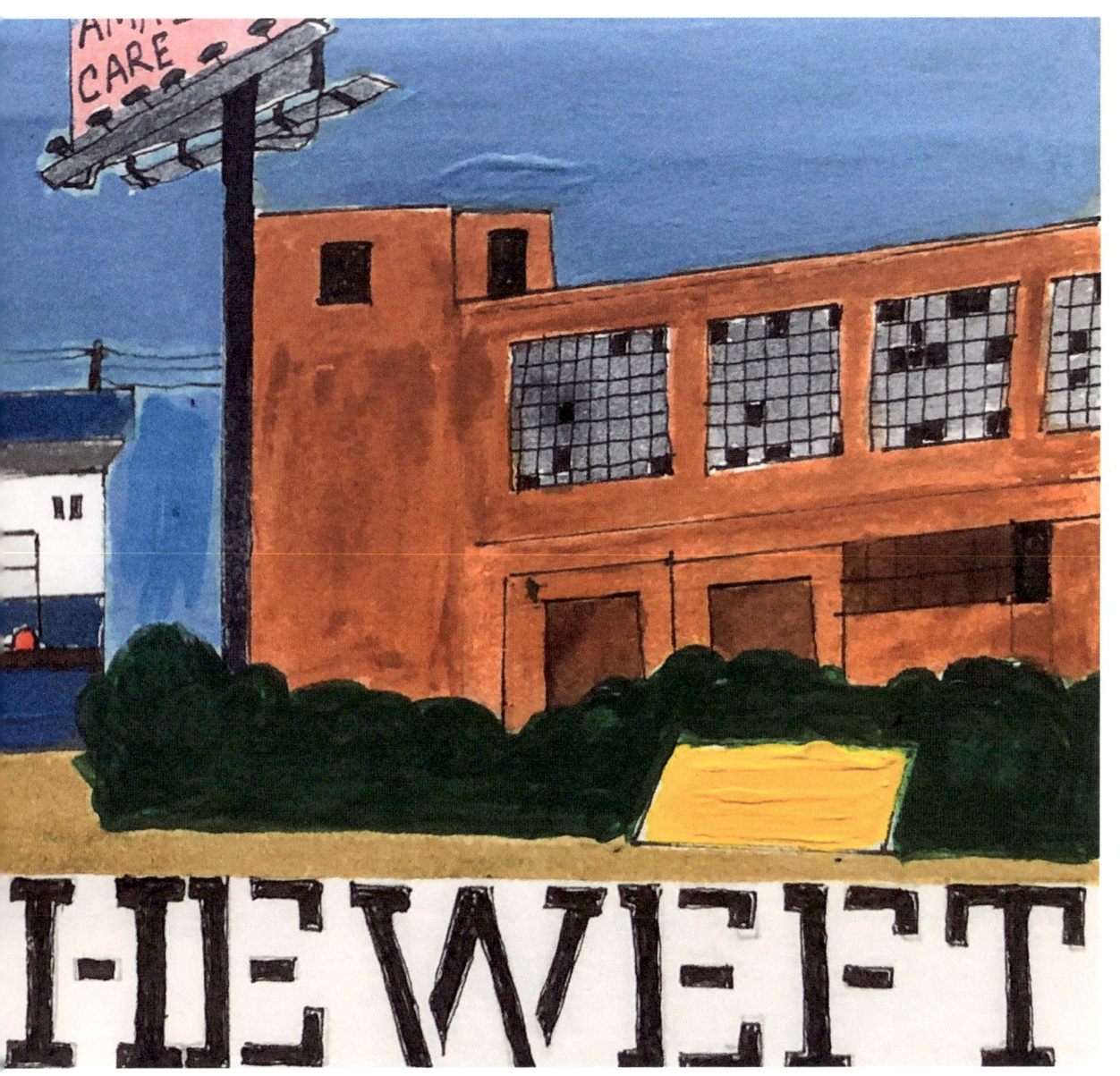

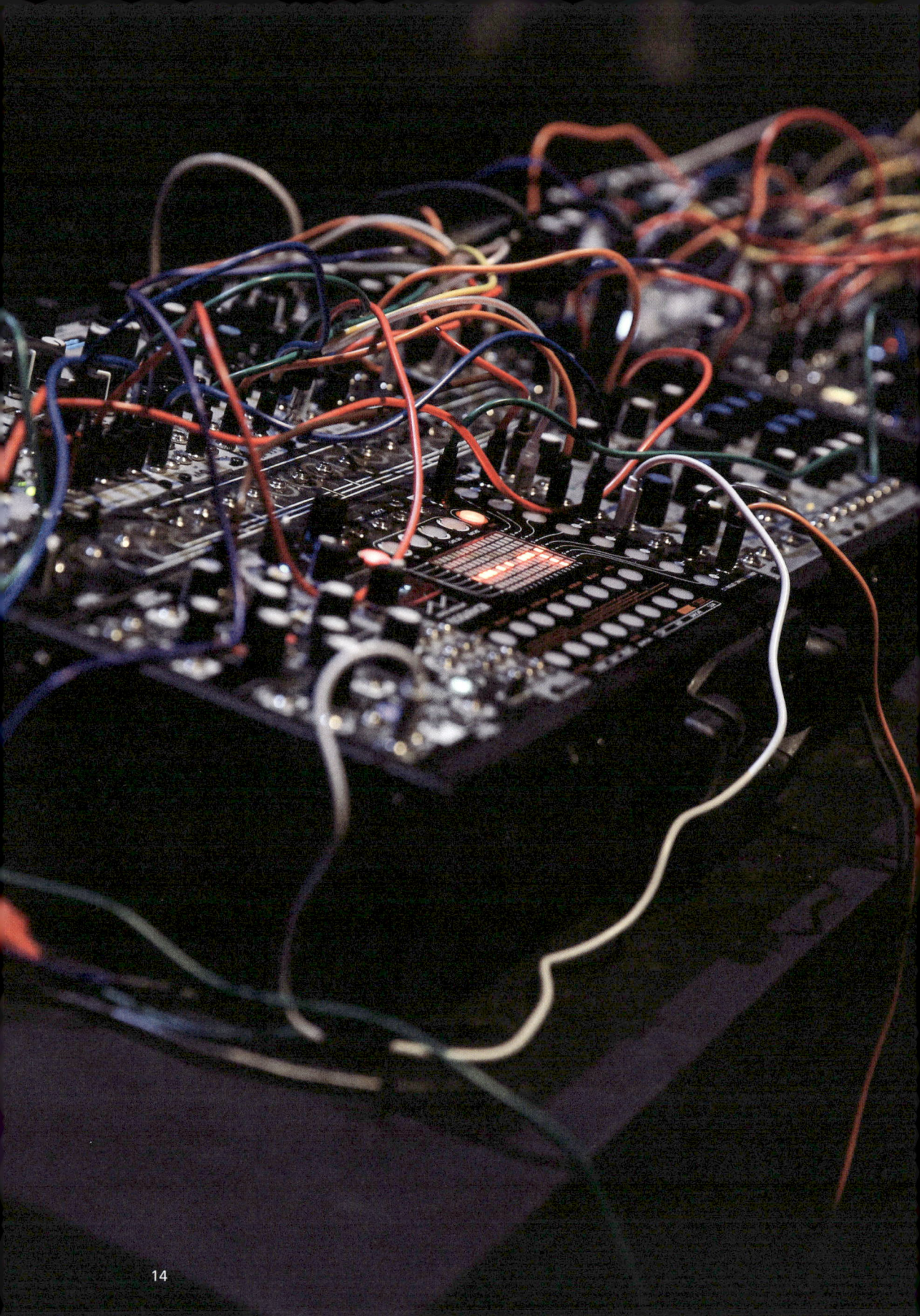

So beautiful
This picture

This implication

Yeah

The only one looking

Yeah

It's arresting and critical

Yeah

And you've blown it up

Yeah

And now you have to do
something with it
But it's wrong!
It's exploiting

Yeah

It's doing it again

Exactly

Replaying that moment
before . . .

Right

The spectacle, terror,
accusation
It's still not giving
anything
You're not saving, there's
no voice

No

You're using
What do you do?
What do you do?

Nothing. This.

Try to tell the story
Try
With terrible earnestness

It will all be for naught

Try to tell it anyway

He refused to tell the
straight story
A stubborn resistance.

The train arrived. A
conveyance was in
waiting. There was
not a shout. A funeral
procession could not
have been more quiet.
He gazed abstractedly
into the faces of the
crowd, never uttering a
word. It is believed
that he told the truth.
Never once wincing.

Did I sing too loud?

No, that's not why

God have mercy

Prayin' won't do you
no good

His petition to heaven
was almost incoherent

Send this dime to my
daddy!

That's it?

Almost

Now he had gone wild
Missouri Negro
A king
Jumping at the air
Jumping at nothin'

Jumping
Jumping the garden wall

What do you do?
What do you do?

Nothing. Just this

OOOOOOOOOOOOO . . .

Lyrics from *Tell it anyway*,
2017—20

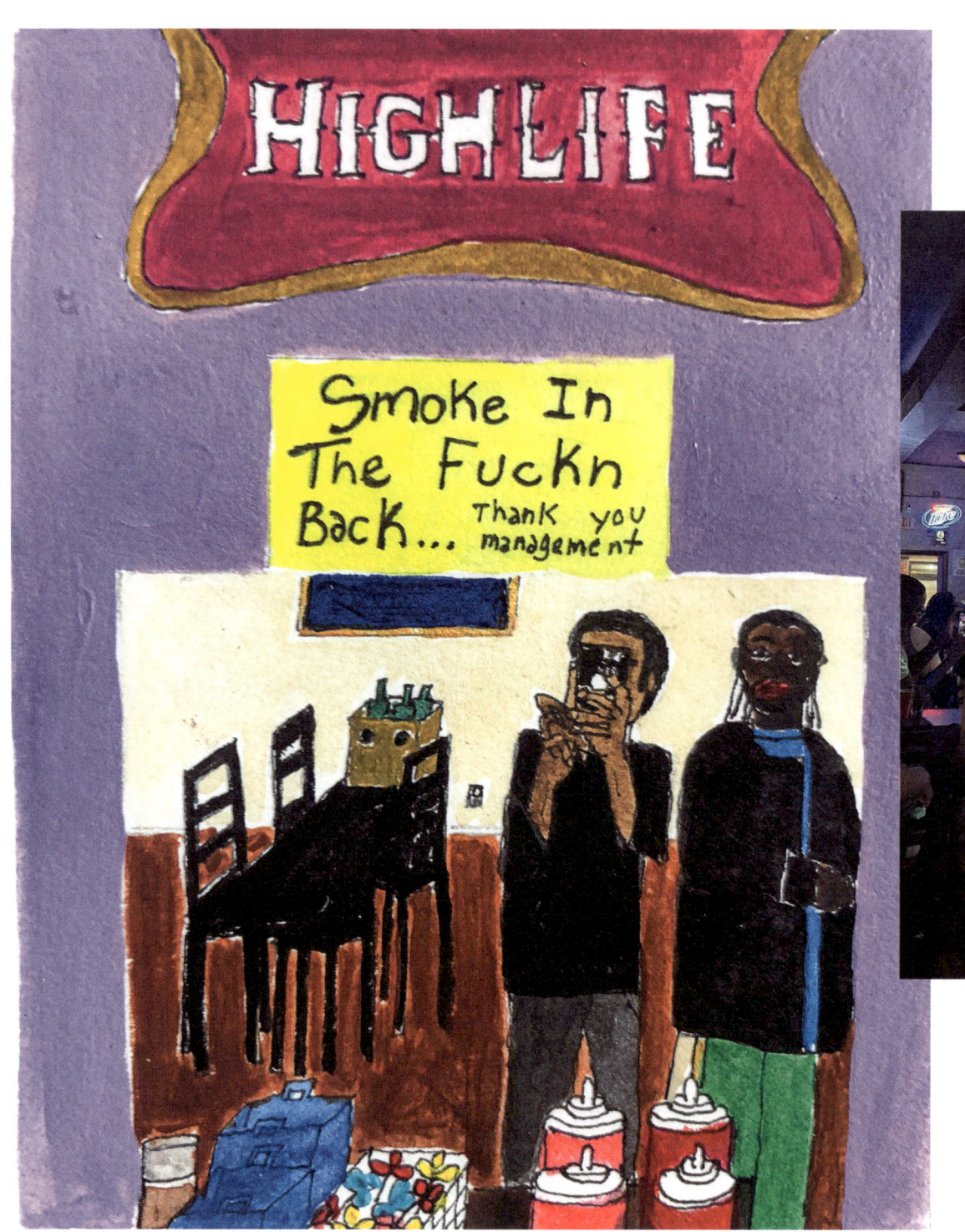

Tell it anyway, 2015—24

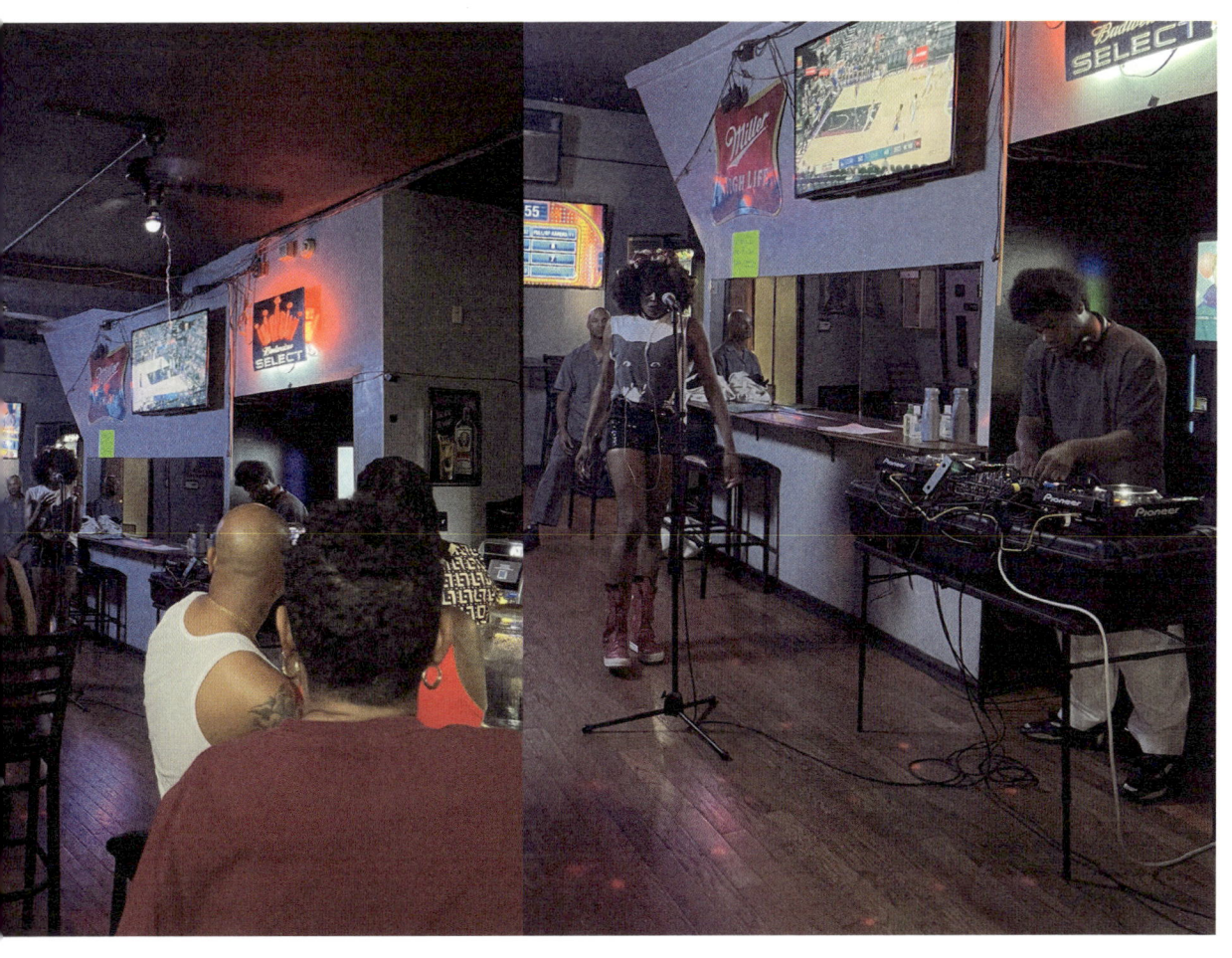

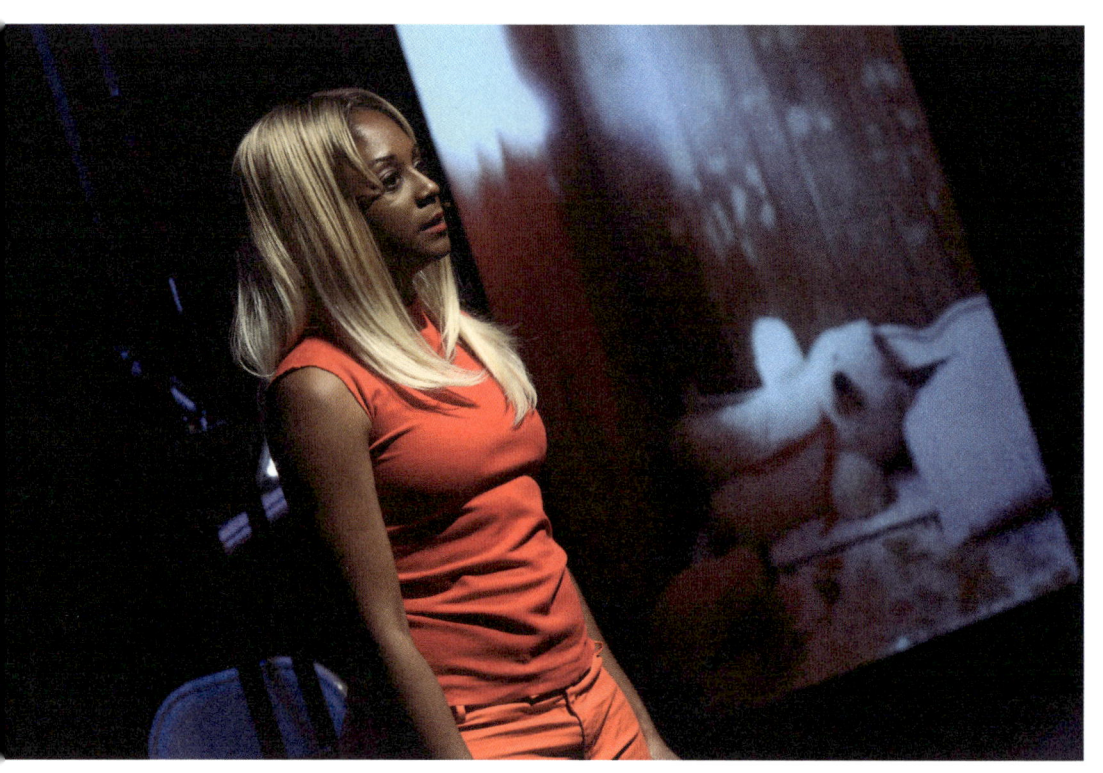

An Intimate Rebellion
Connie Butler

Ralph Lemon pushes hard on the notion of the chorus. Working
with him is an invitation to consider what it means to create
and sustain community: received, given, and reimagined. How
committed are we? What do we bring to the communal moment
of invention? What does it mean to go beyond the body, and
how do we make meaning together?

Ralph is at the center of a diasporic intellectual community
that ebbs and flows depending on the demand of a particular work,
its emotional register, and the seriously effervescent quality
of the iconic artists with whom he collaborates. They are devoted
antagonists, loud interlocutors, and energetic participants in
an elastic practice that is about dance, its problems and possibilities,
and how the body can be pushed to its limits to encompass the
flux and exhaustion and joy of Black life. The body, in Lemon's
lexicon, is a witness to our time with a boundless possibility
for imagining. He understands that abstract movement is, well, an
abstraction: that everything is an abstraction of experience and
emotion, is historical and deeply held in the body but also released,
expunged with some regularity, determined and surfaced by the
problem of living in this impossible time, in this impossible country,
now and every day, for all of us.

Conceived in response to Lemon's own prompt, this publication serves as a devotional handbook reflecting the voices of many of those who have shown up for his work with faith and commitment over its years of evolution. Not a monograph in the traditional sense, *Ceremonies Out of the Air* takes its cue from Simone Forti's 1974 *Handbook in Motion*, a very personal and eccentric diary of movement ideas and sources. Published by the Nova Scotia College of Art and Design at an early point in Forti's career as a post-Judson dancer—a maker of drawings, "dance constructions," and collaborations with musicians—the book traces Forti's early career from when she first arrived in New York from California in 1968. It tracks her experiments with dance that reflected and internalized the social and political upheavals of her time. In an introduction to the third edition in 1997, she describes her handbook as "an intimate example of an artist finding her way":

> The book is about movement. About working with my teachers and my colleagues, about pieces I made and the dancing I did as it evolved through various concerns. And it explores the turning points in my creative life.[1]

Like this book, Forti's handbook is partly diaristic, filled with delicate contour drawings alongside the artist's own words. In Forti's case, but also in Lemon's, the drawings appear to be lines in motion, reminiscent of Paul Klee's poetic manifesto "Taking a Line for a Walk," which appears in his *Pedagogical Sketchbook* (1925). Lemon identifies as an inheritor of diverse traditions—including Klee's lineage of abstraction—that range from line drawing to classical dance to daily, even devotional movement practices. His own evolution as a choreographer and artist has been shaped by both personal and political lines of research. Many of the those who have contributed to *Ceremonies Out of the Air* have been with him since his early experiments and continue to be a part of his ongoing inquiry into the limits of the body as a container of emotions.

I first encountered Lemon's work long after he was on the move as an artist. He had already made his way out of his role as maestro of the Ralph Lemon Company, which he led from 1985 to 1995, working as a choreographer with a troupe and all of the power dynamics and conventions that burden proscenium dance production. He began evolving toward a unique movement-based practice that is polymathic, social, and political, that constitutes an ongoing act of witnessing. Like Miles Davis turning away from his audience (an image he has invoked with conspiratorial relish), Lemon was in many ways ahead of his time in making this move, inventing a mode of creative production that could be based in research but also encompass the vastness of everything he wanted to reflect. Works such as *Scaffold Room*, a lecture/performance presented first at the Walker Art Center, Minneapolis, in 2014 and then in 2015 at The Kitchen, New York, channel the lives and towering performance personae of figures such as Beyoncé, Moms Mabley, Amy Winehouse, and Kathy Acker [pp. 18, 46].[2] Lemon drew on the affects and mythologies around these women, deploying them as a performance archive. Other projects grew out of trips with mercurial goals, for example the *Geography Trilogy* (1996–2004), which took him and a group of young Black male dancers to Côte d'Ivoire and Guinea to study movement within a completely new community of performers. Danspace Project director Judy Hussie-Taylor has described this post-company, more nomadic and exploratory period in Lemon's work as "a decade-long research project . . . at the center of which is the tension between form and non-form, control and release, authenticity and artifice."[3] Beginning with the *Geography Trilogy*, Lemon took up culturally embedded ways of using the body that included the vernaculars of trance, group mourning, and protest—all activities in which the individual gives themselves over to the collective. He began to work in cycles or chapters based on deep study in locales as varied as West Africa, Asia, and the American South to understand how dance and movement function within each of these regions as part of ritual and daily life, including forms of celebration and mourning. He sought to break down and restructure his own understanding of form to arrive at a "no form" in which noise and bodies are infinitely together.[4]

Lemon made his last full-length work for the stage, *How Can You Stay in the House All Day and Not Go Anywhere?*, in 2010. Among its many indelible images was the artist, seated in a plastic lawn chair, reflecting in a lecture/performance on the recent deaths of his life partner, the dancer Asako Takami, and of a key collaborator in Mississippi, Walter Carter. This direct reckoning with loss was as emotional, if less visceral, than the feeling of the first work of his that I saw live, *Come home Charley Patton*, the last chapter of the *Geography Trilogy*, in a performance at the Brooklyn Academy of

Music in 2004. What lodged profoundly in my body then, amid a complex combination of anxiety, empathy, and rage, was the piece's culminating scene, in which Lemon danced desperately, furiously in defiance of a firehose aimed at him by his fellow dancer Djédjé Djédjé Gervais. The combination of actual danger, exhaustion, and fortitude, and the absurd uncanny of seeing this violent image enacted onstage—an image familiar from civil-rights-era documentary photographs of Black Americans in the Deep South being blasted by the police—resonated deeply. It was an example of what Lemon has described as "aestheticized excess," his desire to push the body beyond its limits, to ask what happens *after* a body is exhausted and spent but goes on nevertheless: "I'm interested in what's not there. . . . You get tired, and then what?"[5] The three-minute portion of the performance that the artist refers to as "Fury"—a modality that appears in multiple works —was, according to Lemon, the "physical and psychic beginnings" of what would later become *Rant*, an ongoing series of performances that have taken place five times since 2019, with a sixth planned for the spring of 2025 [pp. 40–45].[6] Staged at venues that have included The Kitchen and an underground parking garage at the Hammer Museum in Los Angeles, these cacophonous marathon dance events mash up voice, funk, text, and bodies moving so frenetically and insistently that they finally expire, spent and wrung out yet indomitable. Lemon's practice of exhaustion and resistance is indeed a sign for our troubled times.

Sometime later, when I met Ralph, he told me he was done with dance (something he's declared periodically for the entire time I've known him). In spite of this provocation—or perhaps because of it—I asked him to participate in the performance component of an exhibition at The Museum of Modern Art that explored the limits of drawing, specifically line, as it moved across the twentieth century, off the page and out of painting into the space of the body. *On Line: Drawing Through the Twentieth Century* (2010– 11), cocurated with Catherine de Zegher, was an eccentric traverse of geographies and chronologies, a path that had been mapped by institutions like MoMA but not yet settled into historical narrative. Our exhibition asked, What if you began the history of twentieth-century art with a figure like the experimental dancer Loie Fuller, skirted Picasso, centered Lygia Clark at midcentury, and found line, abstraction, and movement in the lyrical paintings of Australian Aboriginal artist Emily Kame Kngwarreye?

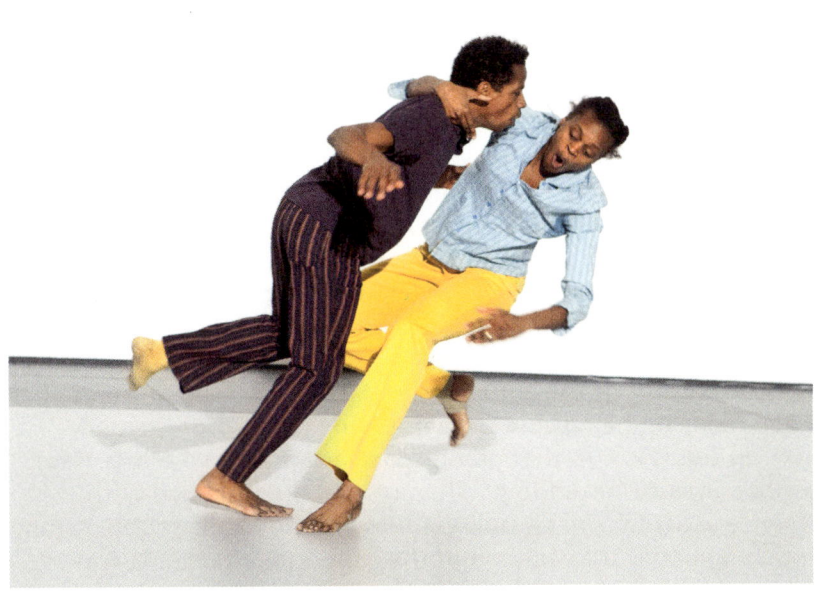

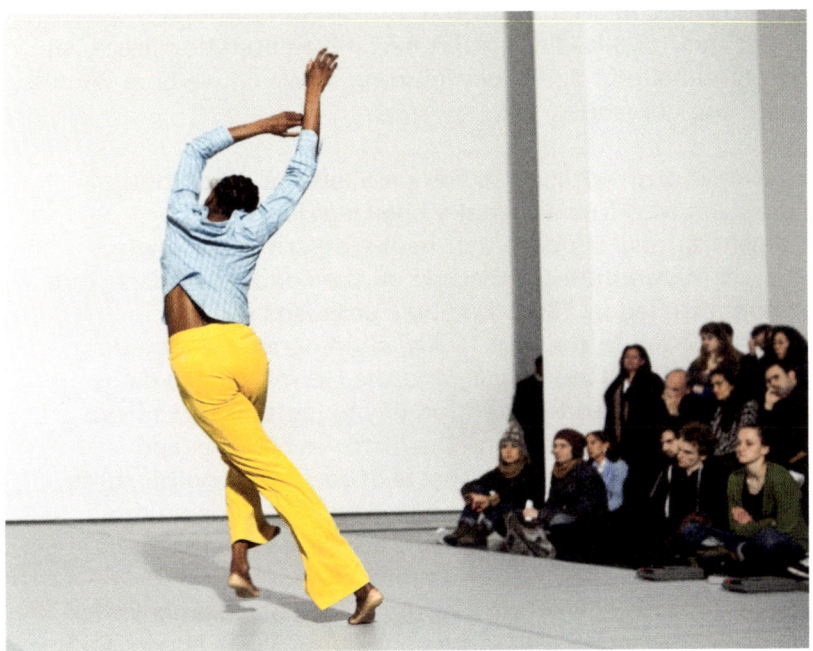

Untitled [2008], featuring Ralph Lemon and Okwui Okpokwasili, performed at
The Museum of Modern Art, New York, 2011

This history—speculative to be sure—was the context into which we invited Lemon. The performance series included his contemporaries Anne Teresa De Keersmaeker and Xavier Le Roy, his forebear Trisha Brown, and conceptual artists Marie Cool and Fabio Balducci, whose interventions were crystalline explorations of space, light, and line.

I recall that, in preparation for On Line, Ralph and I had a series of conversations about MoMA's atrium, its grandeur, and the oppressive presence of Barnett Newman's Broken Obelisk (1963–69), which had stood there inert and imposing since the 2004 completion of the Museum's second renovation. We discussed the scale and whiteness of that space before it became common to speak of the whiteness of museums as a category of recognition and repair. He was excited about the proximity of the audience, and after the production he would comment on being able to feel the breath of those seated, primarily on the floor, in that grand space around a makeshift stage: he described it as Armageddon.[7] The untitled duet opened with performance artist Okwui Okpokwasili in a bunny suit, sobbing—long gut-wrenching howls that echoed in the canyonlike space. It was as if she cried for all of humanity. The entangled, frenetic work that ensued was rooted in grief so deep that it welled through the frantic colliding of their two bodies until it became an ecstatic release, an intimate and rebellious act of communion to which we bore witness. It was wild and gorgeous.

Lemon's career both anticipates and parallels the generation of choreographers who fundamentally changed dance in the 1990s, a generational slippage that he has described as lonely.[8] Few of his contemporaries embarked on the conceptual departure that Lemon initiated in 1995. Led by Europeans and the French in particular in the mid-1990s, choreographers including Le Roy, Jérôme Bel, Tino Sehgal, and the German grand-dame Pina Bausch approached the creation of movement works from a critical perspective, interrogating the histories of ballet and classical forms and introducing aspects of social and political life into the hermetic world of proscenium dance. Theorizing this group of artists, performance curator Catherine Wood suggests:

> Recent art history offers two significant but diametrically
> opposed moments where the concept of dance-choreography
> impacts on the politics of art: one in the '60s, one in
> the '90s. . . . These artists have made works which operate

on a local or personal level and borrow the formal codes of dance performance to highlight the unpredictability or internal illogic which keeps us individual, drives us to disrupt the power of schematic conformist ideologies.[9]

As a dancer, Lemon is an inheritor of the postmodern tradition that takes the women and men—but mostly the women—of Judson Dance Theater and their radical exploitation of everyday movement and then, in his words, "blackifies the situation."[10] He brings history to bear on the privilege of the quotidian, questioning the notion of abstraction and the social, asking how the body holds and communicates meaning. Trying not to differentiate what goes on in the studio from the rest of life, he is indebted to Brown, Forti, Anna Halprin, Steve Paxton, Yvonne Rainer, and others, lifting up that radical, antiheroic set of body-based parameters that forever changed modern dance.

But Lemon moves this archive into the present and a more complicated world that is both in mourning and in ecstasy at any given moment, situating this duality at the forefront of its production. Lemon pushes his collaborators to exceed their capacities to explore the possibilities of exhaustion and control, asking them to "use the body to go beyond the body."[11] He is interested in a kind of group transcendence of the individual, an aleatory experience that generates something larger than the self and interrogates collective experience. What happens as a dancer when you shed everything? What comes next? How do you make a state of exhaustion last? What scholar André Lepecki has identified as the "collisions and crashes" in Lemon's work, a quality of hardness to the movement, is what makes it impossible to look away.[12] It's the not looking away, the transfixing quality of this latent violence, but also the persistence and intimacy of the rebellion, that makes Ralph's offerings linger in the visual and somatic memory. This work, it seems, is never done.

1 Simone Forti, "Introduction," in *Handbook in Motion*, 3rd ed. (self-pub., 1998), 5.

2 See "Ralph Lemon: Scaffold Room," Walker Art Center, 2014, https://walkerart.org/calendar/2014/ralph-lemon-scaffold-room.

3 Judy Hussie-Taylor, introduction to *I Get Lost: Danspace Project Platform* (New York: Danspace Project, 2010), 10.

4 Lemon spoke about this research at the Center for Ballet and the Arts during an event called "'To let things (life) be': A Conversation with André Lepecki and Ralph Lemon," New York University, April 1, 2024.

5 See "Ralph Lemon," interview by James Hannaham, *Bomb* 120 (Summer 2012), https://bombmagazine.org/articles/2012/07/01 /ralph-lemon.

6 Ralph Lemon, email to the author, July 23, 2024.

7 I am grateful to Kathy Halbreich for first suggesting that I consider Lemon's work for *On Line*. He made the Armageddon comment to her as reported in *Ralph Lemon*, Modern Dance series (New York: Museum of Modern Art, 2016), 82.

8 Lemon, email to the author.

9 Catherine Wood, "Extra-ordinary Dance: On the Politics of Dance," *Art Monthly* 252 (December 2001—January 2002), 9–10.

10 Lepecki and Lemon, "'To let things (life) be.'"

11 Hussie-Taylor, introduction to *I Get Lost*, 11.

12 Lepecki and Lemon, "'To let things (life) be.'"

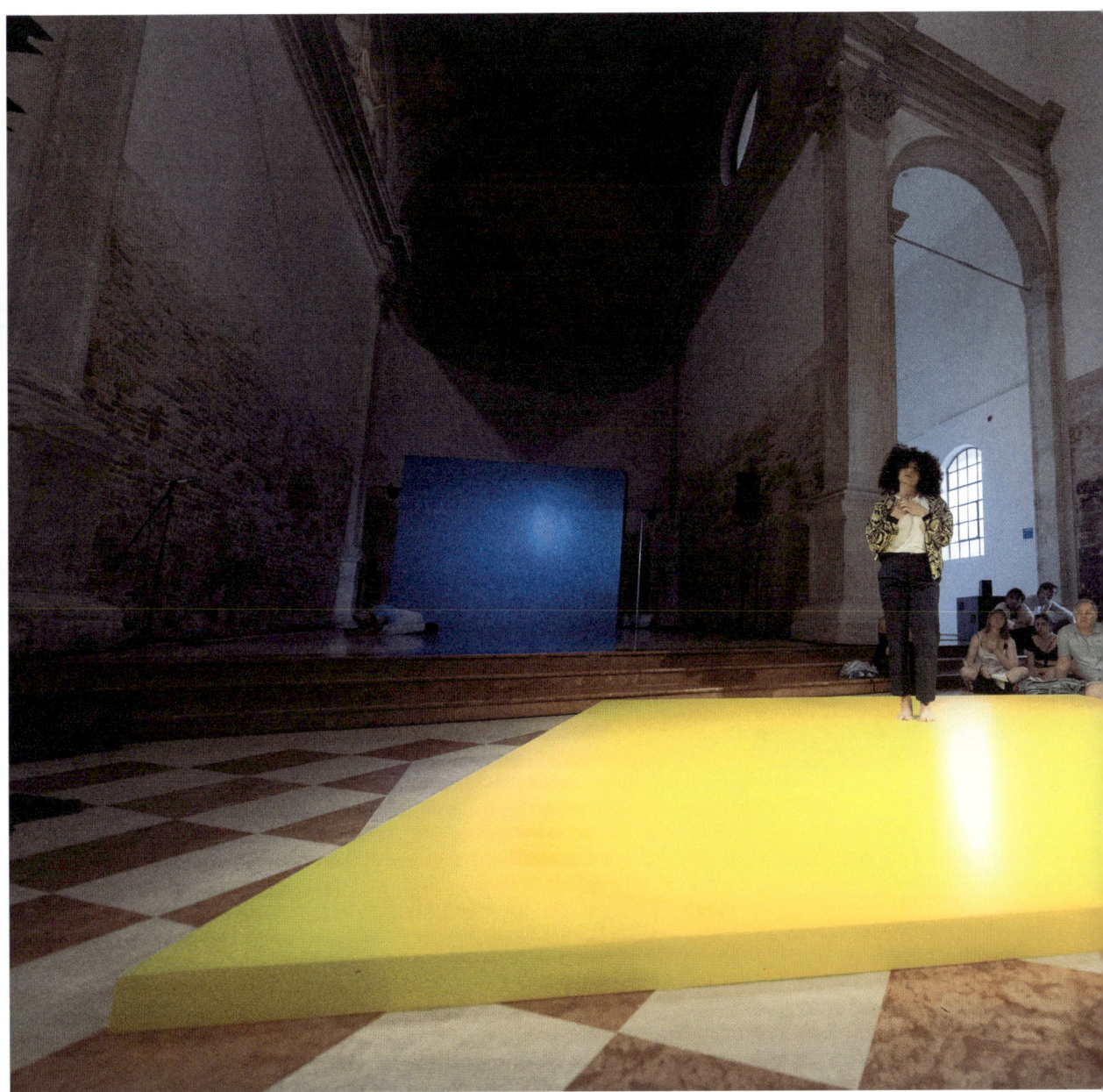

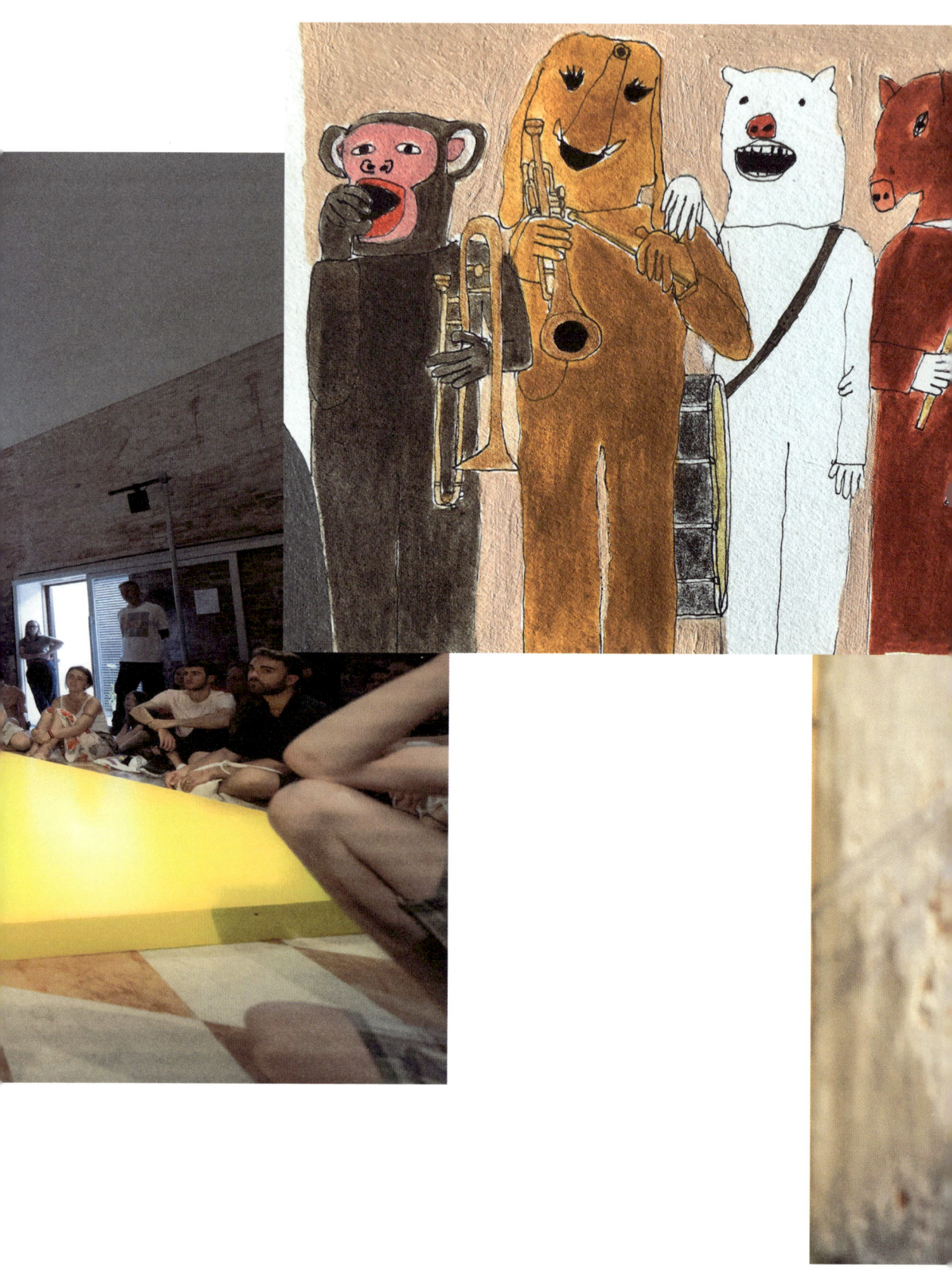

In Proximity, 2022—25

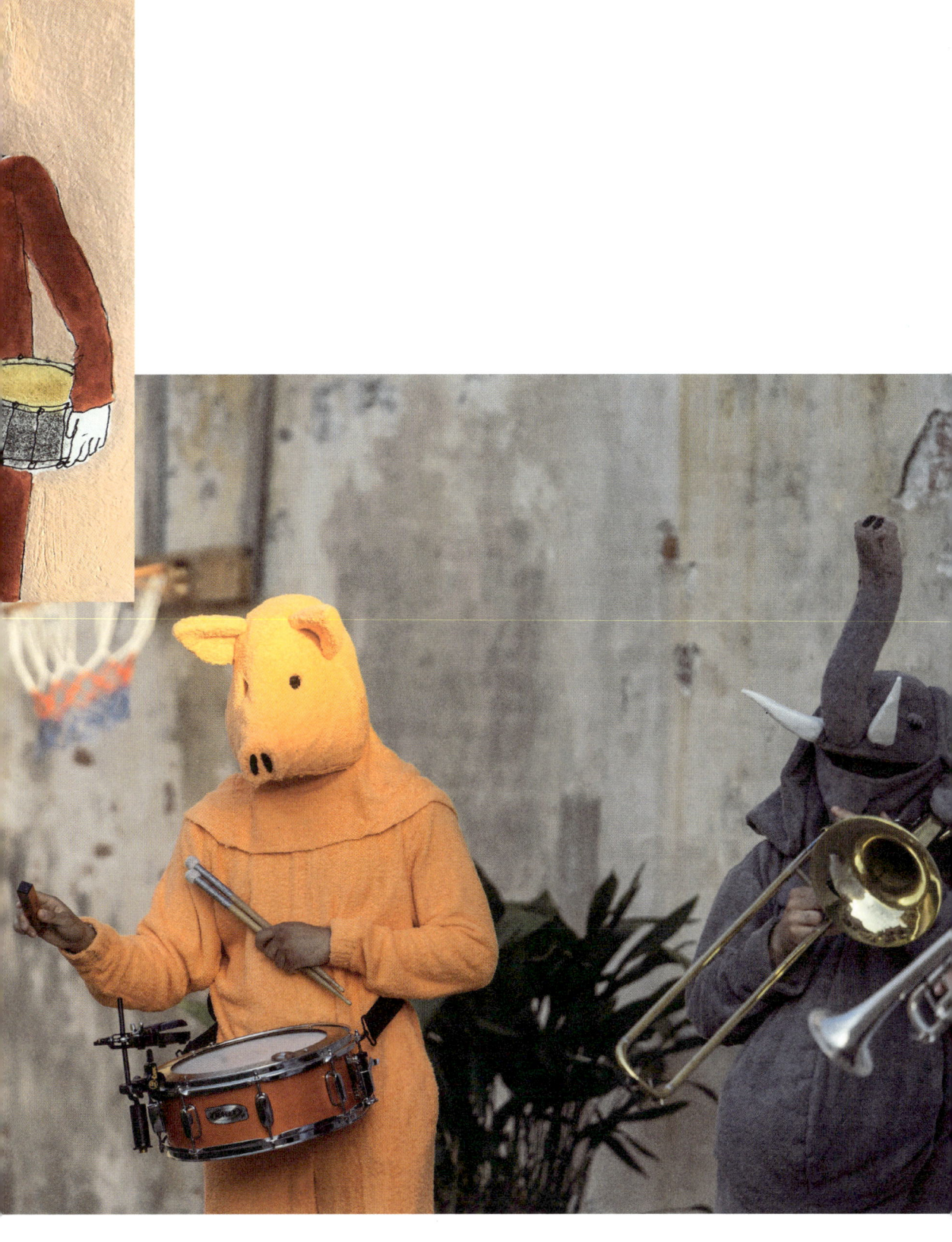

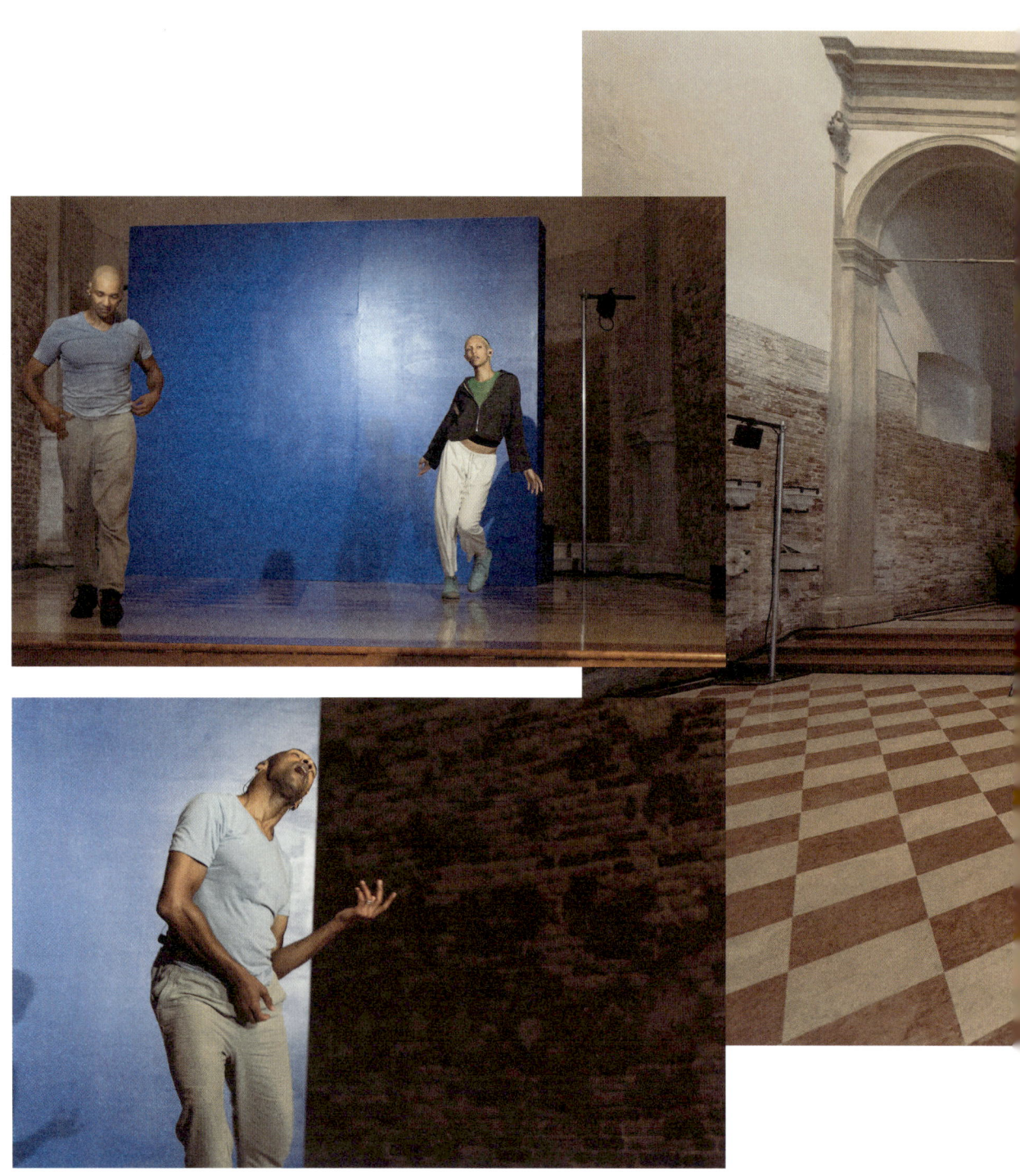

In Proximity, 2022—25

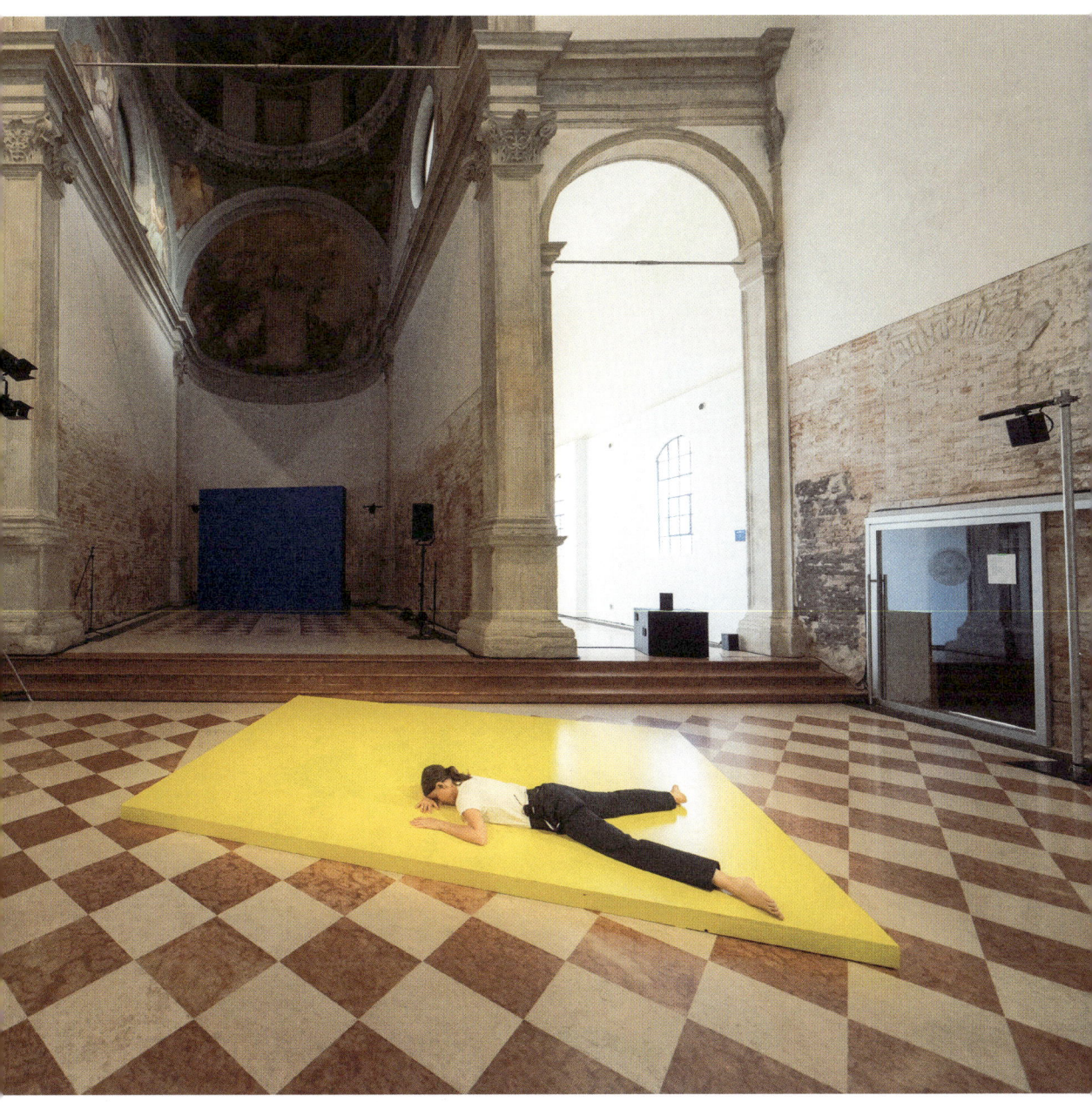

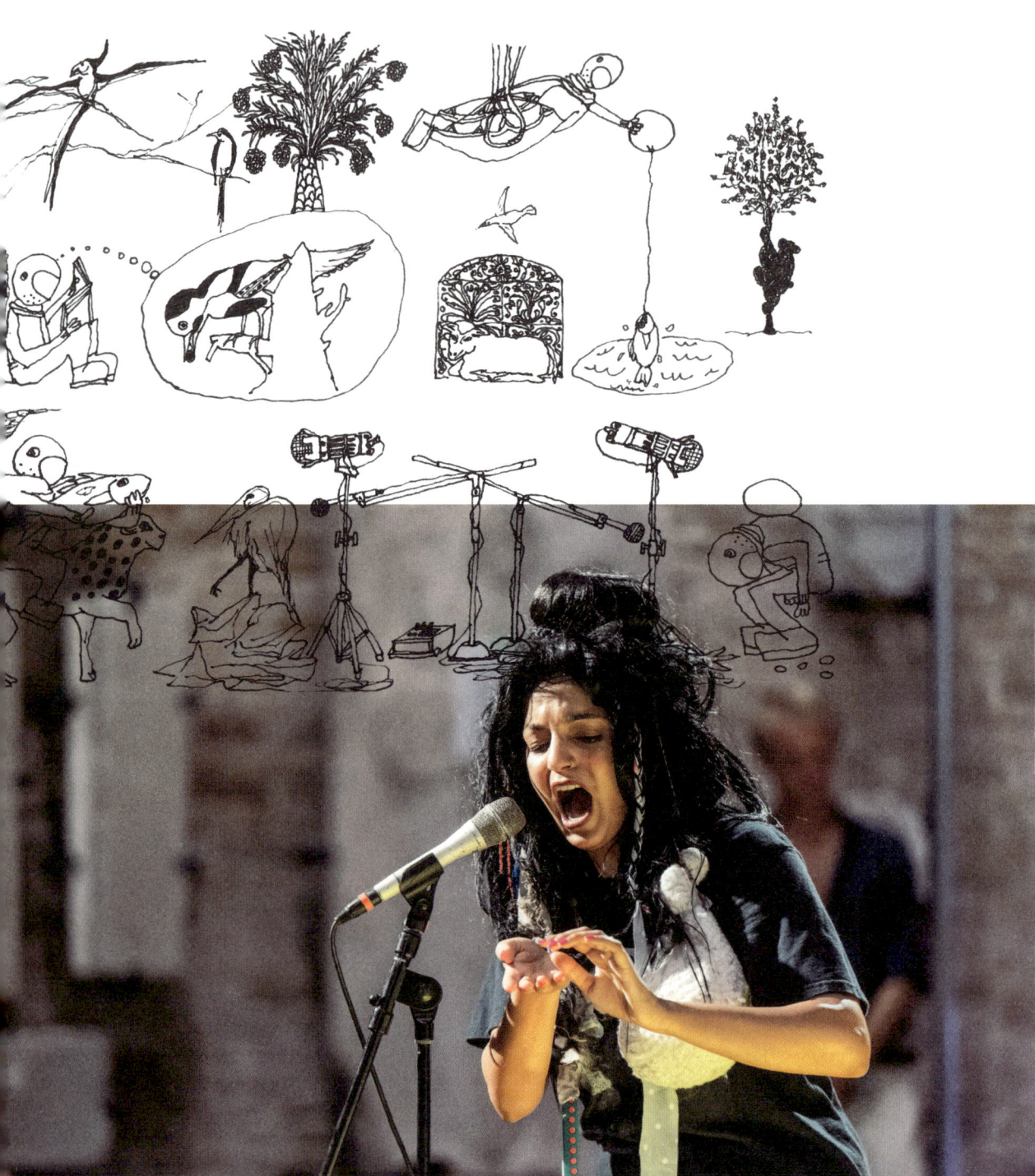

Here: A Lyric Move for Ralph Lemon
Kevin Quashie

She said: "Here," then, "in this here place, we flesh."[1]

This invocation is by Baby Suggs, a character in Toni Morrison's *Beloved*, a preacher, grandmother, and mother-in-law whose intelligence helps to guide her free black community in a small Ohio town. The year is 1864.

We know to whom Baby Suggs, "uncalled, unrobed, unanointed," was speaking:

> When warm weather came, Baby Suggs, holy, followed by every black man, woman and child who could make it through, took her great heart to the Clearing—a wide-open place cut deep in the woods nobody knew for what at the end of a path known only to deer and whoever cleared the land in the first place. In the heat of every Saturday afternoon, she sat in the clearing while the people waited among the trees.[2]

We know the context and what she said, since Morrison gives us two pages of her luminous sermon.

What can we understand about the vocality of her address?

Here: The first move of the sentence marks space and time, though the marking is fantastical, aspirational; it calls on the potency of each congregant, each listener, to settle into their locality, into the sensibility and affect and neediness of their body in that moment as well as the electricity radiating between their body and the ones near them, their body and the air or the trees or the earth beneath their feet. So, the act of declaring *here* is a magic act, performative in the way that speech can announce and enact.

Here, in this here place: Indeed, that demonstrative word *here* is a deictic term, one that points to the impossibly exact place of the speaker's beholding. Deixis, in the English language, is "a word or phrase (such as *this*, *that*, *these*, *those*, *now*, *then*, *here*) that points to the time, place, or situation in which a speaker is speaking."[3] So, the speaker proclaims and instantiates something intense with the word and, especially in Baby Suggs's case, the listener is called to try to inhabit its force. "Here" produces imprecision and certitude, an indexical gorgeousness of a sensibility or feeling that is undeniable and unshareable, belonging exactly to the one who says "here." And still, it is an invitation offered to the listener who bears the saying and who dares to try, unsuccessfully, to find or know "here" as the speaker does.

The magic, of course, is that even in the listener's failure to inhabit the same "here" as the speaker, the listener arrives at their own impossible precision that coordinates to the call. In its failure, "here" makes an offering.

Across this small word are at least three conceptual enactments: "here" instantiates a presence and a present, it gestures to a speaker with a texture of will or urgency or voice or desire, it materializes a scale of intimacy at the same time that its relational specificity is broad.

Here, in this here place, we flesh: Notice, also, that Baby Suggs declares what we are—flesh, life, human. Our commonsense understanding of "flesh" might think this term as something debased, something stripped of social recognition; there are theoretical arguments, too, that debate what such a materiality signifies in the antiblack coloniality of the world.[4] And still,

Baby Suggs deploys the language of embodied mass to register thinking and feeling—"flesh that weeps, laughs; flesh that dances on bare feet in grass"—as well as perhaps to echo the theological resonance between human, spirit, and God.[5] She—and Morrison, in crafting the phrase—inaugurates and rectifies the term "flesh," maybe even imbuing it with an indexical capaciousness akin to "here."

We flesh: She means human and her invocation wrecks language. In declaring "flesh" in the sermonic moment, she handles the word, as if holding and tendering it in her hands so that it can be beheld in the hands of the ones to whom she is speaking—an offering she can gather and pass on. As in *here, take this; here, I give your body back to you so you can break into its (dis)possession*.

Here, we flesh: Notice, too, that no verb is necessary in the phrase, that nothing interrupts the suture between "we" and "flesh," because *we presently and forever flesh*, a demotic formation that elevates the phrase to philosophy and incantation, an amalgamation and throwing of voice.

Again, what can we understand about the vocal force of this sermonic moment, about its act as an address, a devotion, a ceremony, a responsibility, an ethos, a longing, as truth?

/

To me, the force of *here* operates as a lyric address. We know the lyric as a poetic genre, an intensity of voice that the speaker inhabits and struggles to reconcile. Tracy K. Smith describes the lyric as the "primacy of a single speaker whose politics [are] intimate, internal, invisible."[6] That Smith names the lyric as hosting politics is crucial, because it disavows the assumption that lyric is apolitical or neutral or individual, a genre alienated from the expressive traditions of black arts.

If lyric is a sublime enactment of address, if lyric is a "mode of enunciation, where the poet speaks *in propria persona* . . . absorbs into himself the external world and stamps it with inner consciousness,"[7] then it is a form that might aptly designate the enduring complexity of trying to speak one's black human condition.

As a vessel of the vocative, lyric is a site and a performance of address—a throwing of voice where speech manifests dramatically, directly and indirectly. As such, its first-person expressiveness leans on the second person, the you who is conjured as the one who listens, especially if the second person is imaginary or ghostly or implied, fashioned to help materialize the speech moment.

These aesthetic expressive qualities host intimacy and sociality, rendering the lyric's double-voiced intensities a vocative of the political as Smith names it. We might think, then, of lyric as the subject-object dynamic in Du Bois's double consciousness, the hailed black person in Fanon's *Black Skin, White Masks*, the second-person aesthetic in Rankine's *Citizen* or Baldwin's *The Fire Next Time*.[8] In reading thus, we might notice that the doubleness is a function of racial antagonism as well as a reality of trying, genuinely, to express being (and being alive).

Here, in this here place, we flesh: Doubleness, yes, but in truth the intensity of address, the invitation to be lost and found in the call, is a reckoning with first, second, and third pronouns: I who speaks to you, you who might be a they; or I who speaks to you in the context of a they.[9]

Not lyric as a style, not something superficially beautiful or easy, but lyric as force and surge, the voice act that might not (ever) land.

//

In the long tradition of Ralph Lemon's creativity and intelligence resides a thesis on *here* as a lyric potentiality, an art of the body's *here* that incites and twitches, that ignites and demands a risk-full attempt to travel between I, you, them: an experimental clarity that leaps.

His is dance as lyric vocative.

On being presented the twenty-third Heinz Award in the Arts and Humanities in 2018, Lemon asked, "How do I keep this performance, this experiment, this exploration *alive*?" Emphasizing that final word, he is talking about the ephemeral nature of dance, the intensity of its being in a present time; *alive* announces a potency in the fleeting that he exploits exceptionally.

He continues: "I am moving around and I am thinking about this stuff and I am learning all this stuff . . . and then it's gone."[10] The loss is not precisely a loss because it augurs thinking, learning. Lemon understands dance as a philosophy of the body, the way his choreographies exemplify the wildness, the incorrigibility of thinking, the most present action.

Lemon's pronunciation of *alive* rhymes with the idea of *here*—both terms underscore that his kinetic praxis expresses a desire to take his body apart and put it back together. That risk, that experiment, that belief that he is free to imagine the dispersal of the body is quintessentially one of Lemon's gifts. His work invites us into a clearing so that we can enact body-thinking that might give back to us what we don't ever fully possess: the body, this lush animal encasement.

Lemon's choreographic multitude seems to say, *Here, here, the body. Here is wild freedom—it is yours, and you don't own it, and you can fall and fail and flail into it, and it can become you and you can become in it. You don't own it. Here is the body*—and then *here, the body*, without the copula that would imply something finished or static or possessable.

We might want the body, especially the black or minoritarian body, presented in some other convention, something more careful and precious. One understands that need and understands it being fulfilled elsewhere. But Lemon acts as if in accord with Baby Suggs's beatitudes: here, undeniably, the body, engine of thought, movement, ethics, love, fear, danger.

Consider one more inflection: Because Lemon so often films dancers in strange environments—on a farm, in a bedroom, in an astral backdrop—his stage performances conjure up a similar strangeness of space, as if dancers' movements choreograph the air around them into geography, like a clearing.

Such is the case in his piece performed at The Museum of Modern Art in 2011, *Untitled* [2008], a wayward and stalking duet where Lemon and the artist/performer Okwui Okpokwasili engage and alienate each other [p. 23].[11] In their echoes and delineations of shared movement, they are ghosts—ancestor and past and memory. But they also enunciate another sense of ghostliness in the way their bodies reshape the space, clear it out, and then make it small. As their bodies mark and change the space, their bodies mark change—become spectral.

Here, he said, in this dance, we body, we scream, we sigh, we fly. We stay still and hold, we try and tender, taut and loose. Here, devotion; here, a ceremony in the local; here a response and responsibility; here, dream. Here discord, here congress.[12]

Here, he said, with each offering.

Here.

///

The chapter in *Beloved* that houses Baby Suggs's sermon starts quietly and urgently: "It was time to lay it all down."[13] Such a small, even vague claim, though it enunciates a surge, a feeling of right-now, a surrender that doesn't only mean letting go but more importantly announces the need to bear it: to bear what one has been carrying, to assess the carriage, and to decide—to bear the deciding and the decision.

Consider, again, the invocation of work and heft that is offered in a panoramic intimacy, a voice whispering this accord—*lay it all down*—which might be the voice in the winds or of one's neighbor or of one's conscience. A whispering out-of-time voice that is not yours but that speaks to you.

Consider this a lyric condition, an urgency of breath-full scale, a call fractured and specific and (yearning to be) open and (desperately) unfulfilled, language as a harbor housing the sacred in the world.

Like *Here, in this here place, we flesh*, a sermonic invitation, a dancer's instantiation, right here and right now and forever.

Thank you to Domenick Ammirati for thinking with me through this essay; thank you to Ralph Lemon for occasion after occasion after occasion.

[1] Toni Morrison, *Beloved* (New York: Knopf, 1987), 88.

[2] Ibid., 87.

[3] Richard Nordquist, "Deictic Expression (Deixis)," ThoughtCo, updated September 10, 2018, thoughtco.com/deictic-expression-deixis-1690428.

[4] See, for example, Hortense J. Spillers, "Mama's Baby, Papa's Maybe: An American Grammar Book," *Diacritics* 17, no. 2 (Summer 1987), 64–81; Saidiya Hartman, *Scenes of Subjection: Terror, Slavery, and Self-Making in Nineteenth-Century America* (New York: Oxford University Press, 1997); and Zakiyyah Iman Jackson, *Becoming Human: Matter and Meaning in an Antiblack World* (New York: New York University Press, 2020).

[5] Morrison, *Beloved*, 88.

[6] Tracy K. Smith, "Poetry and Politics," *New York Times*, December 16, 2018, https://www.nytimes.com/2018/12/10/books/review/political-poetry.html.

[7] Jonathan Culler, "Introduction," in *Theory of the Lyric* (Cambridge, MA: Harvard University Press, 2017), 1–2. In addition to Smith and Culler, my thinking about the lyric is informed by Anthony Reed, Virginia Jackson, and Gillian White.

[8] W. E. B. Du Bois, *The Souls of Black Folk*, ed. Henry Louis Gates and Terri Hume Oliver (New York: W. W. Norton, 1999); Frantz Fanon, *Black Skin, White Masks*, trans. Richard Philcox (New York: Grove Press, 2008); Claudia Rankine, *Citizen: An American Lyric* (Minneapolis: Graywolf, 2014); James Baldwin, *The Fire Next Time* (New York: Vintage International, 1993).

[9] I am thinking here of the pronoun work in some of the poems in Fred Moten's *perennial fashion presence falling* (Seattle: Wave Books, 2023).

[10] Heinz Awards, "Ralph Lemon, Choreographer Who Redefines the Conventions of Dance—Heinz Awardee," October 29, 2018, video, 3:40, youtu.be/iLK6yz73Q14.

[11] The Museum of Modern Art, "Performance 14: On Line/Ralph Lemon Jan. 26, 29 & 30, 2011," March 25, 2011, video, 3:34, www.youtube.com/watch?v=zD_0VrEV02s.

[12] My prose here leans on rhythms and signifies with three great American lyricists—Lucille Clifton, especially her untitled poem known as "reply," in *The Collected Poems of Lucille Clifton 1965–2010* (Rochester, NY: BOA Editions, 2012), 337; Gwendolyn Brooks, especially her poem "Boy Breaking Glass," in *Blacks* (Chicago: Third World Press, 2000), 438–39; and Aracelis Girmay, especially her poem "Here," in *Teeth: Poems* (Willimantic, CT: Curbstone Press, 2007), 24–27.

[13] Morrison, *Beloved*, 86.

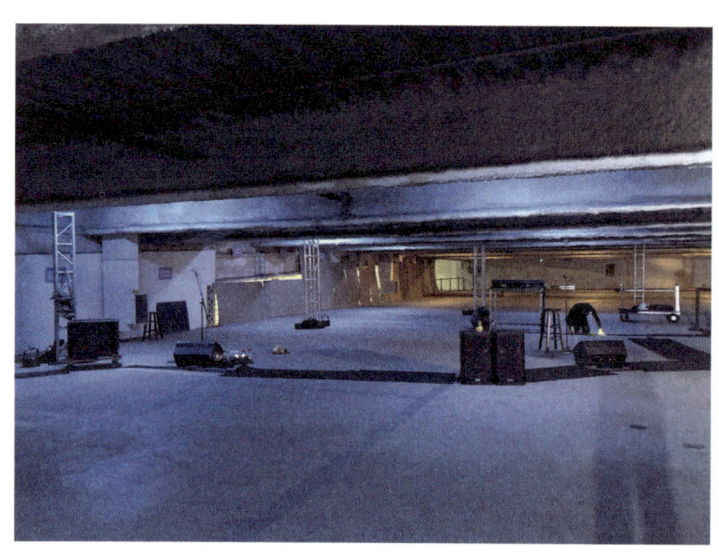

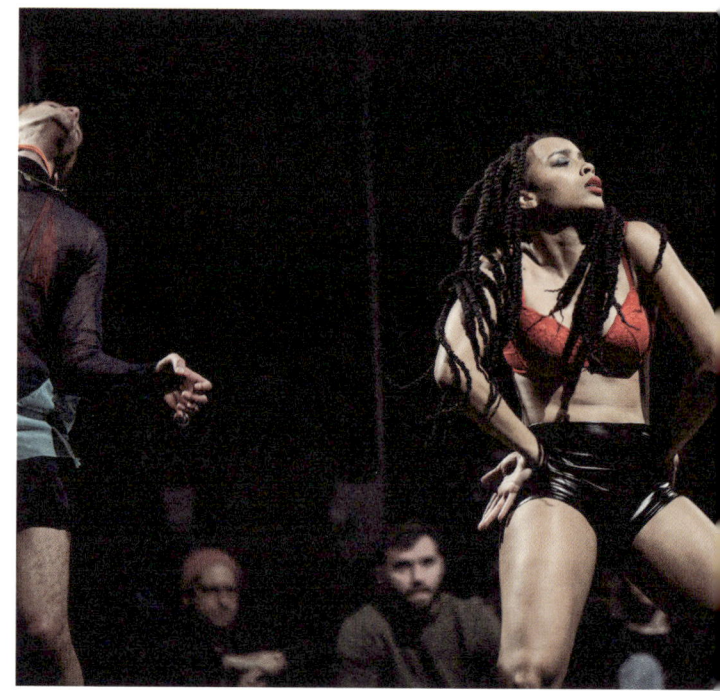

Rant, 2019—

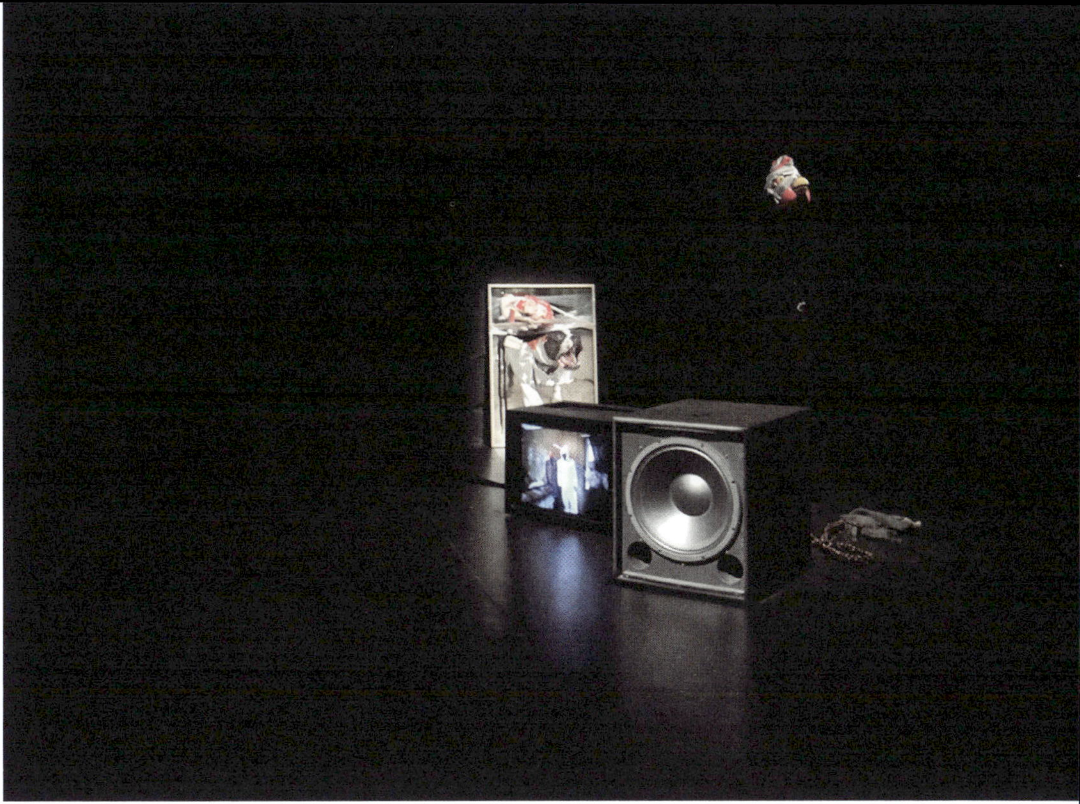

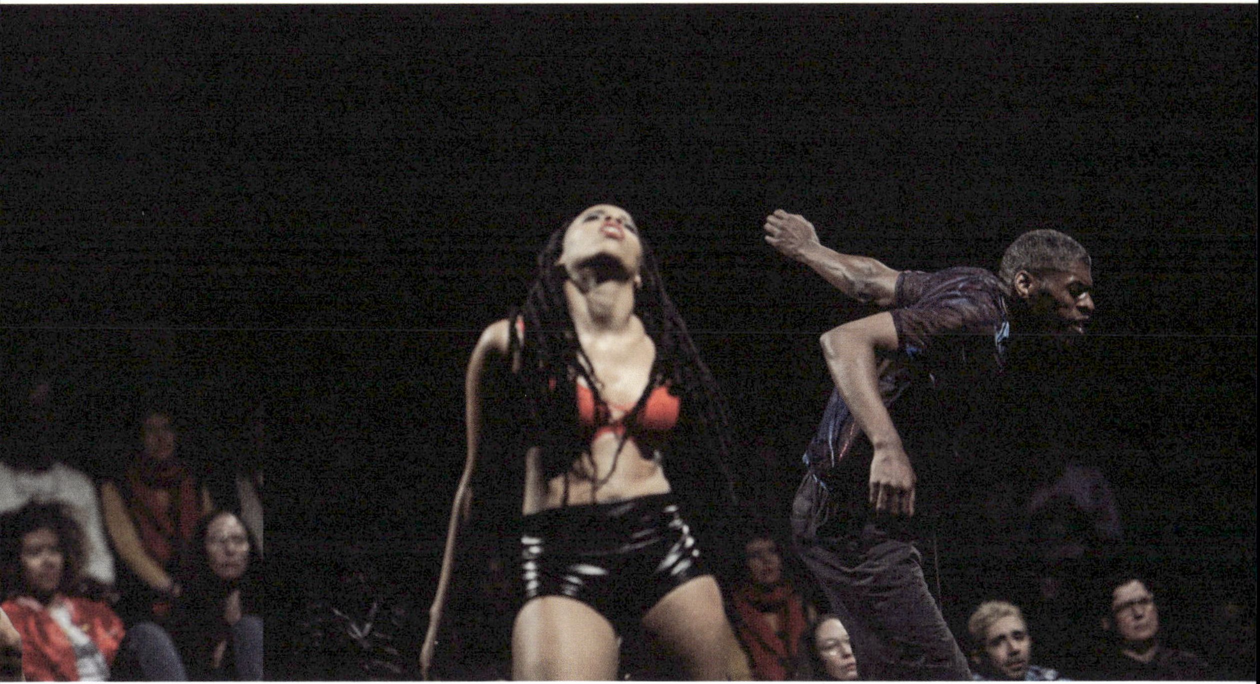

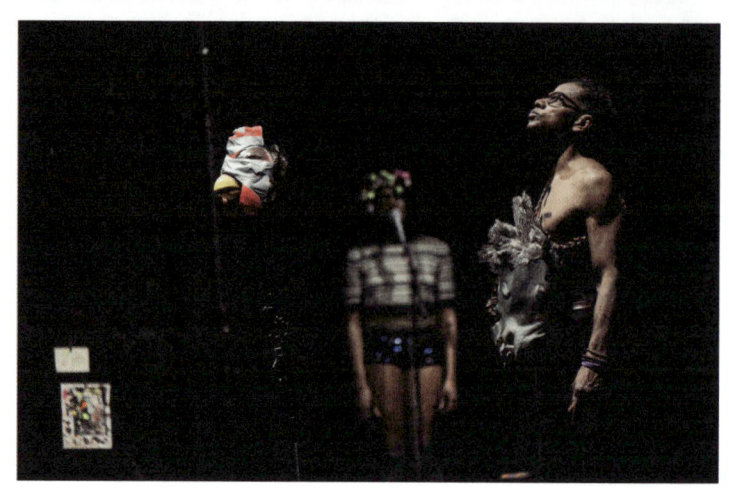

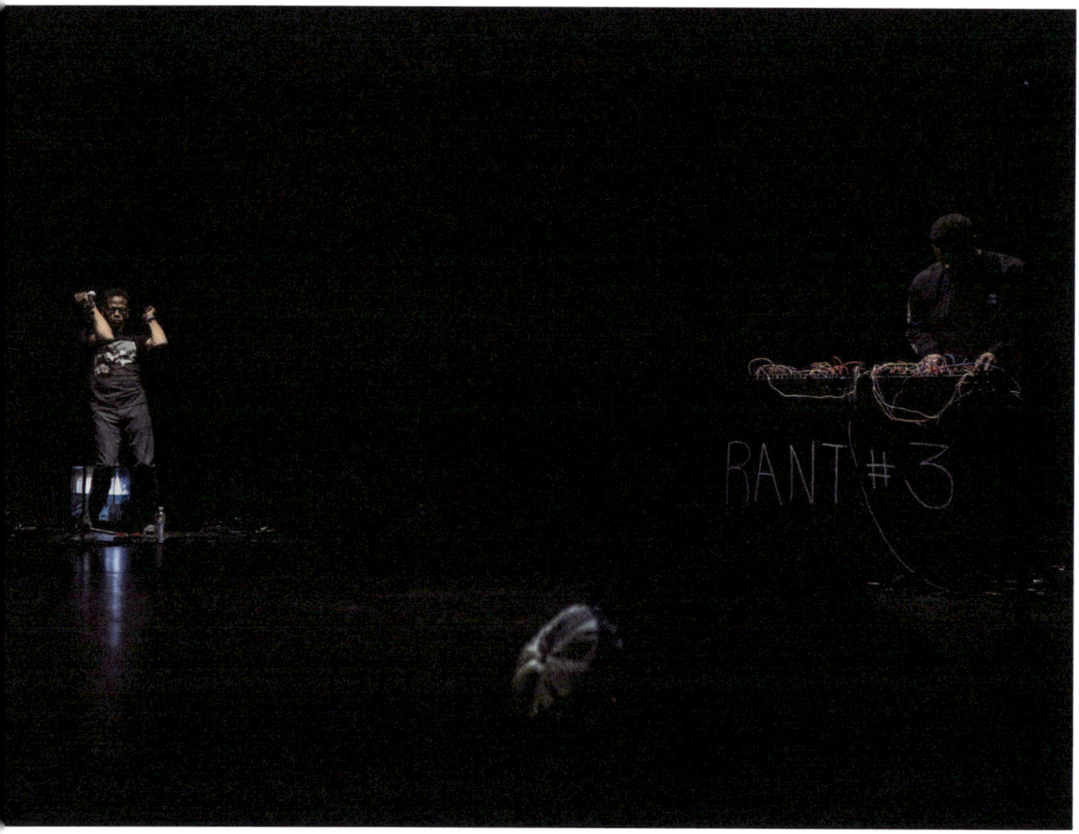

Rant, 2019—

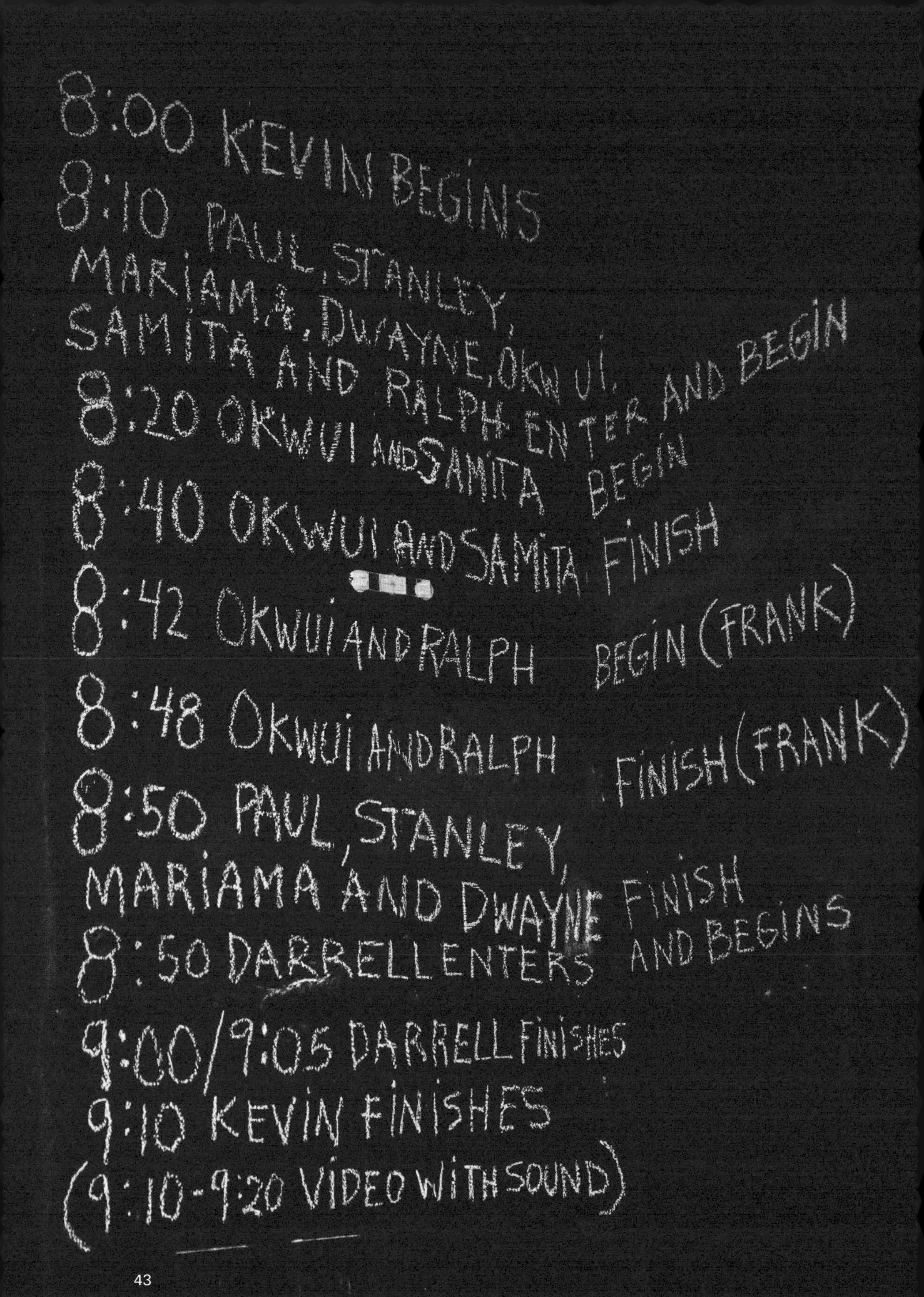

8:00 KEVIN BEGINS
8:10 PAUL, STANLEY,
MARIAMA, DWAYNE, OKWUI,
SAMITA AND RALPH ENTER AND BEGIN
8:20 OKWUI AND SAMITA BEGIN
8:40 OKWUI AND SAMITA FINISH

8:42 OKWUI AND RALPH BEGIN (FRANK)

8:48 OKWUI AND RALPH FINISH (FRANK)
8:50 PAUL, STANLEY,
MARIAMA AND DWAYNE FINISH
8:50 DARRELL ENTERS AND BEGINS

9:00/9:05 DARRELL FINISHES
9:10 KEVIN FINISHES
(9:10-9:20 VIDEO WITH SOUND)

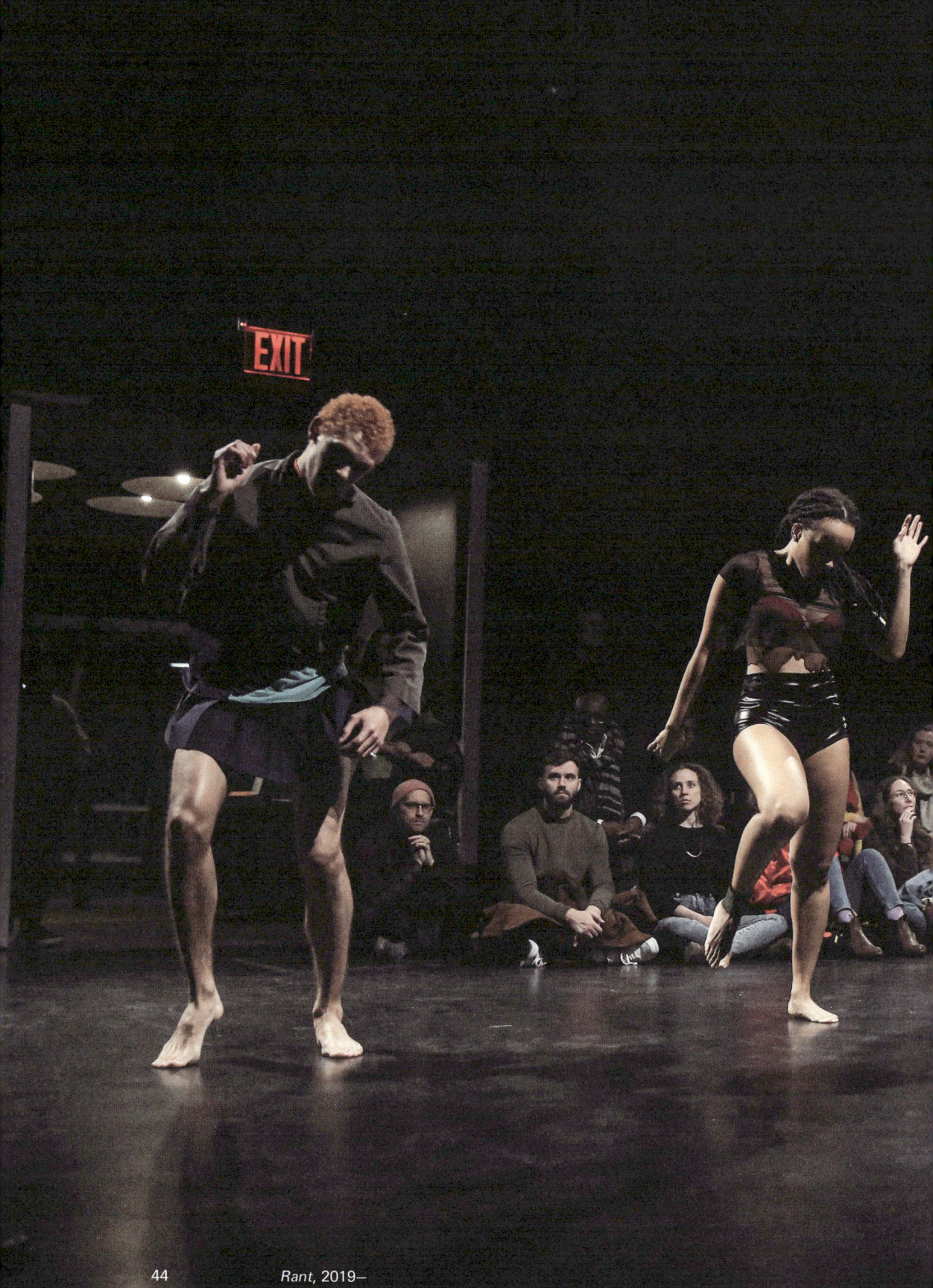

EXIT

Rant, 2019—

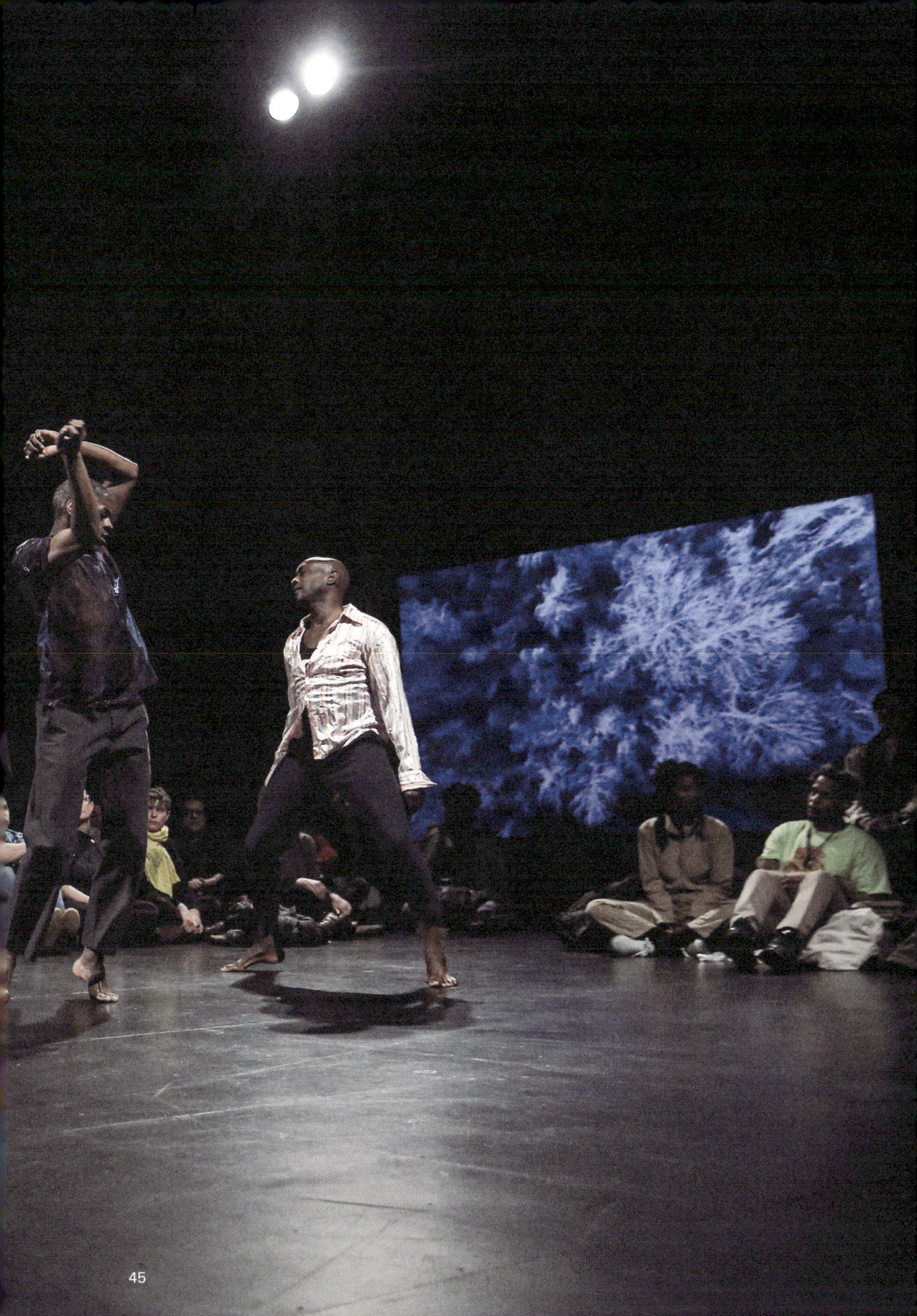

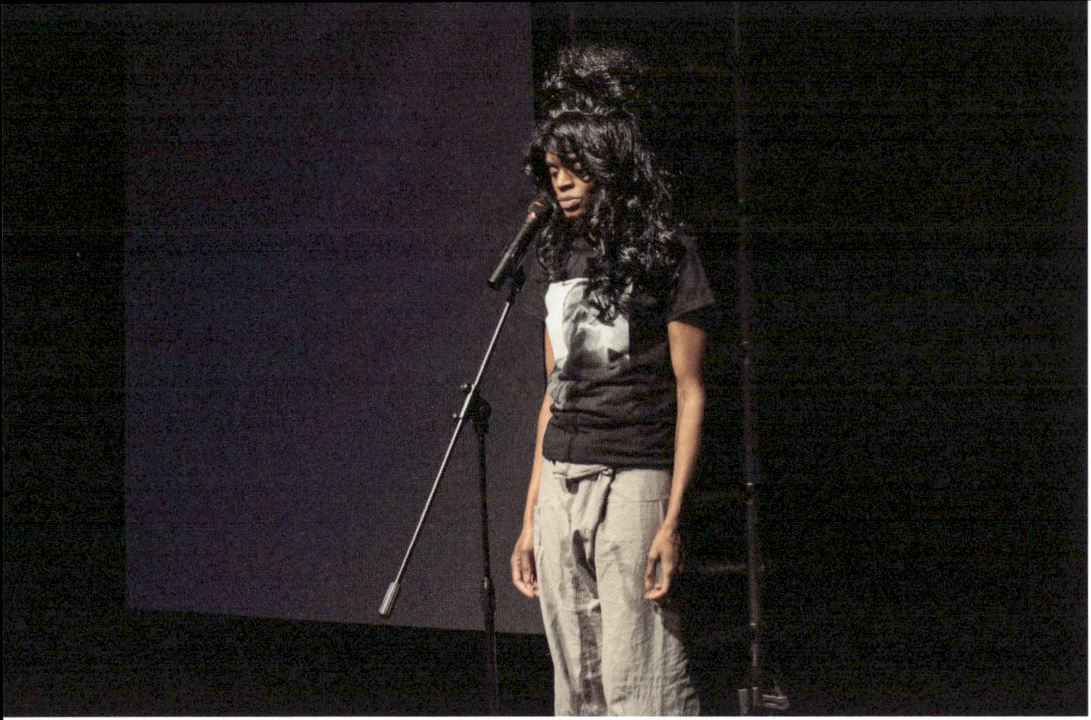

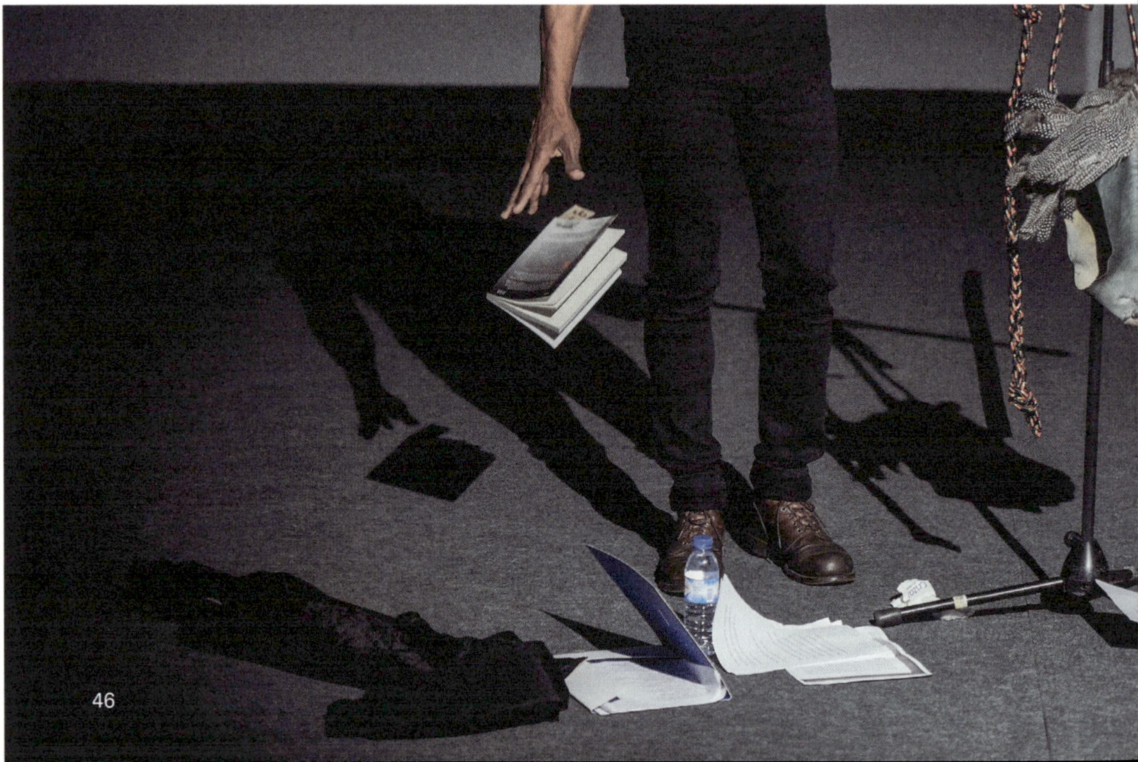

cry for the whole world
Okwui Okpokwasili

He made me cry.
Or he asked if I could.
He said he couldn't.
And I said I thought everyone can.
And he said something to the effect of maybe everyone can cry.
But I'm talking about a wail.
Well.

Hmmm.

We embarked on wailing research.
Not everyone can scream and howl and wail in their grief.
For some, it's unseemly, that loud expression of wretchedness.
Embarrassing.
For some, it would be a beginning without end, the body breaking from the inside out and always. All that would be left of them would be the howl.

But there are people who appear to get swallowed up in the black hole of grief and are able to open their throats right at the smallest and most dense point, right at the singularity, and emit a piercing wail. Then somehow they emerge, apparently intact, and ready to get swallowed up again. Or maybe they just have clear purpose and a refined sense of their craft.

We looked for these practitioners.
K found a book that led us to some of them.

Hmmm.

I said that I wished we could hear them wail. What would it sound like?
He said yes. But maybe it's better to not hear?
I said probably.

Hmmm.

It has to be a wail for the whole world.

Can you wail for five minutes?
Can you wail for six minutes?
Can you wail for seven minutes?
Can you wail for . . . ?
Can you pick up this tambourine?
Can you walk backwards?

Hmmm.

You'll need a crying book.

What is in a crying book?

It is a book that contains the collective images:
of kissing a loved one who is taking their final breath in hospice,
of the bright, piercing eyes of a loved one now passed, giving you
"that look,"
of splayed and scattered limbs along a rutted road,
of square meters of flattened building blocks and knowing that
generations of families are entombed there,
of mass gravesites,
of AR-15s,
of munitions,
of babies being pulled out of the arms of their mothers,
of the body of a lifeless toddler washed up on a Mediterranean shore,

of office workers flying out of buildings that have become infernos,
of the remains of women raped and split open from the womb,
of babies pulled out of crushed mothers,
of people broken by falling aid pallets of food dropped on their
starved bodies,
of people scouring rubble to find bodies or parts of bodies for the
twin purposes of recognition and closure—
each page elicits a howl of grief,
each page touches the suppurating wound.

To move through each page is to move through a wailing score
that holds within it a plea to bear no more death than what must
be borne, and to have some grace when bearing it.

The crying book opens a space to scream and rage and moan and
plummet to the small and dense place within, where the volcanic
ache of loss erupts.

And we cry for the whole wide world.

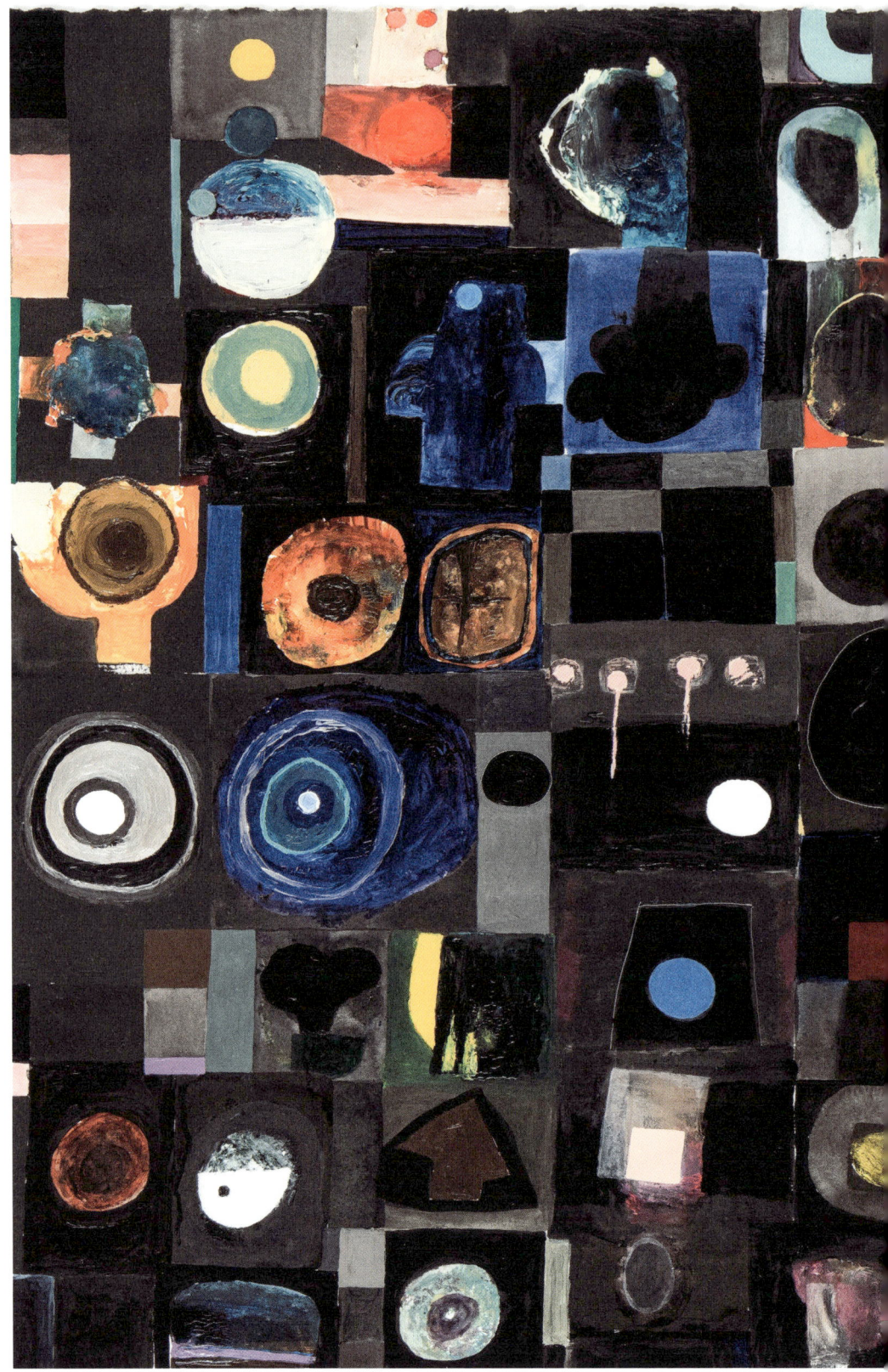

Untitled (Rapture weft), 2020—

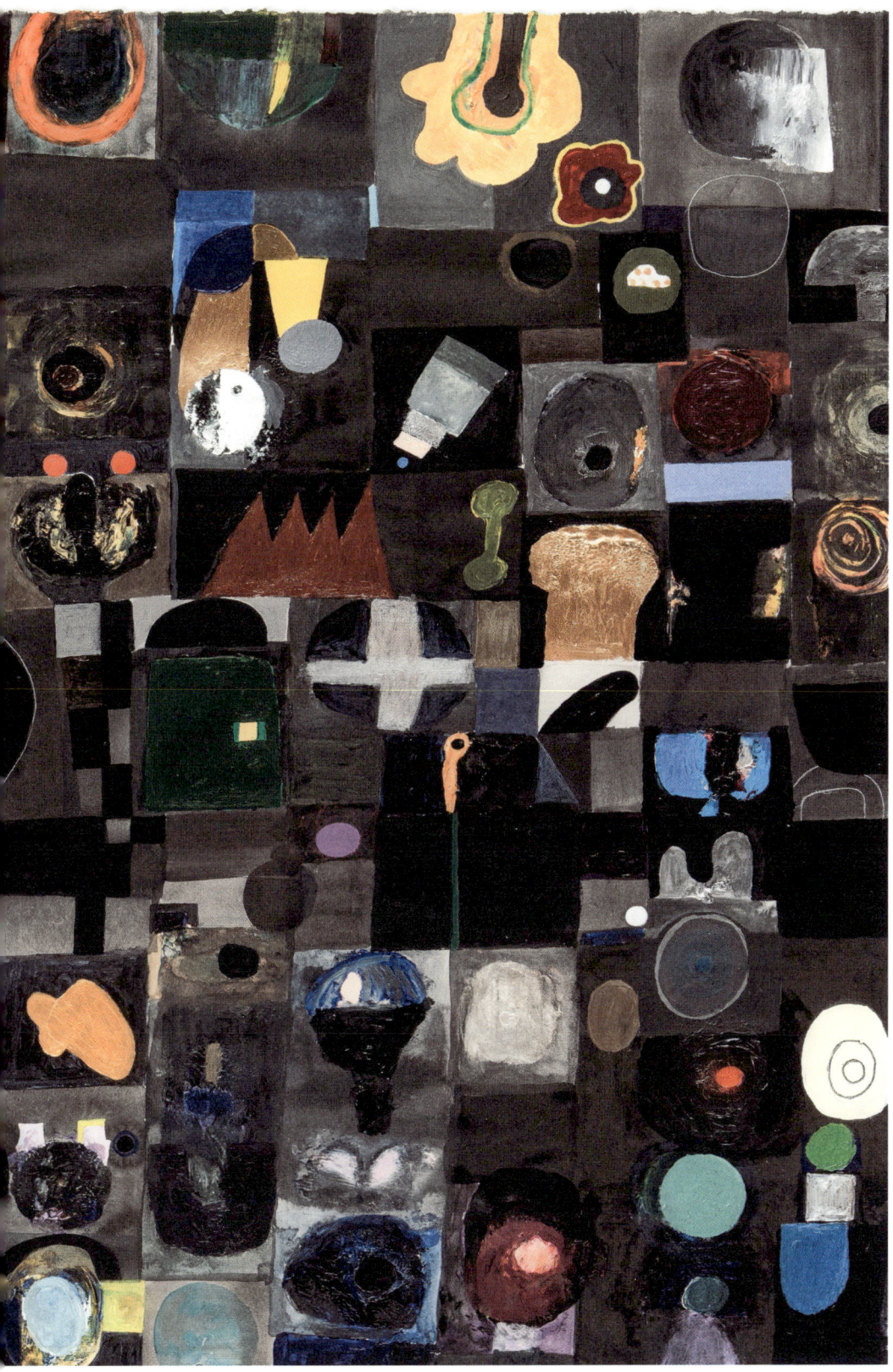

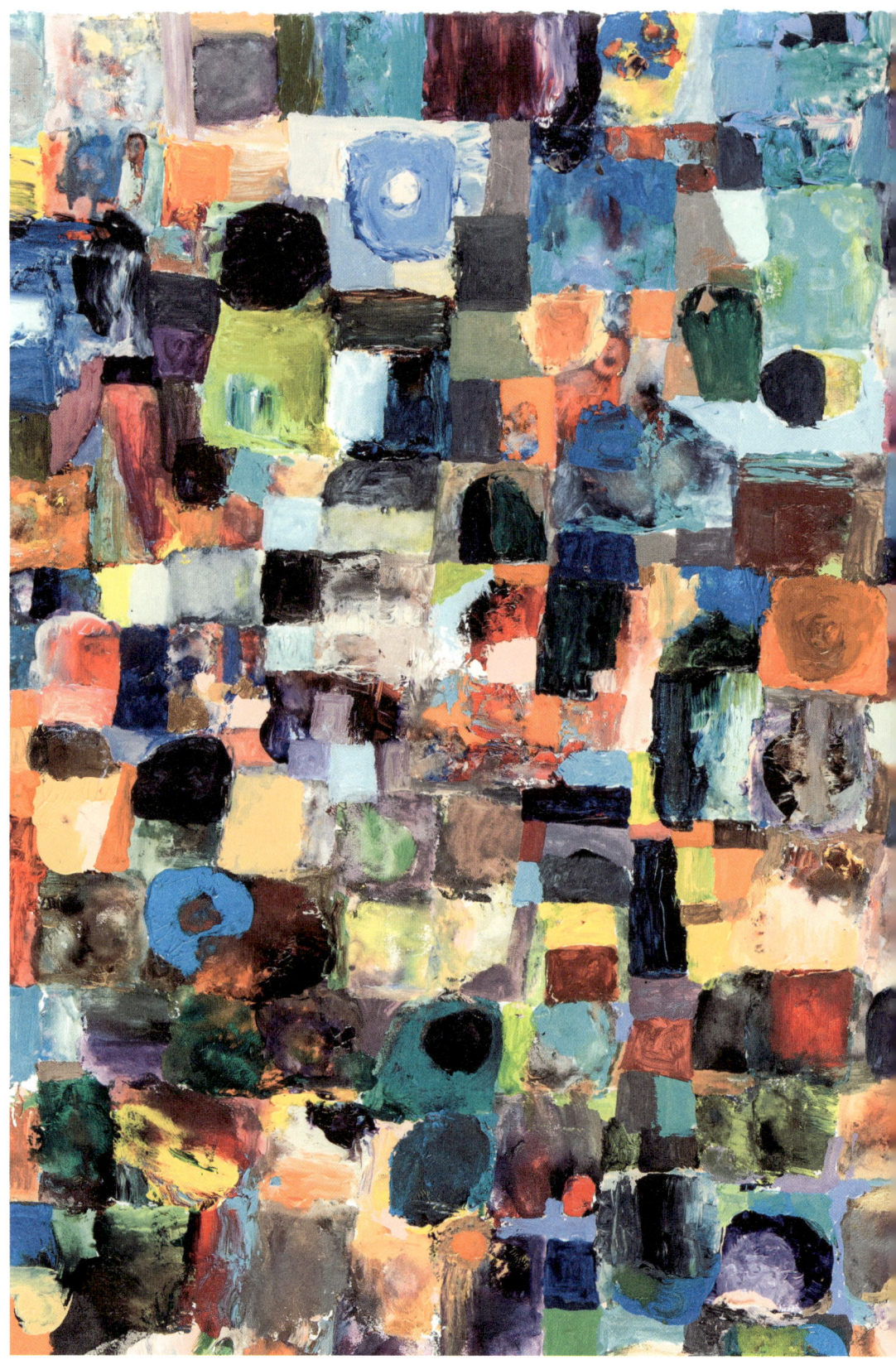

Untitled (Rapture weft), 2020—

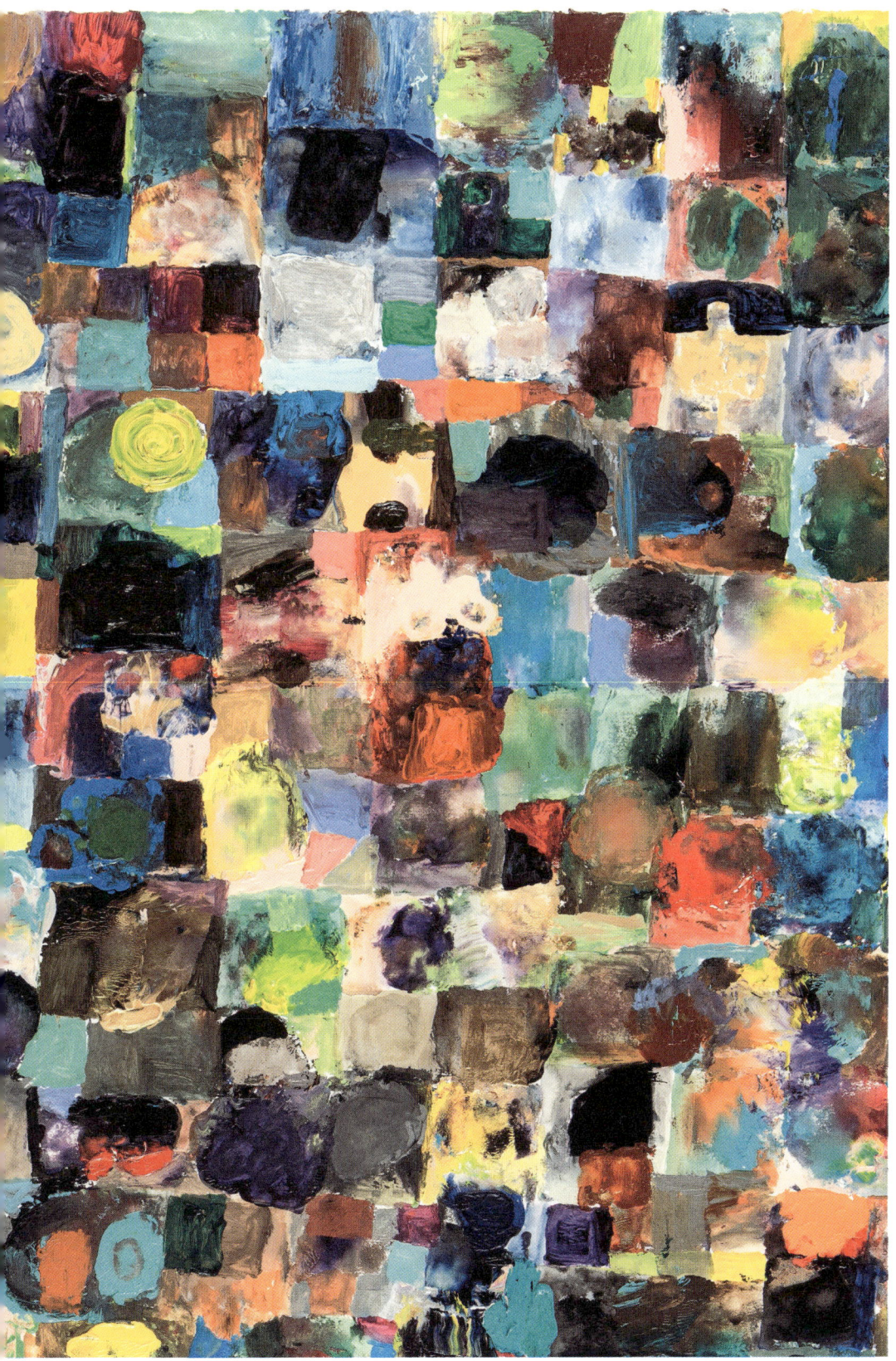

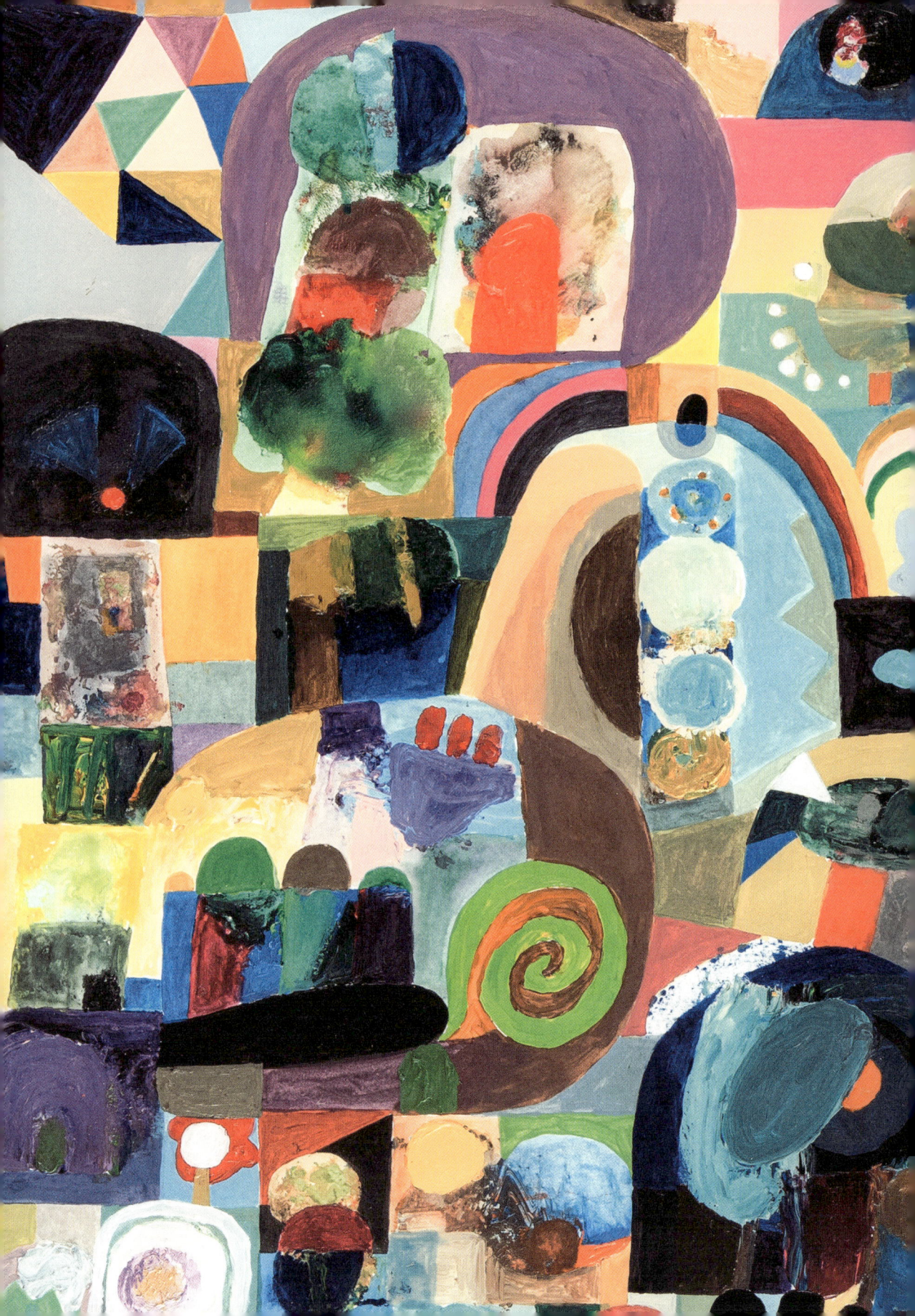

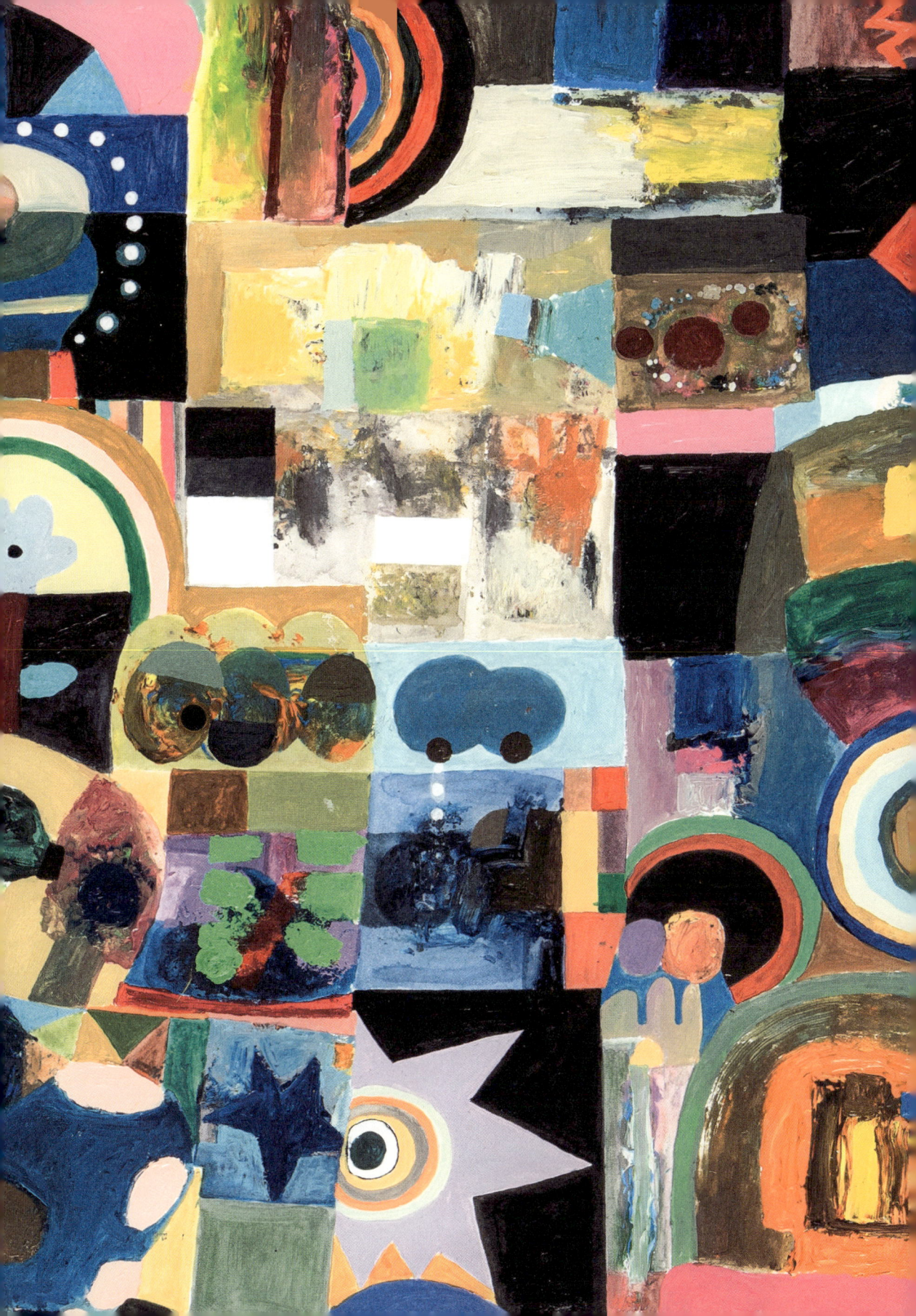

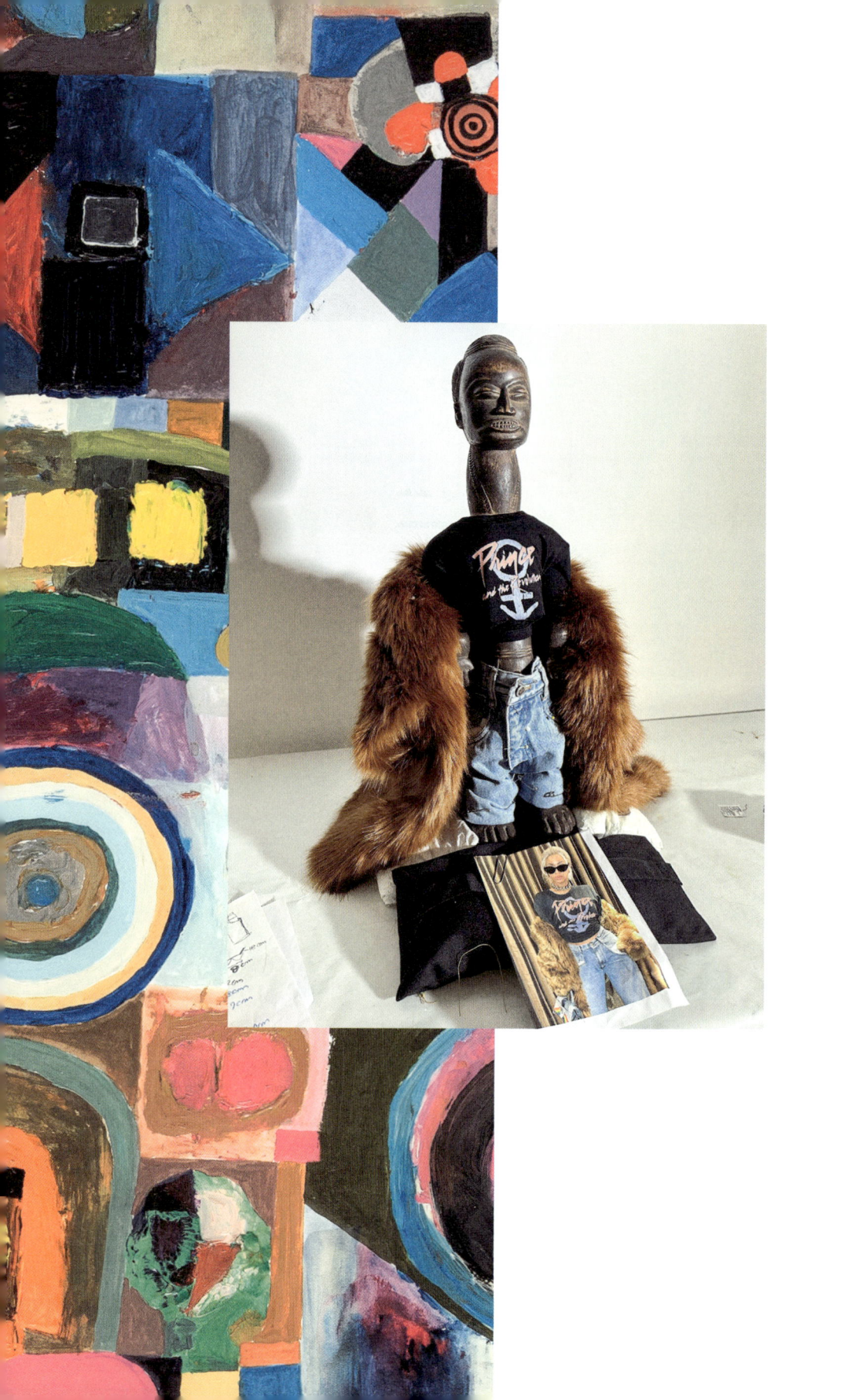

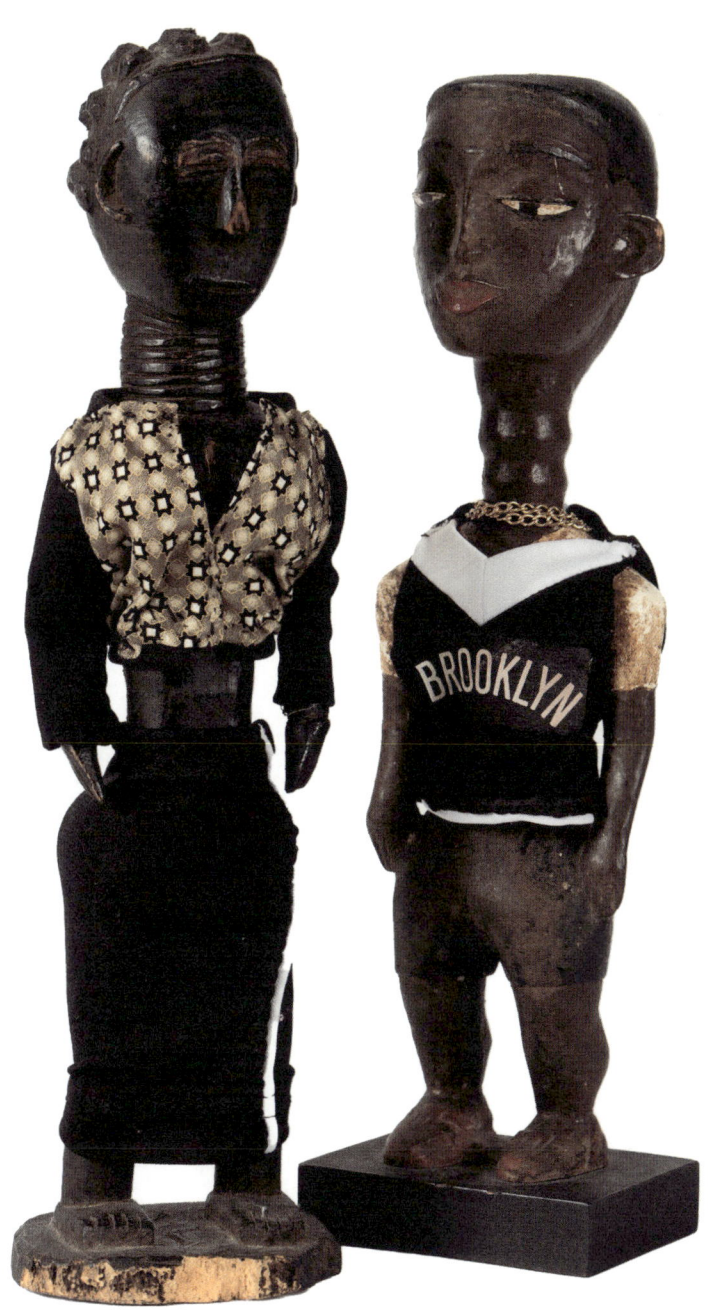

Consecration of Ancestor Figures, 2015—24

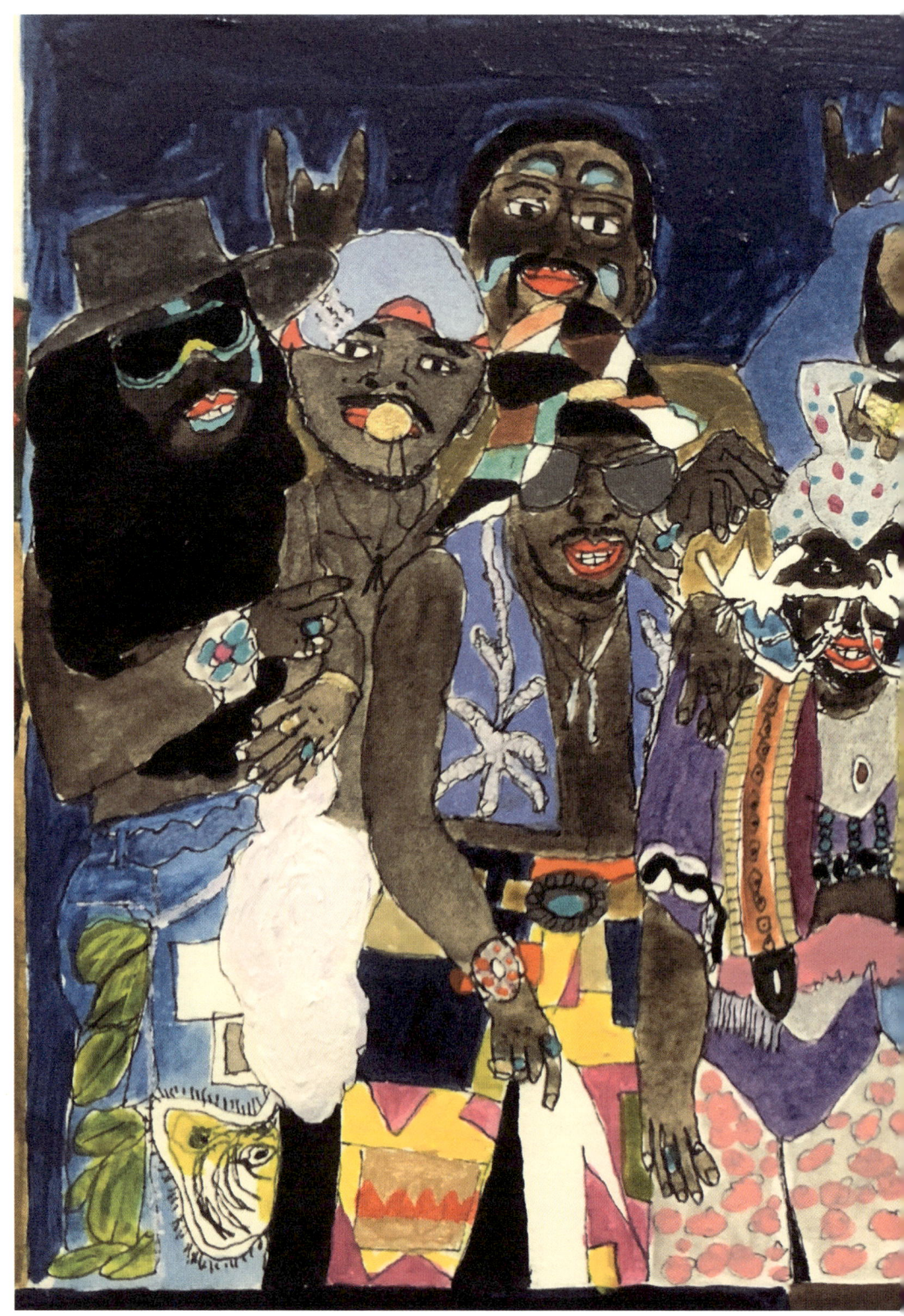

Untitled (The greatest [Black] art history story ever told. Unfinished), 2015—

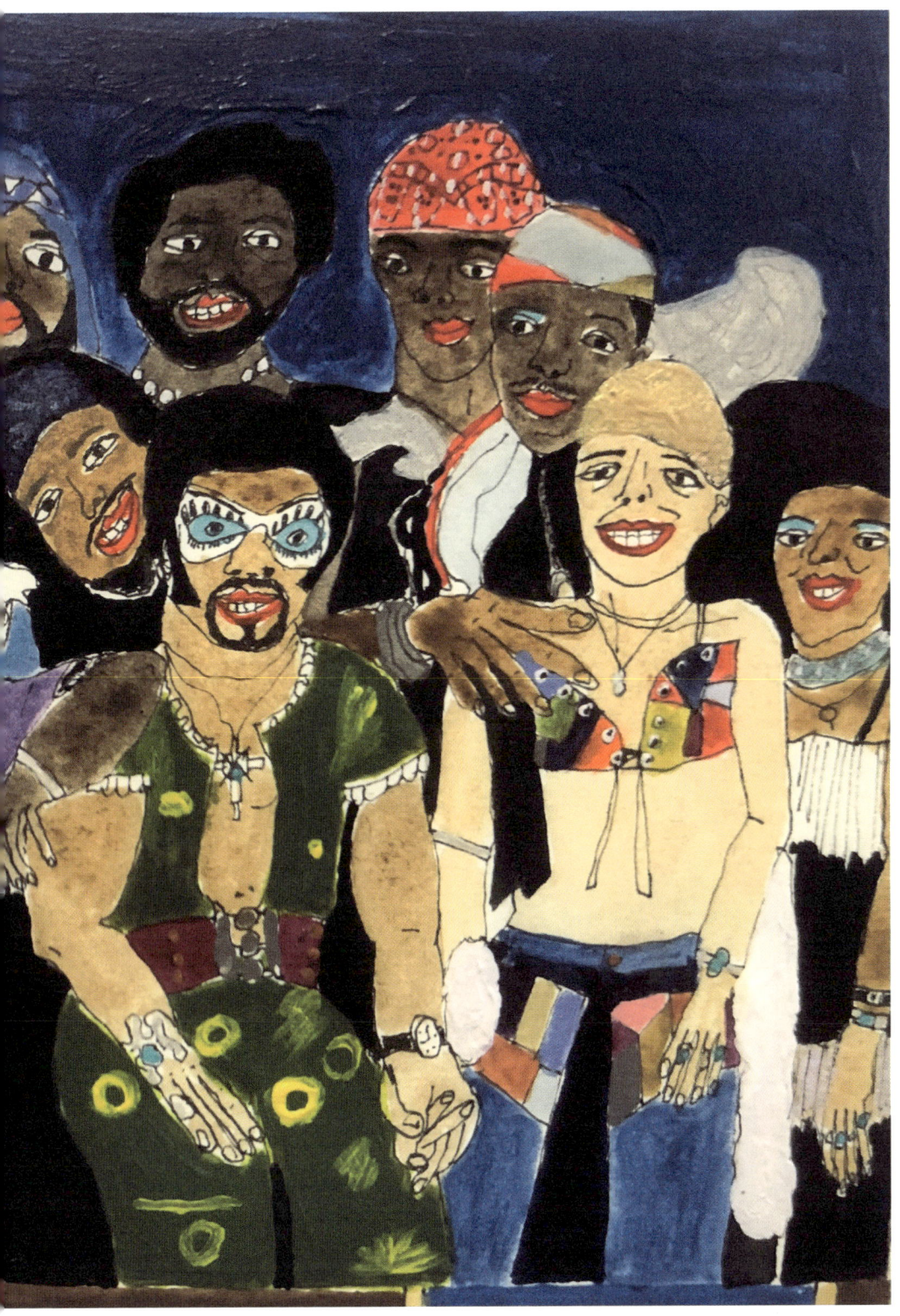

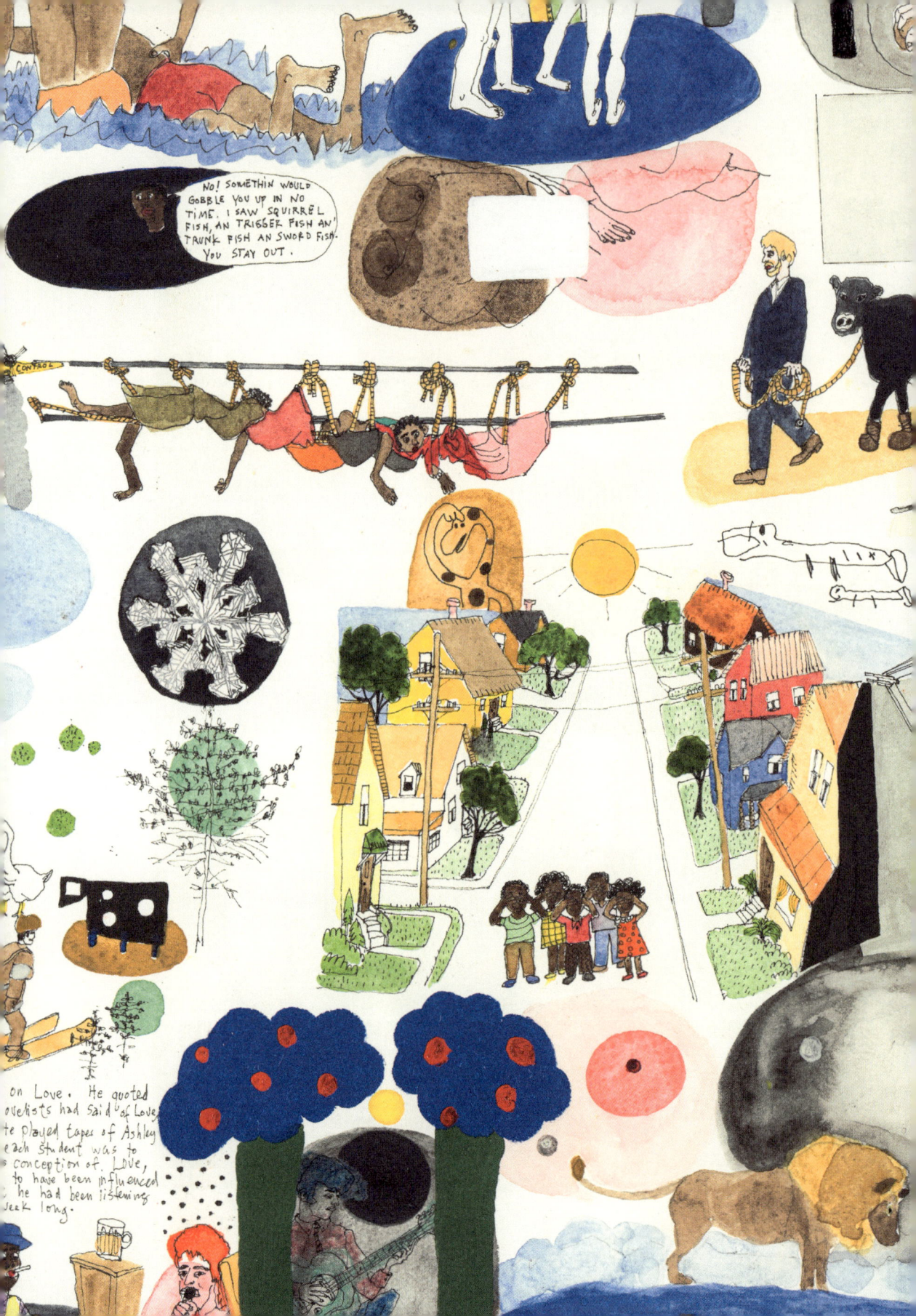

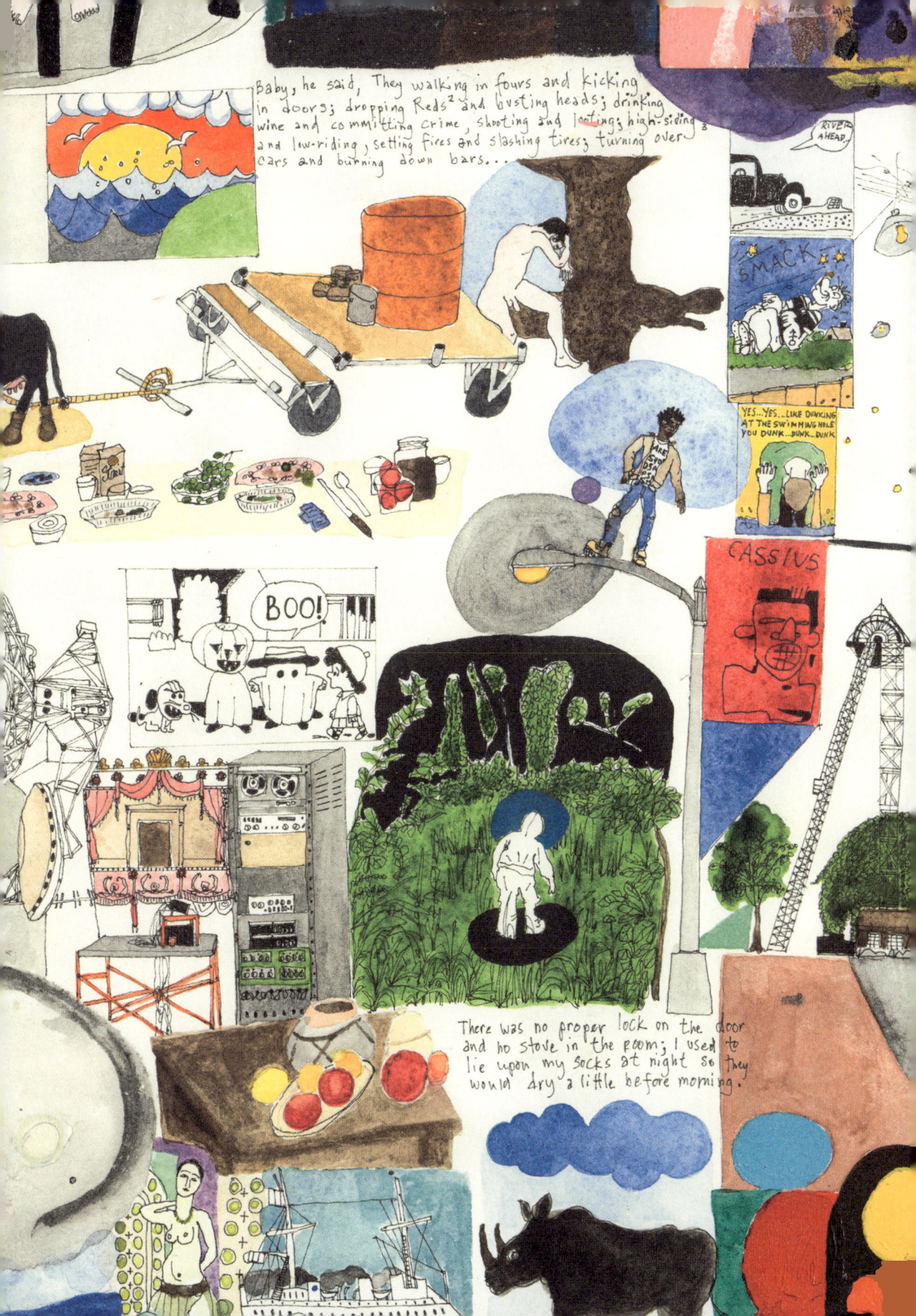

Baby, he said, They walking in fours and kicking in doors; dropping Reds² and busting heads; drinking wine and committing crime, shooting and looting, high-siding and low-riding, setting fires and slashing tires; turning over cars and burning down bars...

RIVER AHEAD.

SMACK

YES...YES...LIKE DUNKING AT THE SWIMMING HOLE YOU DUNK...DUNK...DUNK

CASSIVS

BOO!

There was no proper lock on the door and no stove in the room; I used to lie upon my socks at night so they would dry a little before morning.

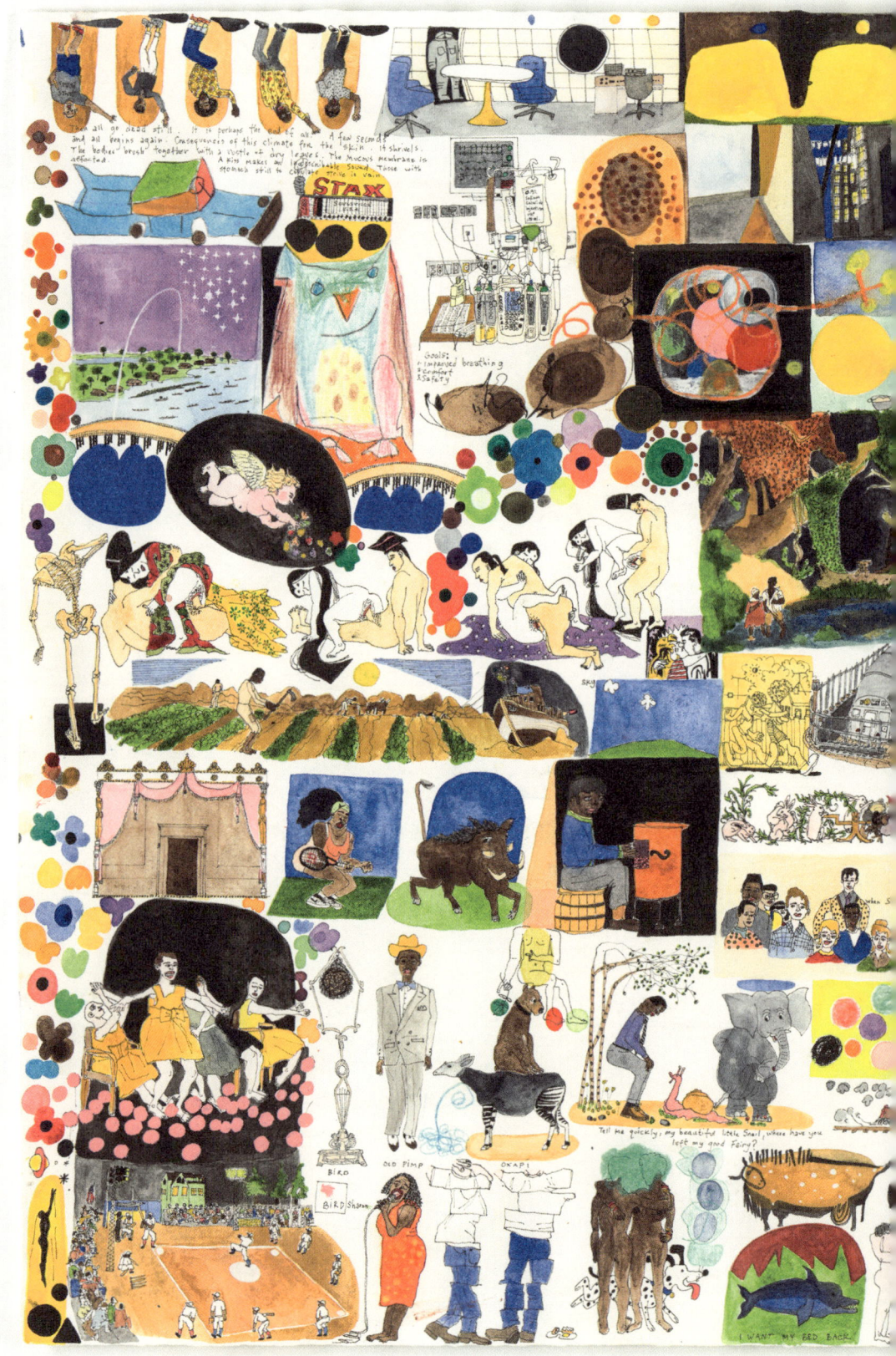

Untitled (The greatest [Black] art history story ever told. Unfinished), 2015—

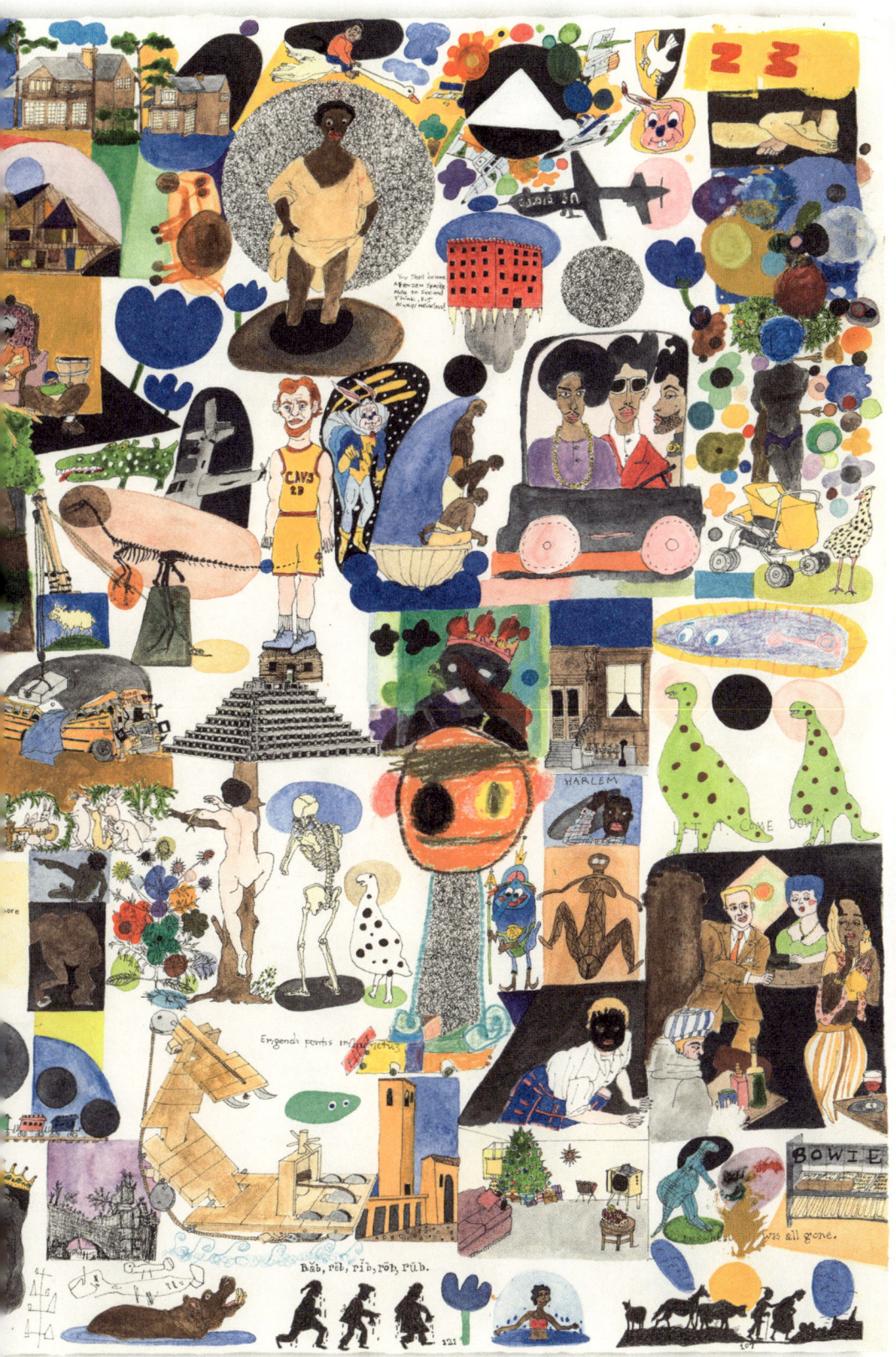

63

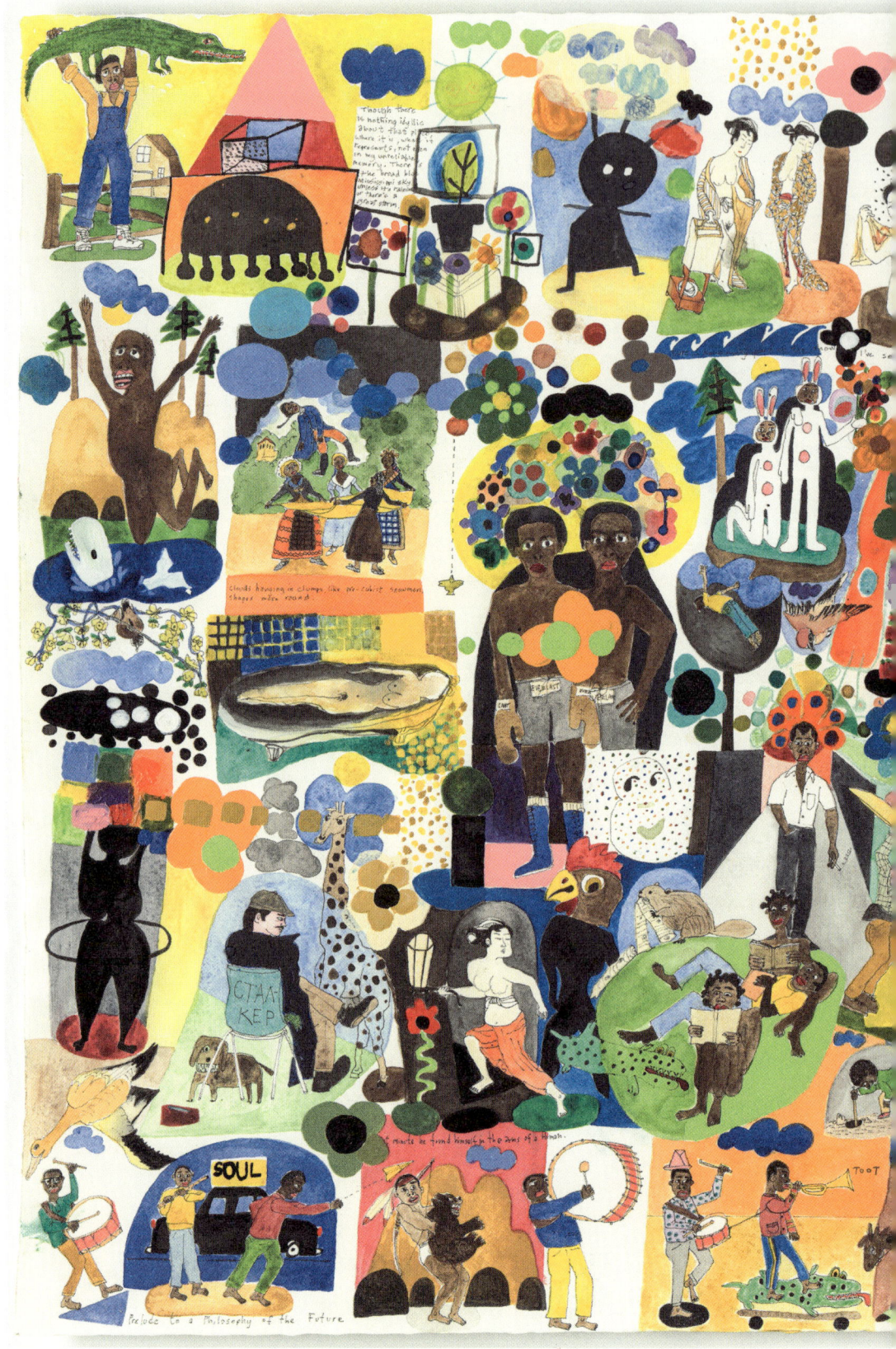

Untitled (The greatest [Black] art history story ever told. Unfinished), 2015—

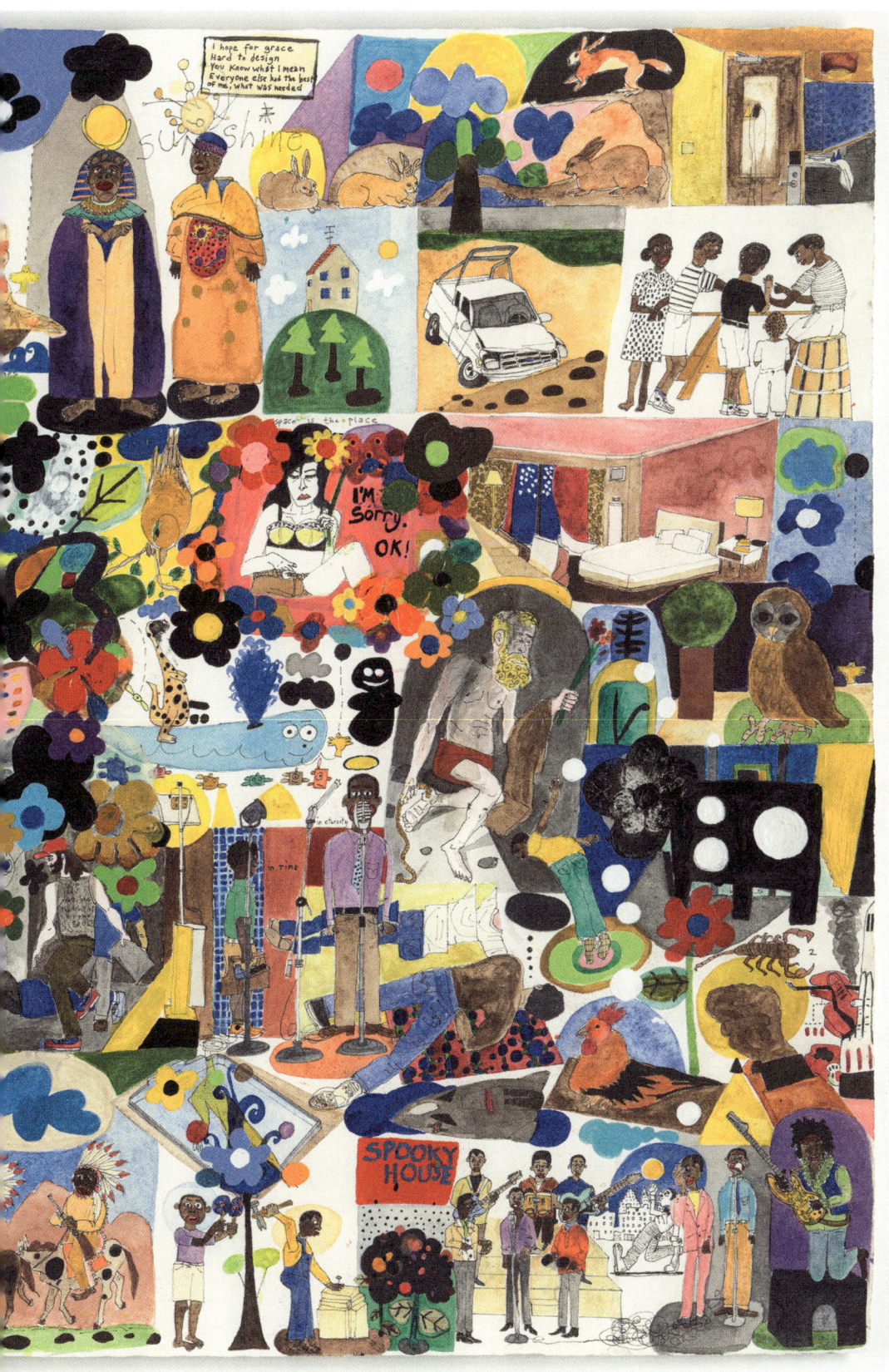

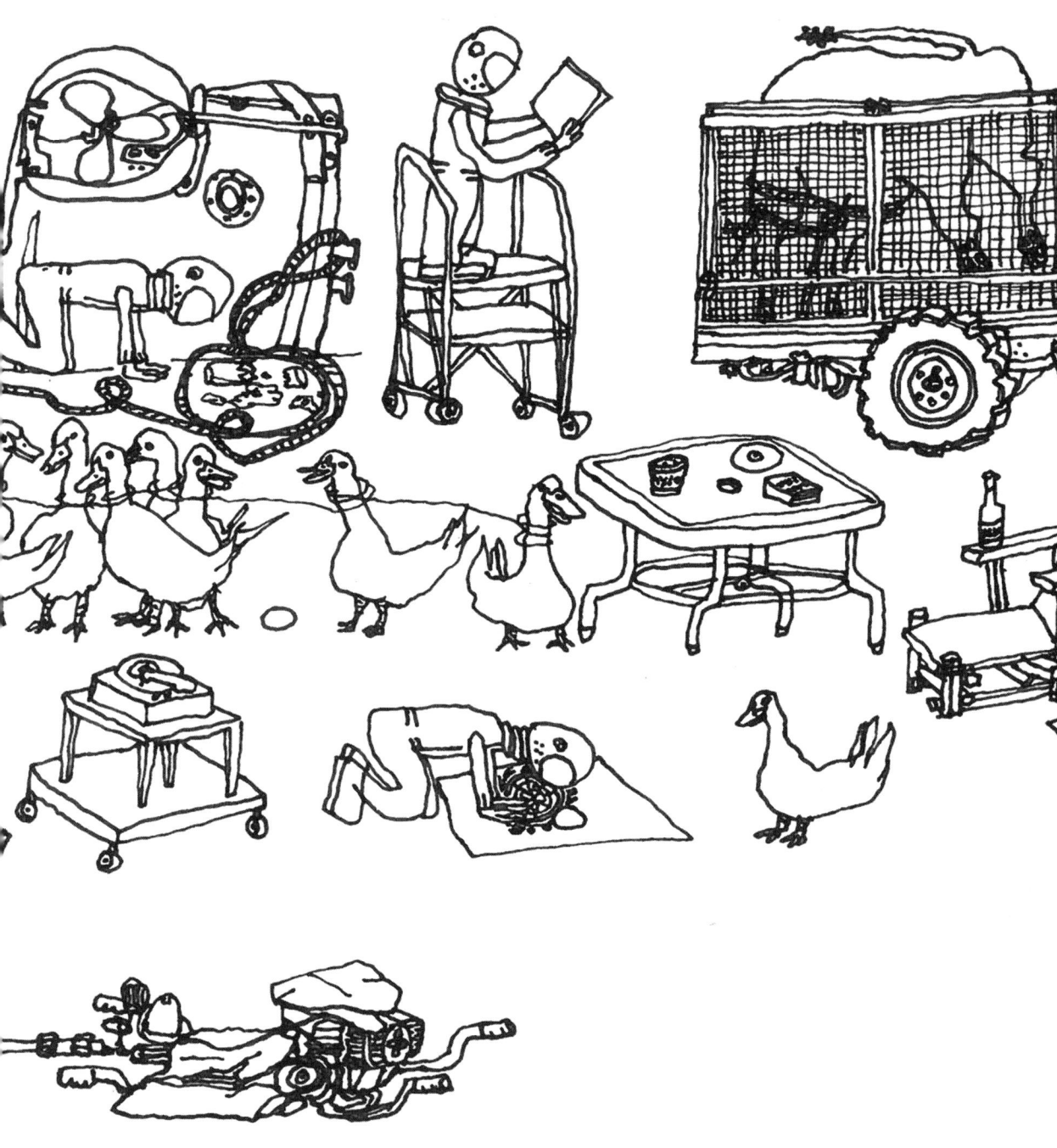

Conversation on Drawing
Ralph Lemon and Kari Rittenbach

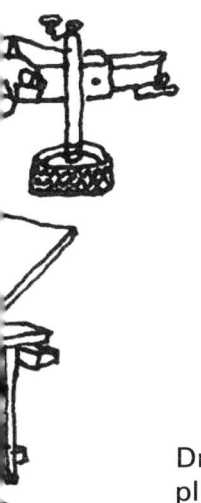

Drawing has long been a critical part of Ralph Lemon's interdisciplinary practice, although carried out in a more diaristic, notational, and meditative mode than his performance and video works intended for a viewing public. *Ceremonies Out of the Air* sets key drawing series in dialogue with contemporaneous artworks, tracing the development and recursion of Lemon's concerns and themes across media. Without the directionality of a score or the system of a diagram, his nonschematic and often tender drawings raise questions about signification, sequencing, and even their own materiality—indexing the spirit of irreverence and ephemerality inherent to his practice. Many of his earliest sketches have been lost to time and circumstance.

Lemon spoke to me about subjects ranging from his relationship to verisimilitude and the color implied by an ink outline to series including the *Spaceman Drawings* (2008–10), which render the challenge of communicating between wildly different universes, and his ongoing narrative epic, *Untitled (The greatest [Black] art history story ever told. Unfinished)* (2015–). His latest works on paper, from *Untitled (Rapture weft)* (2020–), nest concentric mandalas in *ichimatsu*-like patterns, in deepening tones that commence an inevitable, joyful fade to black. —KR

Kari Rittenbach: The first time you worked with Connie Butler was for *On Line: Drawing Through the Twentieth Century* (2010–11), an exhibition that expanded the modernist historical perspective with regard to drawing, which is typically presented as a logical progression of ideas and forms. By considering the line as a point moving through space, the show allowed for dance to enter into this recalibration. A handful of choreographers were invited to participate, including you.

The piece you did there, *Untitled* [2008], with Okwui Okpokwasili, detoured the trajectory of the line into an exchange, or a complex and emotional dialogue that developed between the two of you [p. 23]. What did it mean to be included in a survey on drawing then?

Ralph Lemon: Connie contacted me in early 2010 and asked if I would like to be part of that show. At the time she didn't ask specifically for a performance, so I assumed that I could suggest anything I was working on or interested in. One of my proposals was to assemble a group of professional mourners/wailers who had migrated to the NYC area—public wailers, moirologists, mutes, they're called. I thought that would be an interesting event for the MoMA Atrium. I also shared with her what I considered line drawings that I was working on at the time, from my ongoing practice. The *Spaceman Drawings* (2008–10), in fact [pp. 32, 66, 87, 122, 168].

But Connie wanted a dance—and that was that.

KR: Had you previously worked without a proscenium stage in such an audience-porous space?

RL: It was an audience space that neither Okwui nor I were so privy to prior to this invitation—the surround; some people huddling, fixed, very involved in watching, and other people walking in and out and throughout the space, interested in what we were doing, maybe, or not at all. The Atrium is an entire ecosystem. The space is vast, and it is difficult to determine what is going on from an audience point of view. Okwui and I brought an experiment to the space, and/or an argument. And some crying—elicited by Okwui— so the public wailing proposal wasn't completely lost. My drawings were not part of that experiment-argument. But now they are in this show with Connie years later.

KR: They found their way.

RL: They found their way to a new argument-experiment.

KR: The *Spaceman Drawings* came about while you were working with your Mississippi collaborator Walter Carter after the project for *Spaceship* (2007) began. Associated with this constellation of works is an ink-pen sketch that you made especially for Walter, *Instruction Drawing (Spaceship)* (2006). Can you speak about how drawing featured in your exchange, and what he did with it?

RL: The work with Walter and his community, friends, and relatives, which went on for quite a long time—and continues—is an exercise in the refraction and translation of cultures and bodies and native tongues, or put more simply, how we talk to one another. I went down South as an artist with a particular intention, partly curious and partly exploitative. I can come and go. My being in Little Yazoo, Walter's small town, a town he couldn't easily leave, was initially a research trip that became something else. What do we do, what do I do here? Let's do something together. It was figuring out across very different Black American generations and cultures how to do that.

The specific idea of space travel came from Walter's generational and a more general cultural disbelief—though significantly, not a conspiratorial one—that American astronauts ever went to the moon in 1969. Walter didn't think it was possible. It became a kind of argument that activated the work he and I were already doing. Okay then: What if we build something—an object, a spaceship—and try to make it fly? To see if it is possible or not? We brought his son, Warren (Red) Carter, and his good friend Lloyd Williams into the conversation as well.

KR: That team worked on both spaceships, right? Eventually there were two.

RL: *Instruction Drawing* was for the first spaceship, in 2006. The garden spaceship came second, in 2010 [pp. 118–19]. Lloyd, by and large, built both of them; he became the architect and fabricator of the ongoing project. We began by talking about building something that could (possibly) fly. After there was an agreement to build an actual spaceship, I went away and then sent that drawing in the mail. They adapted the drawing into *Spaceship #1* (2007), which will be in the PS1 show.

KR: The drawing was not exactly prescriptive but rather held part of the conversation you were involved in there.

RL: It has been an interesting kind of play—I would send a drawing as a question and know it would be translated and communicated differently than if I sent it to a fabricator in New York City.

And then there was capital exchange: how much people were being paid, the labor element, was very important too. It became an anchor for all the other complicated things around the relationship and our indeterminate collaboration: the money part. If you work (or play), this is how much you get paid for it, or how much it costs. Figuring out the value of their participation, and the exchange.

KR: Does it seem like that conversation happens in the dance world as well, in terms of bringing people together? You are not building an architecture, but you are building. There is an exchange of labor and the production of value.

RL: I'm sure it has changed since my growing up in the dance world. Back in the 1980s and 1990s, there seemed to be more of a belief system in being together and sharing the same kind of movement, dance, aesthetic styles—that kind of value production. In my case, I was proposing a movement combine/mash-up from all the different movement personalities of the modern dancers I collaborated with, also pulling from Meredith Monk, Merce Cunningham (and John Cage), Trisha Brown, or Pina Bausch, or older (Mary Wigman), or imagined, or something more experimental. It was basically about getting a clear translation of some white modernist movement idea that determined what kind of dance you were making. And in talking, moving, and agreeing on a movement-invention (to sound and/or to silence), you share a point of view. That sharing was also perhaps the currency, the labor exchange. The little money that was paid out and earned was gestural.

In my history of working with dancers, there is a common acceptance of dance as a language, foreign or otherwise. In the case of my *Geography Trilogy* (1996–2004)—which disrupted everything I thought I knew about modern dance and how I valued it—this language spectrum was not completely understood, if at all. It's also about personalities, and getting along. I suspect the same thing was happening with Walter. But the language, and the place we occupied, was another planet.

KR: Maybe the drawing was helping to create that language in a nondance context?

RL: Maybe. I don't think Walter or Lloyd thought of the drawing I sent as art. It was clearly practical. That was one of the more beautiful things about that relationship; was this collaboration art or not art? Does it matter?

KR: It was always a question.

RL: A big question. I don't think Lloyd thought of the spaceships he built as artwork. But they were things he was proud of building. I didn't use the word *art* a lot or at all in our conversations. I did show them Andrei Tarkovsky's *Solaris* (1972) and Jean-Luc Godard's *Alphaville* (1965), while on a TV in another room old Westerns from the 1950s and 1960s were being constantly broadcast at full volume. Neither of us really understood what it was we were doing. There was a certain amount of projection that in my case was purposeful. We liked being in each other's company. That was obviously the center of the relationship.

KR: I'd like to ask a question about *Untitled (The greatest [Black] art history story ever told. Unfinished)* that started around 2015 [pp. 58–65]. How did the first drawing come about? Were you aware that it would be a series?

RL: I would say this for all the drawing, and the rest of the practice: when I start something that interests me, I know it's going to go on for some time until it collapses or is transformed into something else. I begin with something that interests me, and then at some point it becomes a series that ultimately finds a conclusion that opens up a portal to somewhere else.

The *Untitled (GBAHSET)* series is larger and more colorful than anything that came before. What was interesting about the earlier figurative works—my notebooks, the *Young Baldwin Drawings* (2004), and the *Spaceman Drawings*—was the way in which I was drawing, to me, clearly Black characters without coloring them black or brown.

KR: Just using an ink outline.

RL: Creating an idea of Blackness without color (except for the occasional dash of red on the lips). This wasn't an argument I was having with the art world at the time. It was my own musing. What is that? What might that mean, not mean? The drawings seemed complete; nothing was absent. Eventually the evolution of the work required color.

KR: Compared to the *Spaceman Drawings*, the overall saturation of *Untitled (GBAHSET)* is really impressive. The series is also very colorful in terms of the whole chromatic spectrum. And in many places, often because of the subject matter, this brings the 1960s and 1970s to mind—a kind of acid technicolor.

RL: It's an almost sophomoric sense of making something colorful. But if you're looking at the actual drawings, and the details, there are historical and political marks being made as well. I'm appropriating images that are interesting and urgent to me, collecting them, and again, trying to tell a sort of abstract narrative that I invent for myself until it fills a whole sheet of paper. The narrative for a particular drawing is finished once the paper is completely covered and I've run out of room. Then it's on to the next chapter(s).

It is clear to me that the series will never be finished. That is an intentional element of the work that feels daunting but also activating. I've found something that will take the rest of my life to do, because this series is dealing with charged places, architecture, and people historically and presently, and also in some sort of illusory future, and none of that is going to stop. The images keep coming.

KR: It's a bit like *One Thousand and One Nights*, which is also syncretic.

RL: It proposes a certain kind of freedom because it's infinite.

KR: Do you feel the same way about the series *Untitled (Rapture weft)* (2020–), or is that work in a completely different register [pp. 50–55]?

RL: I know that series will have an end, because it's abstract, perhaps. Their unreliable emotional propositions? I think because of the abstraction it is inherent that they disappear. I might reach the point that I don't want to continue *Untitled (GBAHSET)* anymore, but that would have to come at some deep exhaustion with their stakes, which are stakes I will never not be engaged by.

KR: Perhaps that connects to the modality of exhaustion in your work more generally, to the question of how much you can take on or how much the body can take on?

RL: I tell my students that they should know the difference between when they are frightened of something in their art making and when they are exhausted. When you're exhausted, you need to rest and take care of yourself. When you're frightened, ignore it and keep going. The frightened part is the infinite thing, and the exhausted part is when you're done (or almost done). So just rest and see what comes next.

KR: It is a funny thing to ask an artist: When do you know the work is complete? Right? That is wanting to understand where genius lies. It is refreshing to hear you say that there simply is no end.

RL: Every artist has their own view of how and what they do. From my knowledge of dance movement, and dealing with the body, I understand the body is conditional. It gets tired, it gets hurt. It is an instrument. You have to listen to it. A dance as well—a live dance—loses its life, its oxygen. I think that has a lot to do with spirit and psychology and the body, the human tools of dance making. That exchange is very different from an artist working visually, with objects. You go into the studio to make stuff and you can have assistants and fabricators who create things that are solid, maybe permanent. There is more distance. (Even while, as Merleau-Ponty posits, "We give human qualities to anything we objectify.") Different terms are required for when something is exhausted or not, for why that happens.

KR: Is it accurate to say that, for you, the drawing isn't a picture but a practice?

RL: This relates to my performance work also—it's a practice of creating a narrative for myself, and then on my better days a narrative I can share with an audience. An (often unreliable) narrative I'm having with myself in my relationship to the practice of making work, both performance work and drawing.

KR: That brings up the notion of the body at work, and how you draw: Is it on the desk, the wall, or the floor?

RL: Practically, I consider my visual work desk art because it has some relationship to being outside a dance studio, not on a stage, in the privacy of my home. Even as I make art in my studio, drawing for me is about a certain kind of intimacy, with pen, paper, and paint, with art making, with myself, with my home. It has served as a very protected space that is really different from the spectacle of performance as I know it. I am trying to bring a little of that intimacy into the performance work. The spectacle element is coming into the drawing practice too, I suppose, through exhibition, which creates a tension—a generative one, I hope.

KR: Another point about the drawings is that there isn't one way to read them. Especially with the many figures and vignettes in *Untitled (GBAHSET)*, you can kind of start from anywhere. They are dense but quite open to the viewer.

RL: The surprise for me is that once the drawing is done, it creates a narrative that I didn't dictate so much.

KR: You see the narrative after.

RL: I see the larger narrative after. But I feel very deeply about the many highly considered coded narratives within, and how I draw and think about them. It takes a long time, one year per drawing or thereabouts for the larger ones. Time (as a meditation) becomes another certain quotient of the work.

There's also the fact that I do not consider myself a good draftsman. Not that they are bad drawings; I've been drawing my whole life. But I just know how to draw the way that I draw. If I'm appropriating an image, there is tension if it is a photograph or a canonized masterful painting, because I absolutely cannot reproduce what is masterful or photographic about it.

KR: As you were saying before, it's a kind of translation or modification. Your way of drawing is your way of appropriating, or absorbing, another image or artwork. I would say these tableaux can often be recognized; a viewer can understand it is a reference that you've been thinking about.

RL: As craft, I'm also confronting the value systems of these images. I'm pulling from these long historical canons of what is valued as remarkable work, excellent work, or good art. And I'm appropriating photographs that have been selected and published. All these images have been graded in a certain way. I feel the tension between its original value and my more indeterminate value system. I'm doing the best I can to recreate the original, but it's morphing. That is a big part of the work.

KR: When you describe appropriating an existing image or episode and putting it into another composition, it reminds me of dance works like the *Rants* (2019–) [pp. 40–45] or *Chorus* (2015) that take passages of movement that we might recognize from one situation—displays of frustration, grief, rage; or even *Soul Train*—and unexpectedly cast or recombine them into your choreographies. Is that a parallel to the drawing practice?

RL: Structurally, there is a clear sense of reconstitution, not repetition. This thing I am working on has yet to die, and I am honoring it by continuing to work on its liveliness, or aliveness, or urgency, or joy.

KR: Reframing what that urgency can be?

RL: I like the word *refracting*. How much of this can I refract? *Rant* can only be refracted a little bit because it is so clear and loud about what it is. This is not discord or rage but something beyond those things, freer. Certain works dictate to me what needs to happen. The *Rants* do that. Kevin Beasley and I speak about this all the time. The format is so loud there's not much else we need to do other than stop it, stop the doing of it. With *Tell it anyway* (2024), we are beginning to refract *Rant*—or *at least making an attempt to stop it* [pp. 9–17]. The timing feels right; we have the space and mind and wherewithal to do that now, but it has taken this long. When *Rant #5* was presented at the Hammer Museum in 2022, the space kind of broke it, broke what it was, in a parking garage sixty feet underground, claustrophobic and dark, a place not built for human beings, and certainly not for a dance [p. 40]. That generative breakage has dictated the next phase of whatever *Rant* is, which is in part *Tell it anyway*. I think.

With *Untitled (GBAHSET)*, I don't know how to break the flow unless I start destroying the drawings, or painting (black) over all of the images to obliterate the narrative. And then what? Whereas with *Untitled (RW)*, painting (black) all over the image, obliterating what is there, would be a natural extension of what is already happening in their serial transformation. It's interesting.

KR: In terms of refraction, Darrell Jones described *Low* (2003–25), which will be performed in the winter, as a mode of working that developed from a past performance [pp. 130–32]. Another element of your work is precisely that reworking: focusing on certain themes, motifs, or sections that are transformed through greater, even collective, concentration.

RL: I started work on *Chorus* in 2014 (with dancers Paul Hamilton, Malcolm Low, and Omagbitse Omagbemi). That dance became *Rant*. That has now become *Tell it anyway*. It's not like I have a plan for this temporality; it's just, what's the life of this thing? And then letting outside forces help that process, with some disciplined observation from me—it's a responsibility, in fact.

Darrell and I have been working on the modality of Low since we first began collaborating. It also feels infinite. A couple of years ago, it became clear to me—and this is now my hope for more of my performative work—that the work evolves to somehow not be my work anymore. I feel that Low is fully Darrell's practice now. He has taken it over in a very organic way, over a long period of working together, and through a long physical and verbal conversation about what it is we are doing. It's his. My work on Low now seems to be: How do I ask the right questions to keep the flow of the work out of my hands? I'm trying to do that with *Tell it anyway* as well. I would like its authorship to be more collective; it works sometimes and sometimes it doesn't.

I suppose the drawings in *Untitled (GBAHSET)* have a similar intentional trajectory. There is some idea of collective authorship, if perhaps more perverse, more to do with love and thievery. I've also been appropriating my eleven-year-old daughter's drawings into the work, because they are amazing and absolutely impossible for me to recreate.

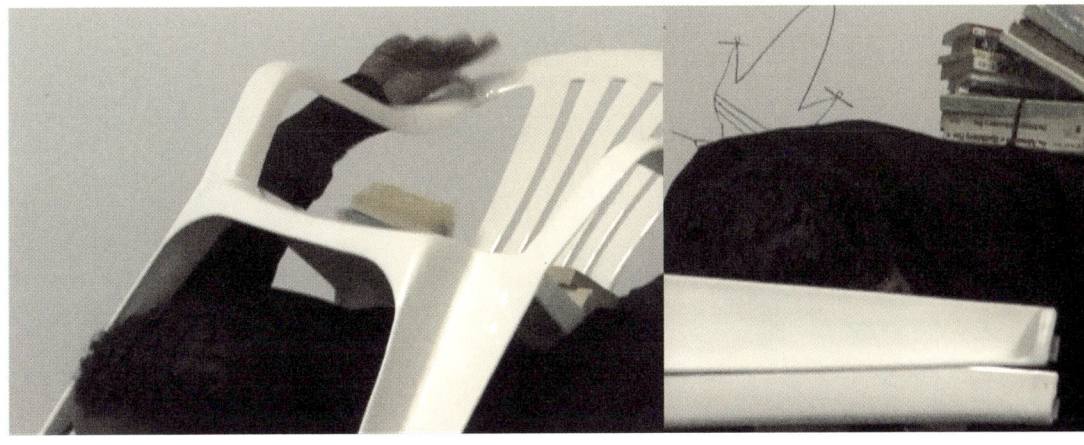

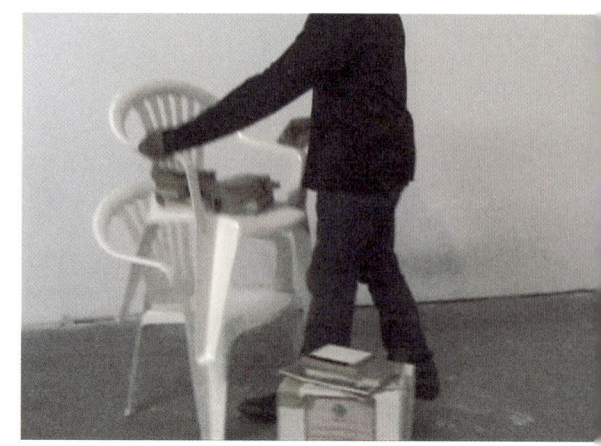

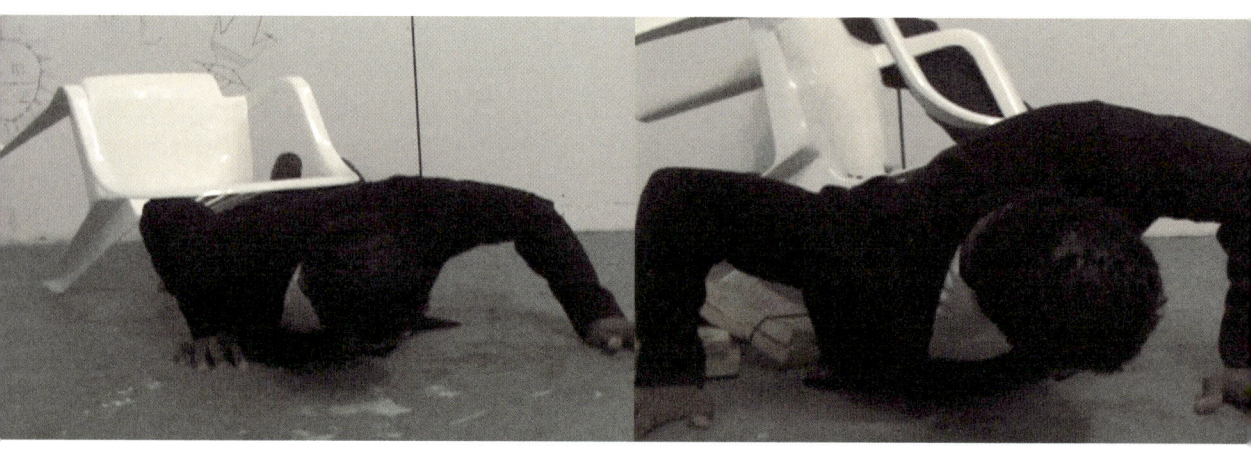

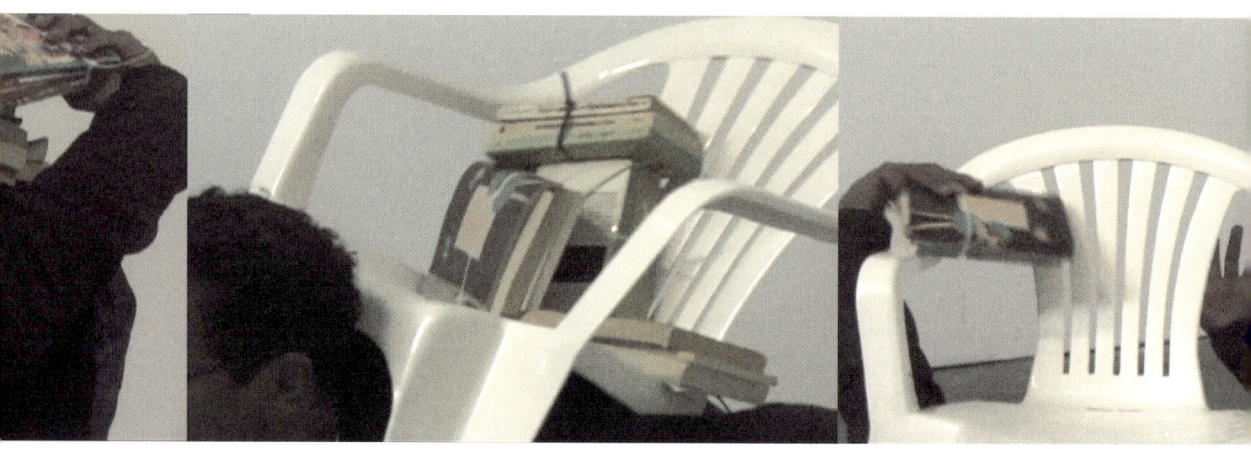

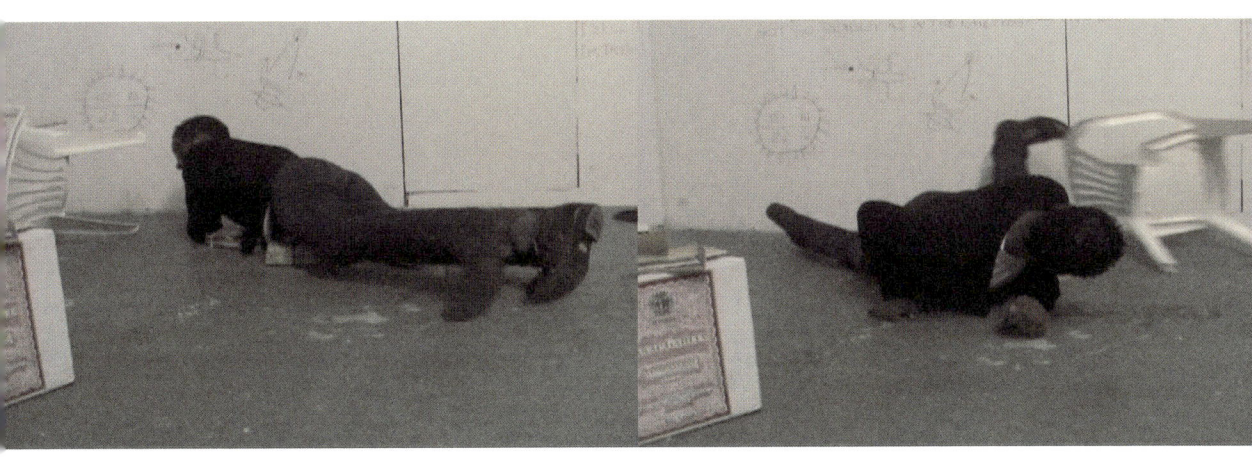

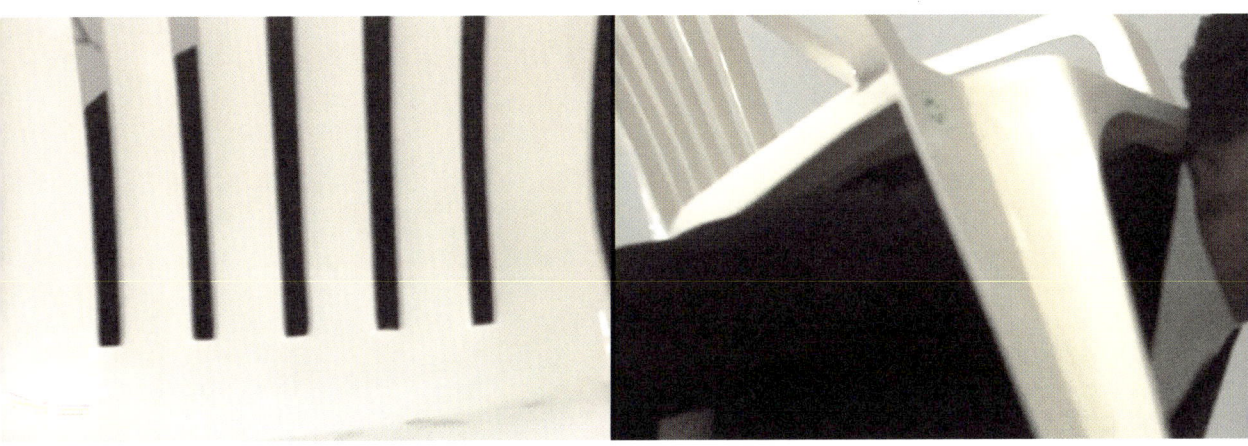

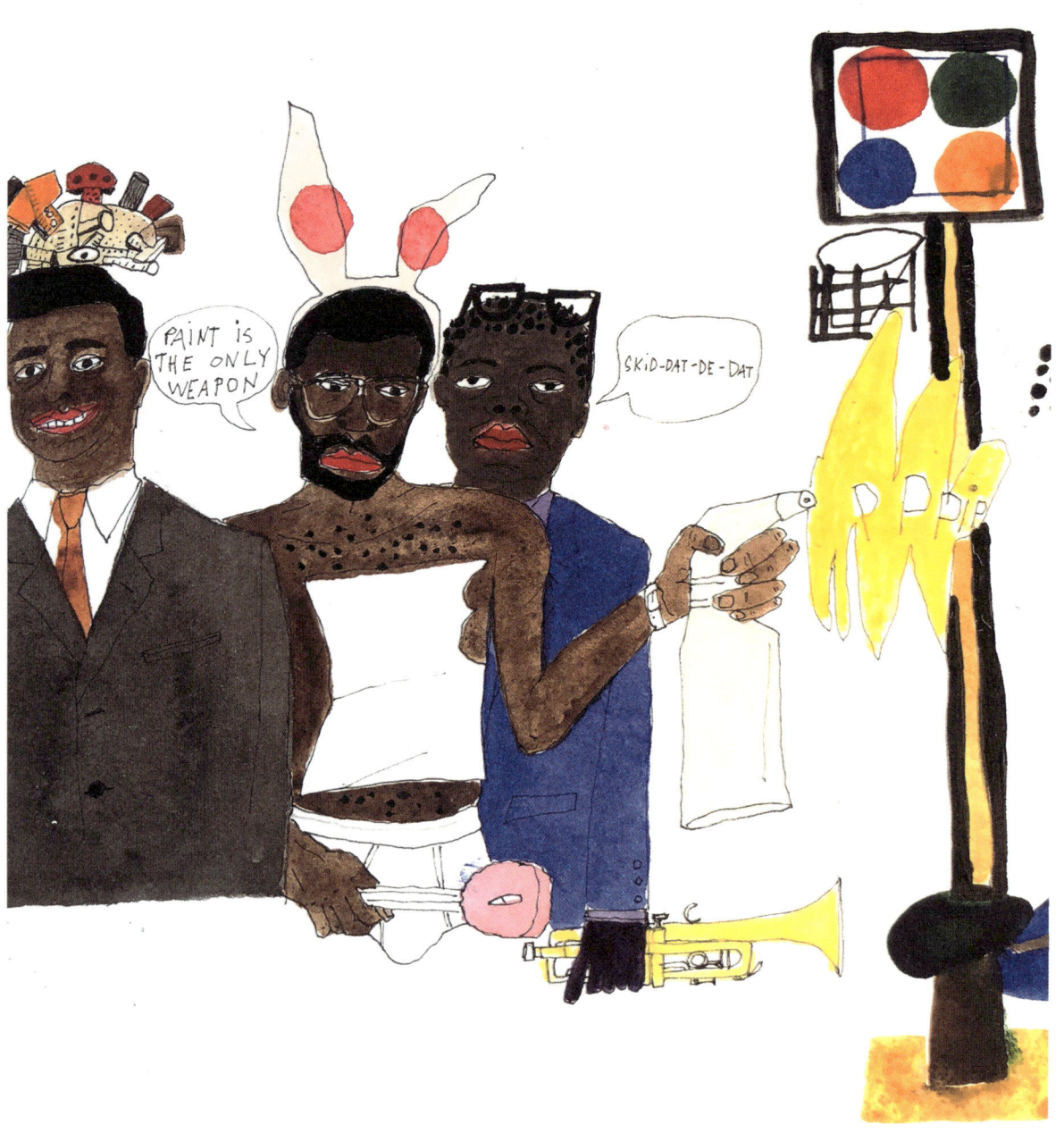

Uriposia Story; or,
Little House Where I Used to Live In
Pope.L

The following is one of Pope.L's many "Mr. Brown-Guy Stories," a family of writings he began around 1980. Commissioned for "An Evening with Ralph Lemon and Pope.L"—a program organized on the occasion of the exhibition *Bruce Nauman: Disappearing Acts* (2018–19) at MoMA and MoMA PS1—the text was read to a live audience at The Museum of Modern Art on January 28, 2019. After studying Nauman's *Wall/Floor Positions* (1965/68), Lemon invited Pope.L to expand upon questions of the body, race, and the confines of the studio that Nauman's work raised for him—contextualized in the tumultuous political climate of the 1960s and subsequent histories of performance art. The version published here has been adapted to include spoken divergences from the script. The original script was first published in *My Kingdom for a Title* (Mitchell-Innes & Nash and New Documents, 2021), a volume of collected writings by Pope.L.

For a a uh.

Long long time I lived in a house or a hosue on a hill. A house. Or or should I say it lived in me. Hard to tell. I am alive in that lag way, you see . . .

So so—for. For a long long time I lived in a house on a hill. For. For um. For for—

The house the.

Was made mostly of uh wood on the exterior, liquids between the seams, clapboard style rusting gutters watery windows to to see out of or over over for example . . .

Ample . . . Tample . . .

The the—the pre-previous owner of the house was an amous visual artist. Not just an artist but an amous visual artist. Amous as in immaterial. Uh uh uh a visual artist. As opposed to a non-visual artist. The artist's ame had been secured by making things no not associated purely urely with sight with light with—

Zeit.

Vision being always a nigger to some thing or other vision being always a nigger it shall—what sort of artist is that? Who makes an art not obligated to the lenses or the princes? Sounds more like a non-visual artist anyday now gray say how? How do you how do you how do the corollary hollow? If so, how briskly rafter, crafter?

At times I I if I may I I may I I remember the house on its hill as a picture picture postcard setting but but but in reality it was something totally other, a gift, a scene, a set upset its perch of nil, and woe, and clod while while while I lived in it I disappeared there in that cloud I I was afraid I was going through something.

I was I was uh being next to something. Being next to . . . to . . . to. To the floor and wall of something. To floor and wall of something. An ation, an ation, a relation in this case: land and sky do not make the same decision. I'd I'd I'd stand on the back porch, I'd stand on the back porch, always the back, never ever the front, always the back, always the back I'd stand on the back porch and take in the scenery . . .

Now behound behind behind the house was a was a a uh dump. The factory whose dump it was produced liquids for a distributor in E-E-Eastern Europe. A kind of a kind of paint in small ffflat metal containers. Cans. Cans.

Only awkward paint was discarded.

Discarded behind the factory creating a nest of valleys, of cresting flat tins of discarded paint. Apparently this this this had been going on for decades because the valley is stretched out into an ecology far far wide and deep. Wha-wha-what can I see . . . see . . . see . . . le Bruce . . . le Bruce wha-wha-what-t can I see what—what-t—wa-wa-what can I see—

Sometimes I'd visit the dump and I'd stab the metal staff into the sea of cans, methodically, always methodically leaking as a metaphor for synecdoche herself itself letting the paint run out down into the nound the mound the underground under what is bound. All all sorts of colors, many unfamiliar to me. Fulvous. Smaragdine. Wenge. Glaucous. Psilocine. Sloss.

I'd I'd stand there shivering while poking, stabbing who is that
weeping p-p-p-piercing the tins finding myself lost in something more
than reverie looking back at myself looking at myself in the dump
staff mitt wit hand finding myself seeing myself standing standing
standing on the porch of my one time synechdo-bode the door of the
housue vacant hide wide open behind the portal behind the screen
door gaping wide wide wide leading down into the effacement—

Or what I sometimes called my cellar I'd constructed long ago in
a panic of squalor and squander. Adorno and his bastard hunchback
son lose the key to his hejira now now I call it my basement, or
the crucible fe-fi-fuck the meaning of two ideas or or or or the pond,
I call it the pond walk past by the towering stacks of magazines,
love letters, mirrors covered with tafeh taffeta bills and newspapers
through the labyrinth of wrapped objects—

[pause]

Quick mysystems until finally fe-fi-fo-finally I am standing before a
metal door with its um its its—

Its lock.

And so and so I undo myself and enter I enter the room. First
impression upon entering is it's not so spacious. In fact, it is
cramped. It is cramped. Low ceiling. Unforgiving un painted cinder
block walls. Liquid between the lathing. No windows. A smell,
in what air there is, a smell rich yellow bitter. This is where
I keep my stash, that is one of the names I get for it, I call it my
stash. My collection. Or my lash. My confection. Or my task.
My pamerambulation. My gash. What I get for it—

Now in the room, in the room—picture it, picture it: jars and jars and
jars of lant on gray coated metal shelves casting an incandescent
glow over the room like the inside of a certain kind of telly fish. The
kind you dream about in your asshole. The kind the kind that
sings inside your asshole. Now lant is fermented urine once used in
preindustrial processes such as tanning or embalming, my use
equally emblematic diagrammatic teleological performative illusory
—I—I—I—I—I—I—

I am trying to re-create a charge you see, a helpless charge. Just just the dust of the image by itself in in insignificant. If if I wasn't so lonely I'd—I'd—

So . . . so . . . so the room on its immediate entry appears limited, in fact, the lant, on its many, many gray coated metal shelves extends projects the length of the room underground seemingly indefinitely to a subterranean instant but but but this this this this this is yet another lie because the first room on the first entry is only a quarter of a mile in length. However at some point, say say another eighth of a mile, say, say the room makes a sharp desperate left-turn moving off swiftly a third of a mile more-or-less ending suddenly without preamble, without warning without poetry without mucosa exactly the way Yvonne would have wanted it, longed for it. This this stopping point is not arbitrary but exactly exactly underneath the westernmost valley of the dump behind the paint factory.

Now the westernmost valley is a particular nexus of—containing specific complexion of paint, awkward like the rest but specific all the more because its quality. Oh oh-ho-ho over the years I began to add paint to the lant to produce a rabid drawn out gradation of 134 shades of a certain color, a certain use-function of pallor gradation of a certain dolor color; my thesis, one nested inside the other but at least one urine hewed to diagnose several bodies as well as sine as well as sine-ety—for example, red urine indicates projection, white urine indicates saturation, black indicates intramuscular iron injections, blue is pissing away your ectoplasm intrauterine visions way back before seawater—I—I—am a drive-en to color I do not know why before the word I do this this this this gradation à la para-para-practice cause ultimately i have no I have no use for this sort of theater this this sort of a gimmick being so sick in mind body my-myself and society already i am beyond the pale as demonstrated in the long long drives I had begun taking in those last past few years when I lived in the house or were they I was feeling the seepage even then even in the vehicle filling up with the yellow pillage my fellow spillage even when speeding along the against the tollbooths, drive throughs and concrete embankments I could feel it. I could feel it. I can feel it—

Now on one such drive I'd been collecting my liquid as per my usual, almost enough urine to return to base, the hosue, but but but the hosue this this time the situation became a season of its own arrival.

I am not normally a sad person, I do not believe in one hand before the other, I am intractable such that during these drives I never ever left the vehicle, never once no matter what, catheter shoved deep into my bladder like an like an oil derrick and beyond until blood flowed through the clear plastic tubing, at some point the timer on the catheter must have malfunctioned, just happened no alarm like it's suppose to human error what you going to do what you going to do so suddenly I'm back at the hosue in the driveway catheter-bottle halfway full other times over-flowing, I'm a little bit more than nuts got no idea how, who, what and so and so and so and so and so and so this this this time it happens again but it happens when I am out and about gathering the liquid and the catheter-bottle groins over-flows and I panic to see a tiny yellow dot blooming on my trouser mesmerizing disturbing soul searching the very—

So quick I find a highway rest-stop, I lock myself in a toilet stall in the men's room, why do they call it the men's room? What what what am I doing? I am in there a long time. Eventually I hear a noise, a knock on the door. It's the attendant. He's knocking on the toilet stall door, he says: "Hey buddy, you monopolizing the facilities."

He says, he says, "Hey buddy, if you don't clear out, my manager's going to call the department."

Well.

I tell him my name is Mr. Brown Guy, that I am a very handsome man and highly complected. I have a very gashing chin vermillion, etc. etc. etc. I give him the usual description.

Slight pause.

So I reassure him, I tell him in an overly loud voice I say, "I have had a little spillage."

[pause]

"What?" says the attendant.

Pause. Longer pause.

The attendant leaves. The waft of his cologne remains. Alcohol and feces.

I escape the stall and drive home with my eyes closed in the rain it is night at night in a rainstorm. I drive up onto the lawn, apologize to the *Dichondra repens* ground cover wishing it was wisteria. Enter the house hosue only to grab my metal staff from its metal cousins from the metal rack in the metal kitchen, climb, climb climb slide slip down the hill directly out to the dump, moving methodically always methodically from valley-this to valley-that, I climb and scrabble arriving at the designated-designated and begin poke poking fiercely at the cans, then the paint in the cans, then the very very thing in the paint in the cans, the paint itself forcing the liquid down underground drip drip dripping drip talking talking to the lant like it's going to change anything like it's going to change anything like it's going to change anything, my face turned up to the lightning my face turned up up up with against the firmament—

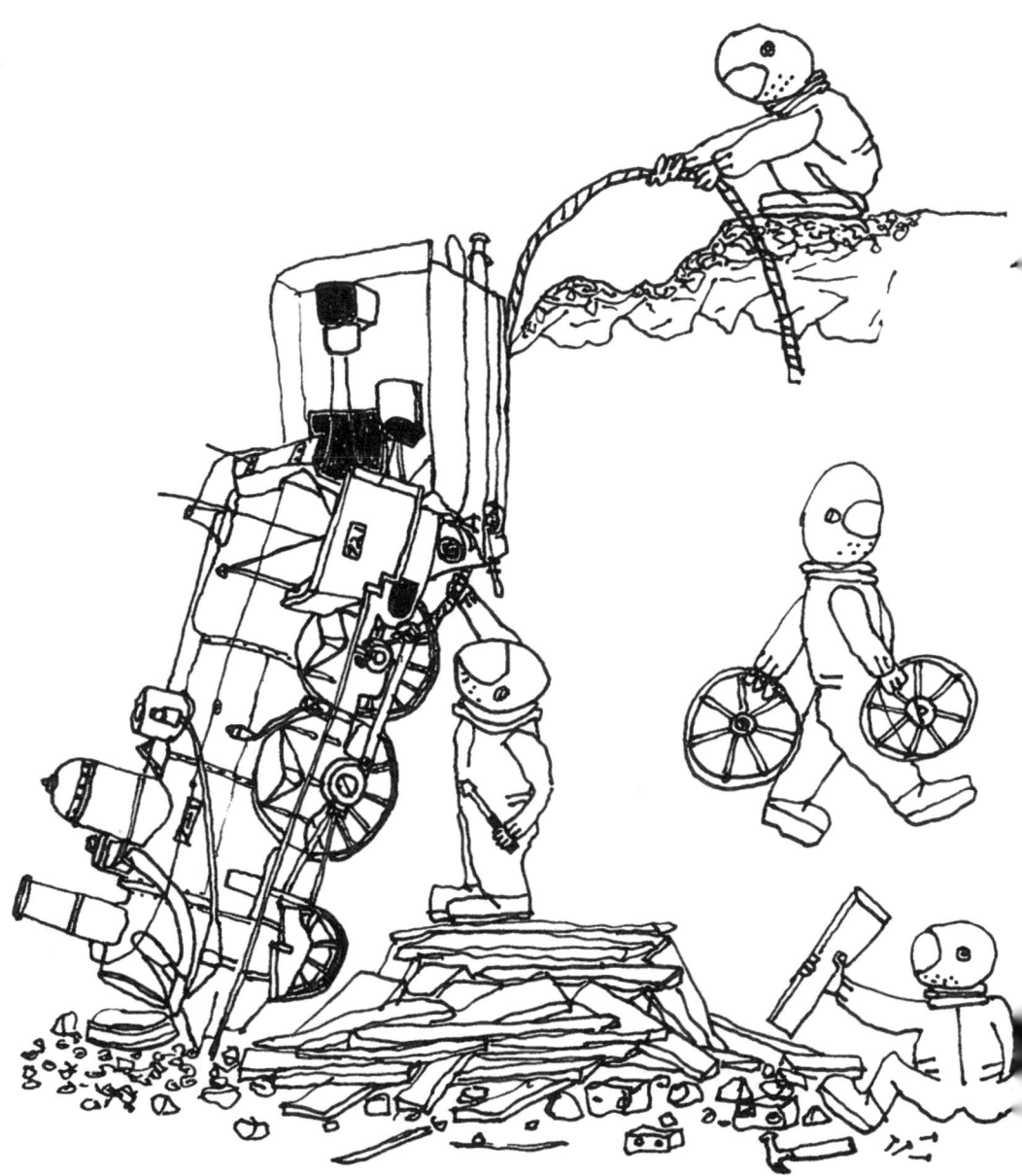

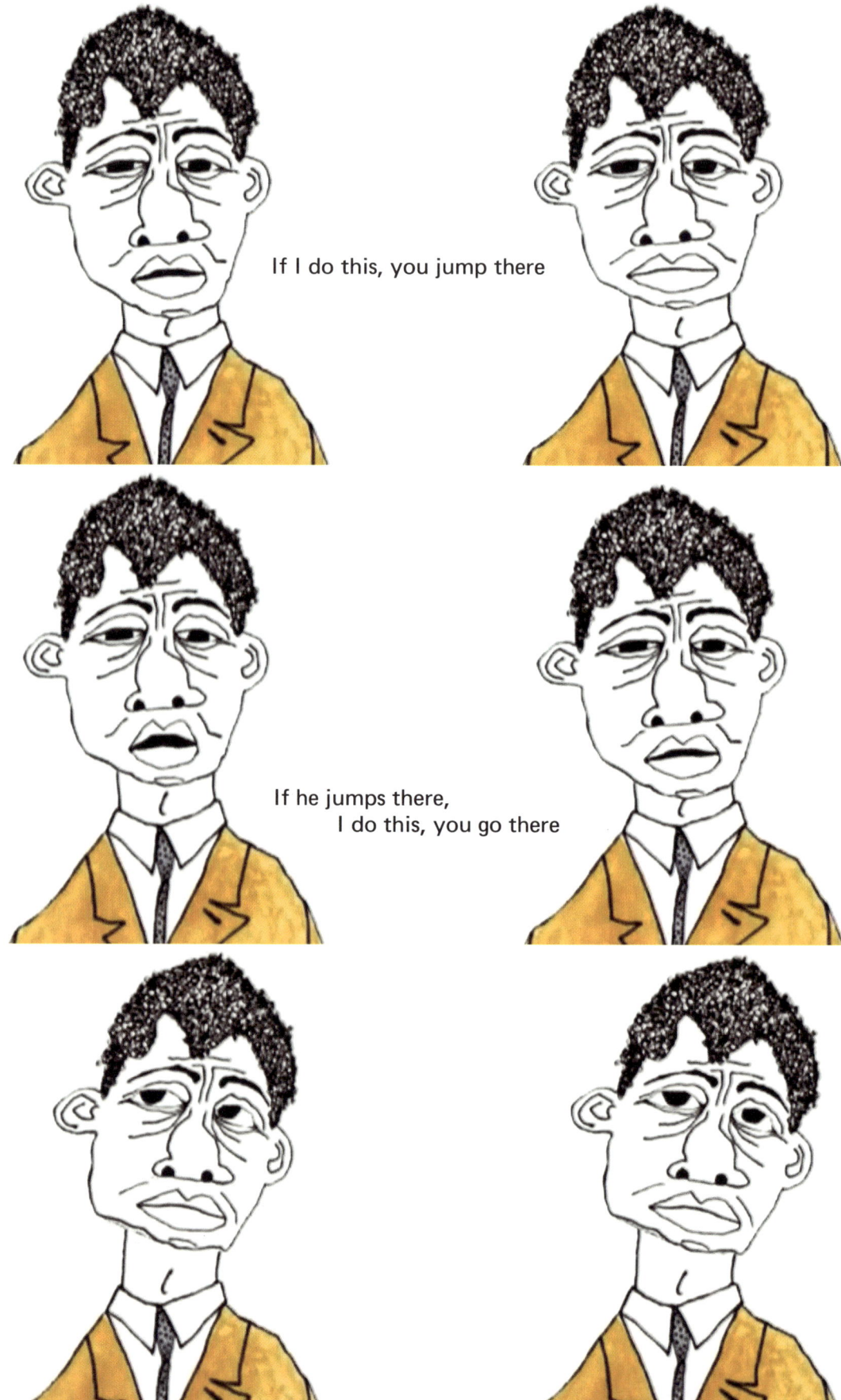

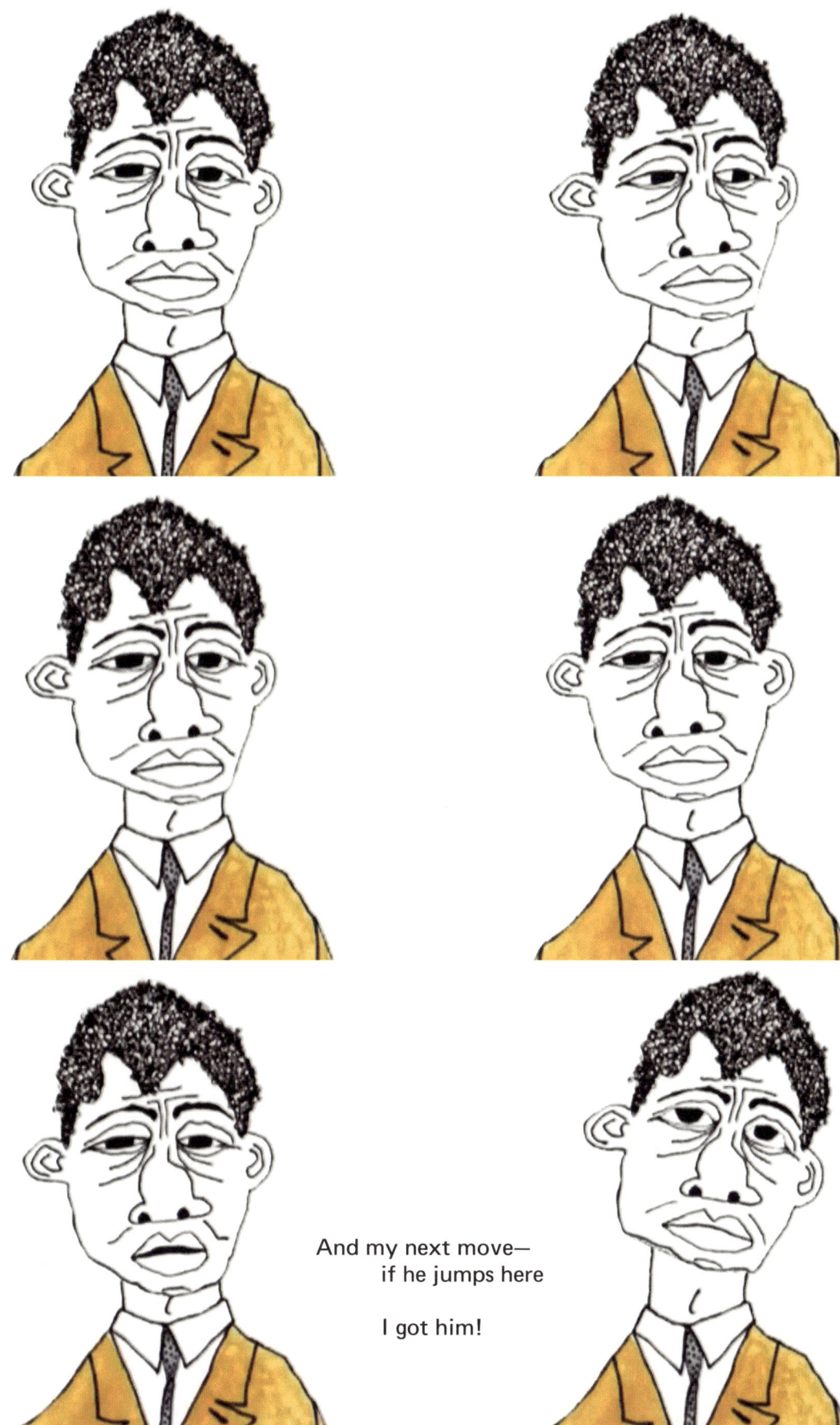

And my next move—
if he jumps here

I got him!

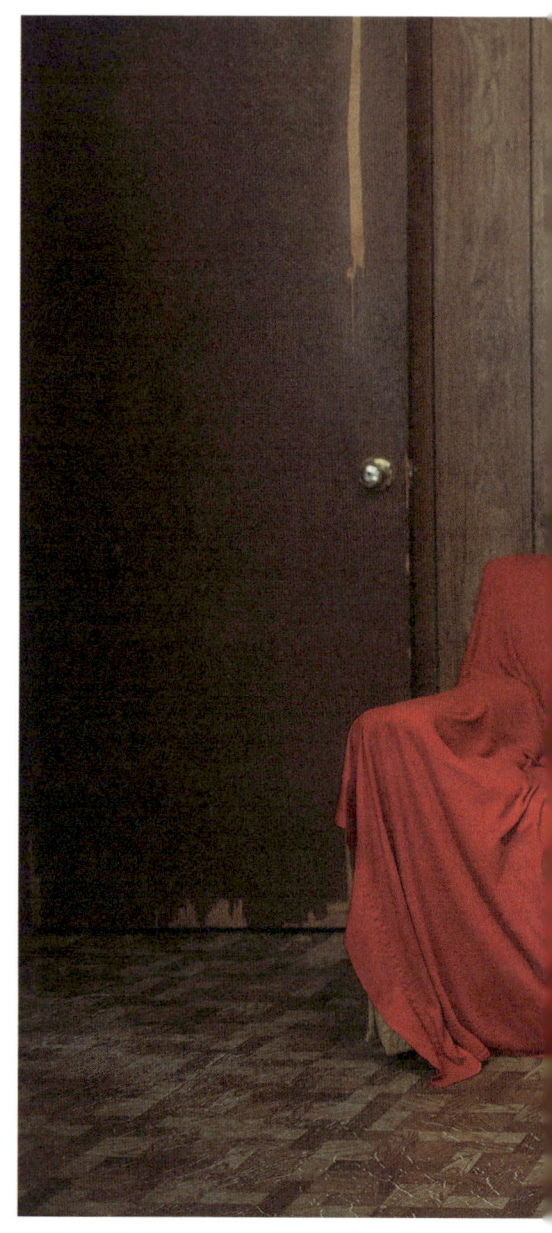

Walter Carter Suite, 2002—24

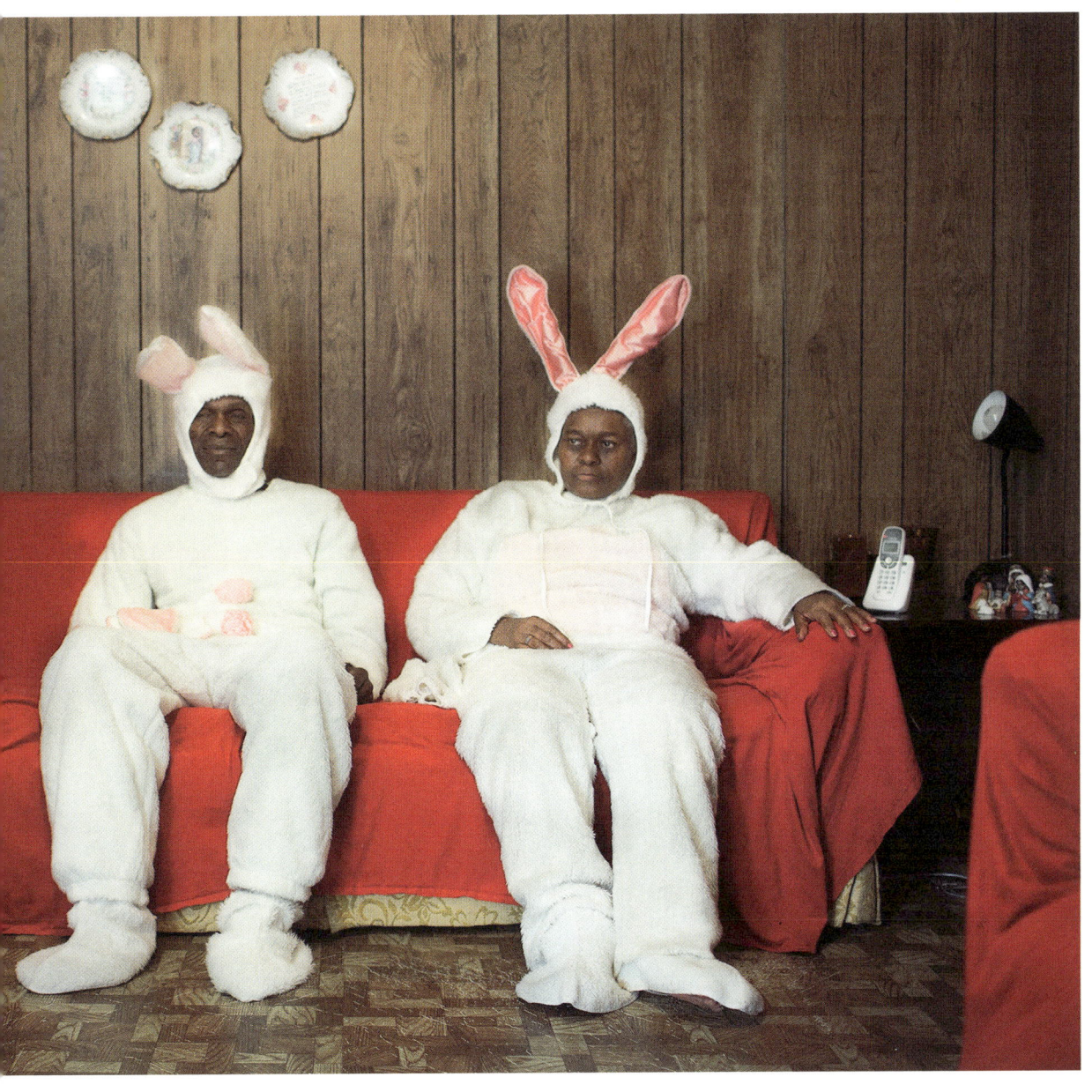

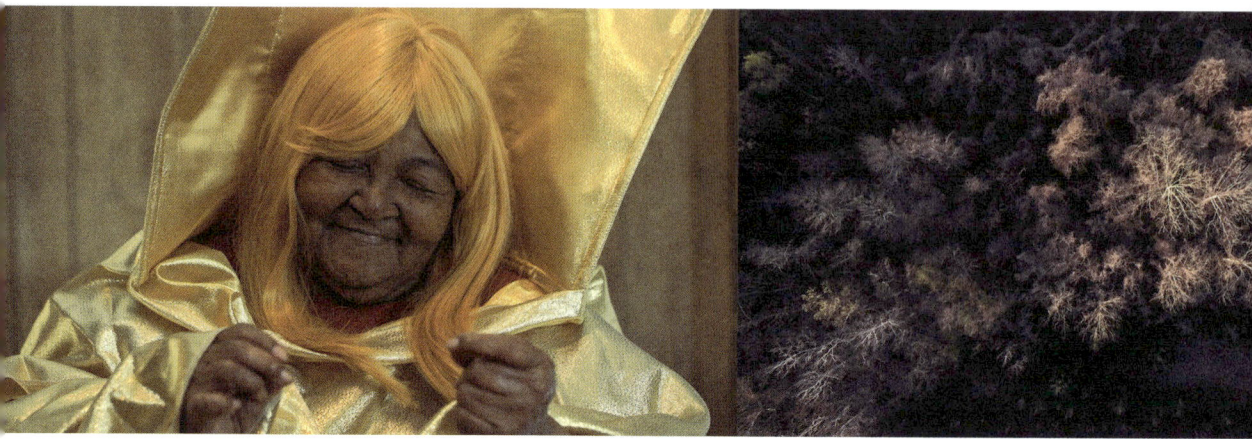

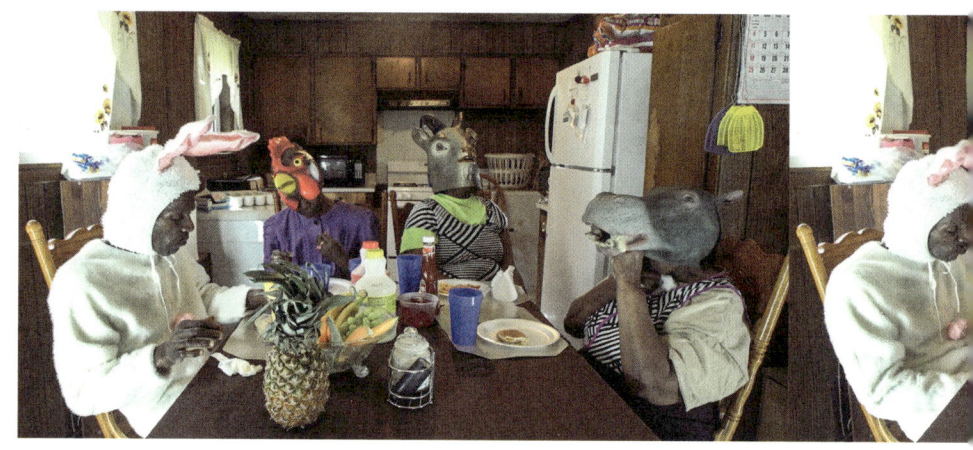

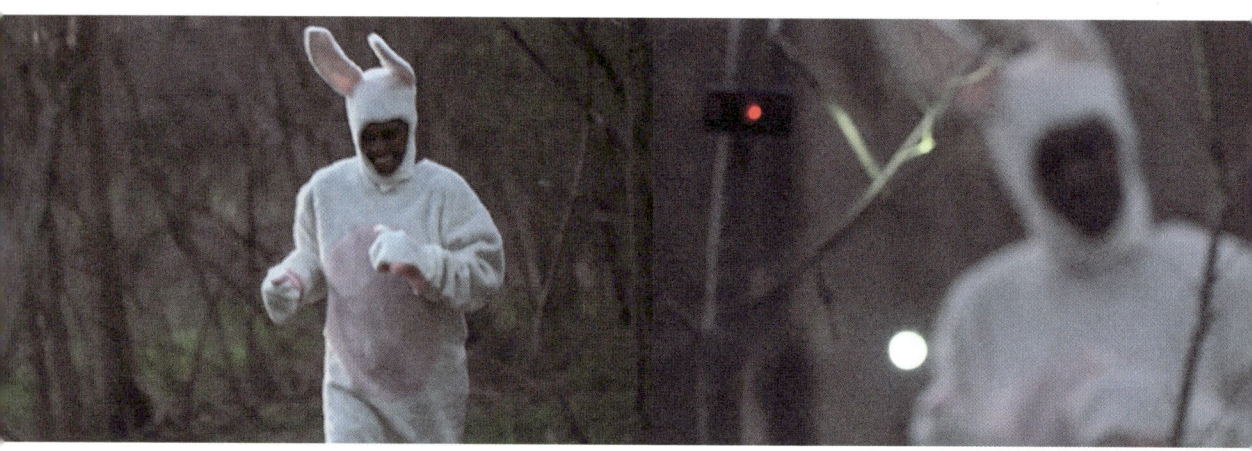

Walter Carter Suite, 2002—24

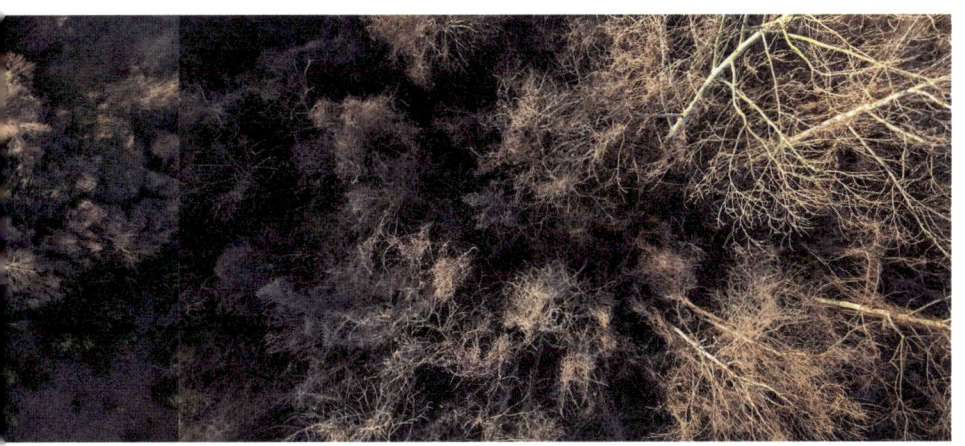

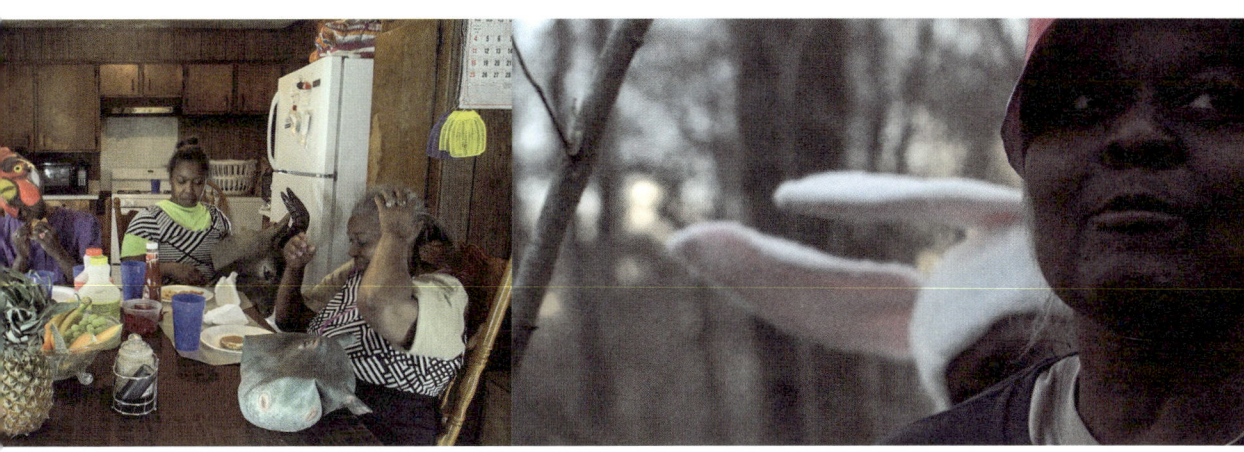

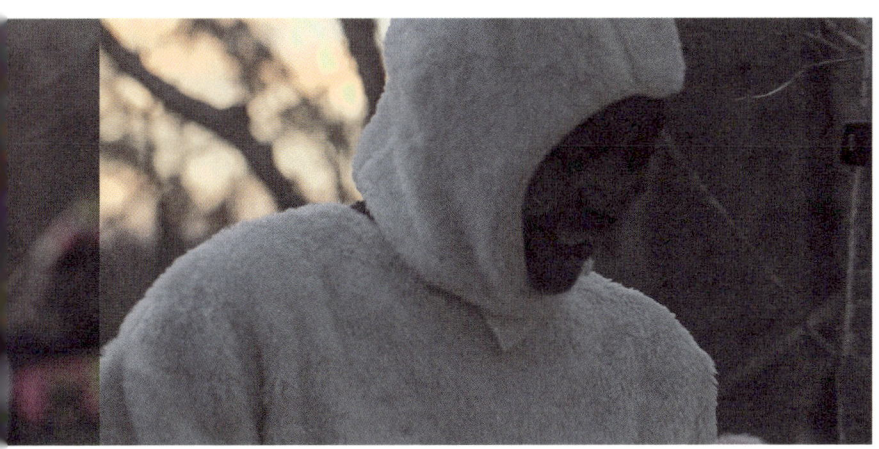

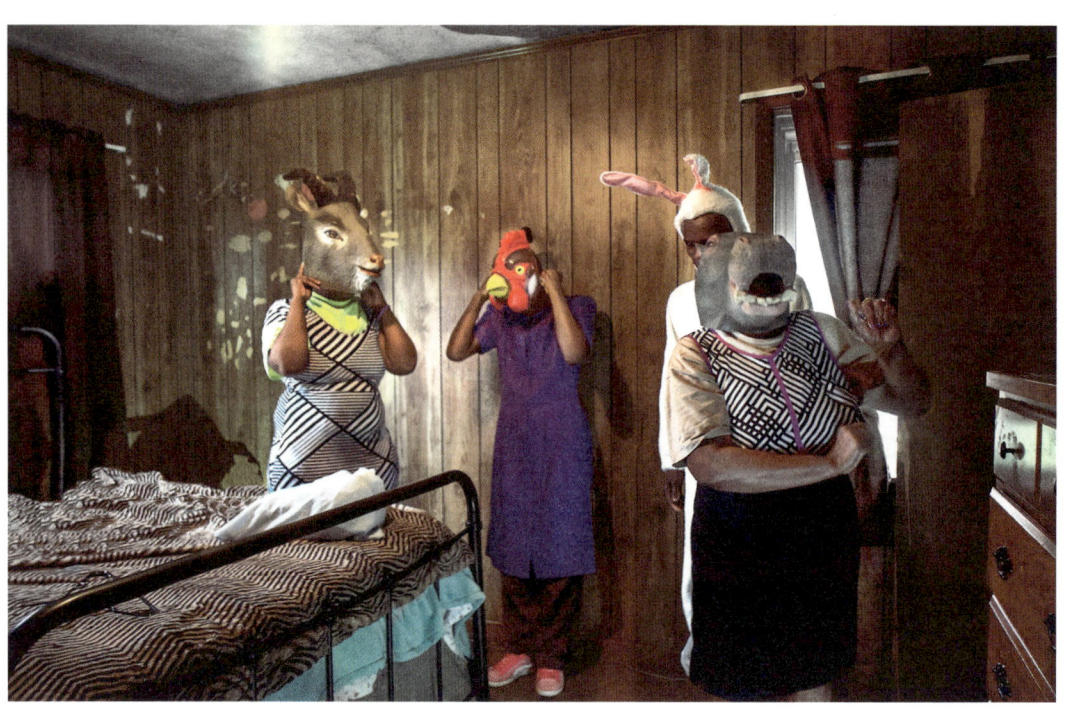

Walter Carter Suite, 2002—24

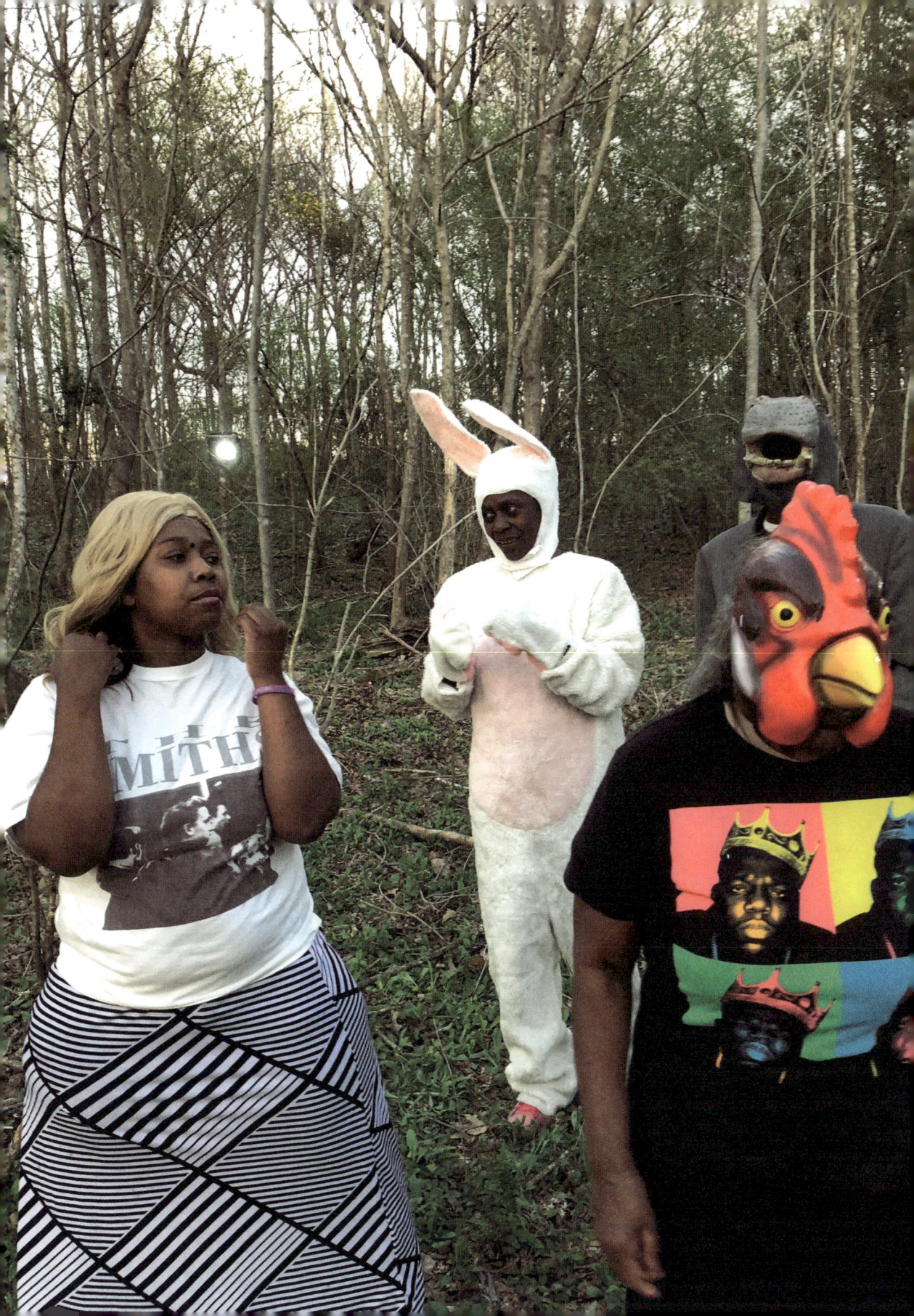

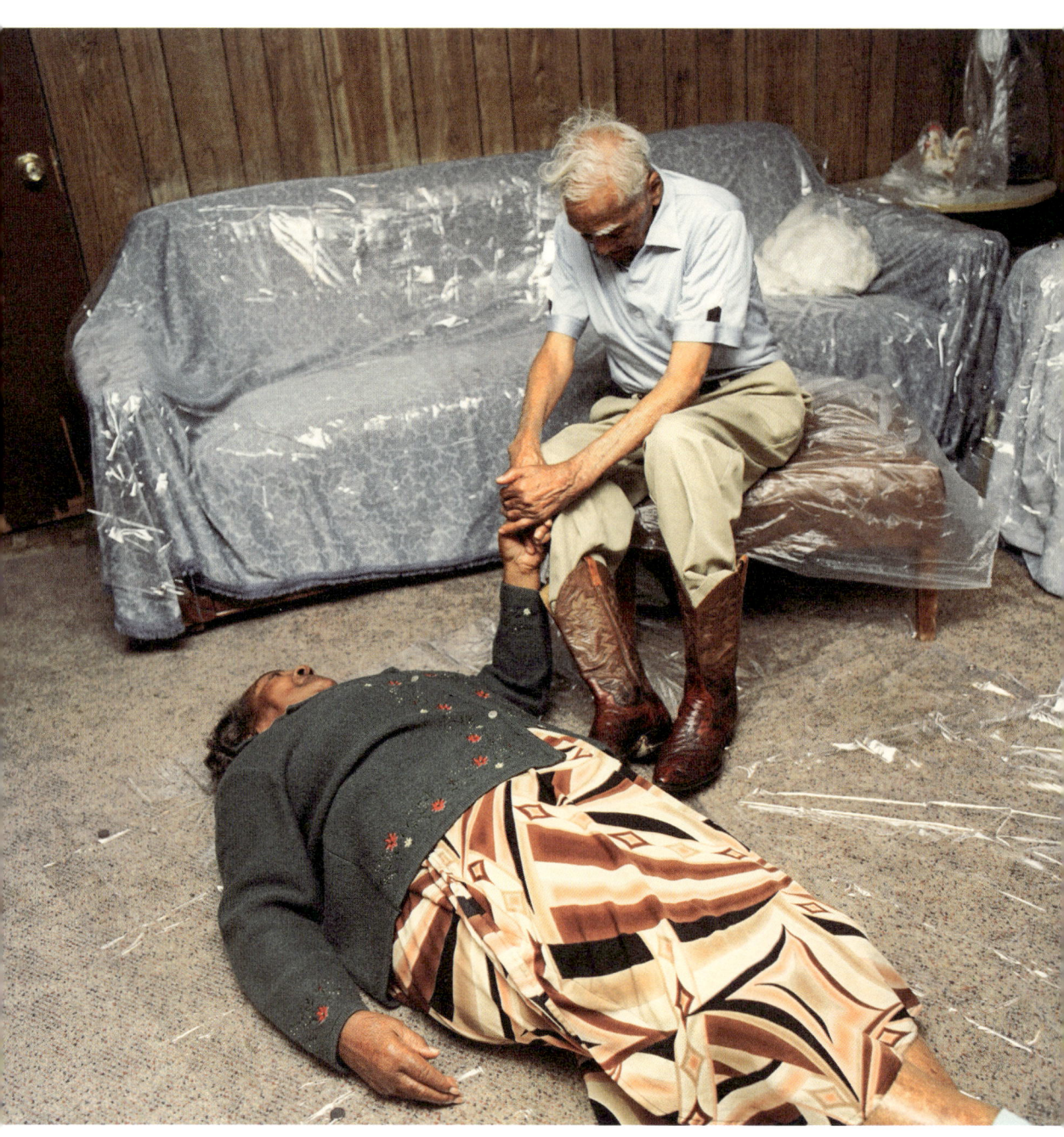

Walter Carter Suite, 2002—24

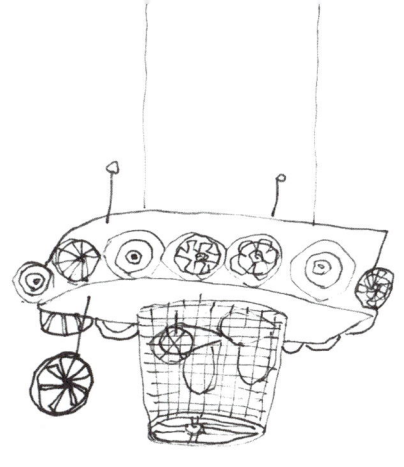

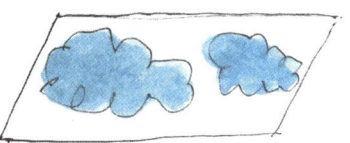

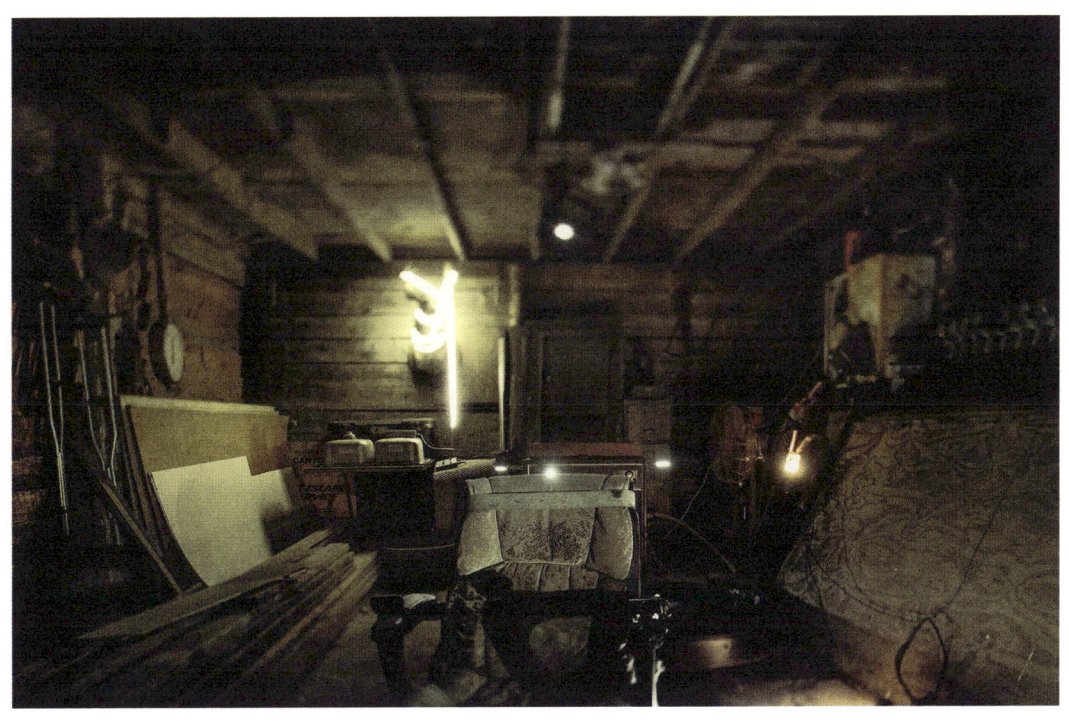

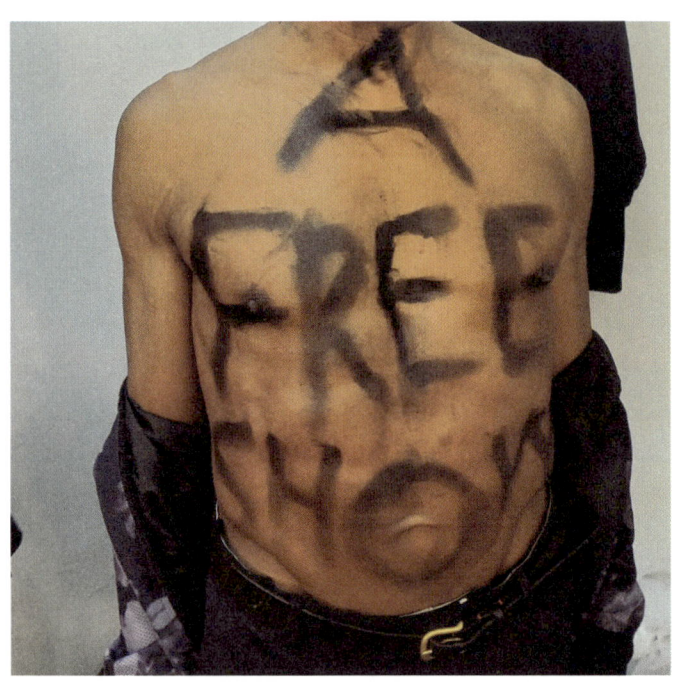

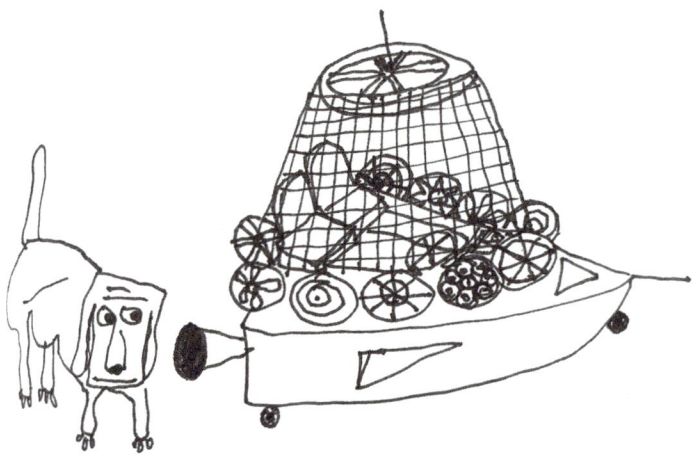

A.P.EX.: Always Planning Excursions
Adrienne Edwards

I first saw Ralph Lemon dance in 1997 at the Brooklyn Academy of Music's Majestic Theater (now named the Harvey Theater). It was the New York premiere of *Geography*, the first piece in what ultimately expanded into a trilogy of works bannered under the same name, which included *Tree* (2000) and *Come home Charley Patton* (2004). *Geography* inaugurated what had not been up to that point but would become Ralph's fundamental questioning of what it means to be Black, to explore what it means to create works of art about Blackness. The piece also pointedly queried the complexities of diasporic relationality in general and artistic collaboration in particular, as well as the power of structured tension as part of the creative process. Such interests aligned with the globalist tendency of the political moment, but they also harkened back to the anthropological thrust of dance research and movement we can mark in the choreographies of artists such as Katherine Dunham, Pearl Primus, and Alvin Ailey. I know all of this history now, but I didn't at the time.

I had recently arrived to New York to attend graduate school in art history and museum studies with a focus on the Italian Renaissance, steeped in iconography, formalism, perspective, and the political and economic interests that buttressed it. I had happened across an article by Ann Daly in the *New York Times* titled "Conversations about Race in the Language of Dance" that introduced me to Ralph's work, how he had radically disbanded his modern dance company to embark on movement research in Haiti and countries in West Africa, so I got a ticket to the show, which he described as his version of *Revelations*, Ailey's 1960 tour de force.[1] As someone who had danced for many years, I was intrigued by the idea of an artist who was not merely willing but needing to let something go in order to save the very thing he loved; that is, what we might readily characterize as art itself but what actually is its driving force—curiosity, questioning, desire; the impulses and impetuses that make us want to make.

In retrospect, I realize that the coincidence of reading that article and seeing *Geography* was the first dawning of an interest in art that I would tilt toward years later, after leaving a career in arts administration and returning to graduate school yet again, this time for a doctorate in performance studies. That step followed extended travel in India and my beginning to seriously study Buddhism, which I would later learn Ralph has also practiced extensively. My interests, which traverse genres, were less about performance per se but rather a journey into what art does in the world and how certain animations of Blackness in their most opaque manifestations pressure the being of the world in dynamically distinct ways. I now wonder if this commitment was somehow seeded in *Geography*. Writing for *Variety*, critic Markland Taylor described it as "far too opaque to welcome audiences into its world."[2] The matter of performing insularity, withholding, and inexplicability before us, the audience, is singular to the Ralph experience. Like any gift, his works always want something of us in return. That demand is that we return to ourselves—the stakes of being inextricably coterminous within the I, among the we, and in the melee of the things of the world. The confounding fact is that he doesn't make it easy for us. The troubled is a kind of sublime; the being-in the undoing, the unknowing required of his work, and therefore us, destabilizes in its faceting, and that is precisely the point.

My first studio visit with Ralph was in 2012, when he was in residence at the Park Avenue Armory and I was beginning my PhD coursework; there, I saw laid out on the tables piles of drawings. But unlike the eccentric colorful ones of figures real and imagined from his research and travels over the years, which I had seen in his books on the trilogy, these were composed of finely drawn black lines that recurred, unfolding, skirting, enfolding one another. They were, I recognized, meditations. I recall feeling almost embarrassed to ask about them—to do so seemed to me too invasive—but their resonance lingered. It would take years more for a genuine creative intimacy to evolve between us for me to engage him about those works. Ultimately, we displayed them as part of *Quiet as It's Kept*, the 2022 Whitney Biennial, which I cocurated with David Breslin. Ralph and I decided that we would survey his drawing practice, which spans nearly thirty years and reveals the profundity of his imagination, by changing the system of display and the works themselves nearly each month. Ralph takes pleasure pressuring art institutions and their mores as much as he likes pushing the bounds of choreography (not to mention the boundaries of those who perform it). These metabolic installations were a performance even more behind the scenes than in the gallery itself—his suspect propositions, unending questions, and most importantly, unbounded generosity—in many emails and phone calls as well as countless meetings with framers, registrars, exhibition designers and coordinators, art handlers. We were all in it together. Each iteration of his contribution had one work placed elsewhere in the museum; the last one was installed within the gallery dedicated to writer Steve Cannon and A Gathering of the Tribes, the interdisciplinary arts hub and publisher that Cannon founded in his apartment in the East Village (a tribute that I coarranged with artist David Hammons). During the run of the show, two incidents took place. One concerned a painted-over postcard, a Courbet seascape titled *Marine* (1866), which had been used as a blotching tool for Ralph's *Untitled (Rapture weft)* (2020–) series of drawings [pp. 50–55], that was stolen on the opening night of the Biennial. With some effort, we ultimately got it back. Later there was an attempted theft of a small drawing of a "naked man." Someone ripped it while trying to remove it from the plexiglass shield, but it was, remarkably, repaired by the conservation department. Ralph is now a legend at the Whitney.

The Biennial was not my first sojourn with Ralph at the Whitney, however. Shortly after my arrival in 2018, I worked to bring *Fuck Bruce Nauman* (2009–19) into the museum's permanent collection [pp. 77–79]. I had previously shown the work—the 2009 version, as it were—in an exhibition spotlighting the Walker Art Center's holdings in conceptual art titled *I am you, you are too*

(2017–20). Ralph became fascinated with Nauman, in a complicated way—a productive entanglement of ambivalence, antagonism, and admiration. The first variation of the work included a video that references Nauman's recorded studio experiments, shot while Ralph was on an artist's residency in New Orleans shortly after the devastation of Hurricane Katrina. Ralph can be seen and heard writhing, falling, and laughing among formerly waterlogged books and a white plastic lawn chair. The video was shown on a small CRT monitor installed in a small black room, placed at a slight angle on the floor alongside a black-light neon featuring the title of the work. Ralph was asking a profound question: What else was going on in the world at the time Nauman made his iconic *Wall/Floor Positions* in his studio, first in 1965 and later when he recorded it on video in 1968? In these years, Malcolm X was assassinated and Martin Luther King, Jr. had the same fate; there was Bloody Sunday in Selma; Norman Rockwell's painting *Murder in Mississippi (Southern Justice)* (1965) was published in *Look* magazine as a memorial to civil rights activists James Chaney, Andrew Goodman, and Michael Schwerner; the Tet Offensive occurred in Vietnam; Bobby Hutton of the Black Panthers was murdered; and so on.

When I approached Ralph about acquiring the piece for the Whitney, he said sure, but he was emphatic that the work was not finished. Since we had acquisition funds but not commissioning funds, some magical thinking and institutional maneuvering was required, which Ralph relished. The elements he added to round out the multi-faceted artwork included a square aluminum sculpture, a kind of sarcophagus that referred to Nauman's *John Coltrane Piece* (1968), a memorial to the jazz innovator who had died the prior year. Ralph was intrigued that Nauman had polished only the underside of his work, leaving the shine facing down, unavailable to us. For his take, Lemon employed another neon, a riff on the spiral-neon series *The True Artist* that Nauman began in the 1960s, which he embedded into his own aluminum sculpture, similarly obscured from view. It states, "The true artist is (un)seen the true artist is voluminous emptiness the true artist answers the tyranny of what seems to be external." The black-light neon capstoned the piece. Ralph arranged a choreography for the work that involves art handlers turning the neon off and on at specific intervals during opening hours.

At the 2022 Whitney Biennial, the labyrinth of the sixth floor's installation unfolded from a single antechamber. Triangulated there were an ephemeral trinket of an inventor's life, preserved and ensconced so as to encourage us to believe not only in its very possibility but also in the overestimation of its value (Henry Ford's vial of Thomas Edison's last breath, captured in 1931); a reverb of/from centuries of occupation and surveillance presenting the evidence that the land, its waters, and Native people are unbeloved by this nation (Raven Chacon's *Silent Choir*, 2017); and a memorial-relic of withholding of the unspeakable terror against Black life (Ralph and Kevin Beasley's tribute to Frank Embree, referred to as an anonymous contribution to the exhibition).[3] Ralph and I had been in conversation about Frank since 2017. Our conversations took place in intervals, some just between us and others publicly, as in the Biennial (even though most missed it) and in his November 2020 special issue of *The Brooklyn Rail*, where the piece's origins are explained in depth. Intervals and precipices have come to define my excursions with Ralph, and have profoundly shaped much of my work in general.

It matters how we arrive at the precipice, and it matters that there are things we cannot escape in the interval. The labyrinth is said to protect us against supernatural powers; it is a path we must take to enter the spirit world when we die. Because one loses a sense of direction in these mazelike structures, they are spaces of disorientation, leaving one feeling unmoored. Within the high walls and narrow corridor of the antechamber, with its sharp angles, we sense one of the distinct characteristics of the labyrinth: it conjures a sense of being betwixt and thus is where we marvel. An interval, the labyrinth is the space-time-pitch of a resplendent betweenness that situates one always at the precipice of the Other, and with others. The interval was, first, a space of enclosure, of defense; it was the bridge between the fortress and the wall that protected it from the world beyond. To make things for a moment—the interval performs the times, animates difference within and of the times, meeting the conditions of arrival, which in the labyrinth always concerns another world and the limitations of the body acknowledged in the present one—is always precarious, insatiable, and also full of wonder. Deliberately designed so that one finds oneself in the act of wandering, it never concerns the end, that is, locating the center of the labyrinth, but rather the process—the process of the interval through which we begin again. Here at the precipice, we perform our ablutions, sending off and away the embedded violence in our surround that incessantly reverberates in and beyond our times. In Greek mythology, the labyrinth symbolized sacrifice as well as change and the possibility of transformation. The Hawara labyrinth in Egypt served as an enclosure, and also a space of transformation, within the funerary complex of a pyramid, with its countless connected rooms, halls, and courts. It is a space of obscurity, darkness, and transitions. In the labyrinth, we acquiesce to while also troubling self-discovery on the existential journey of life itself: our relations and grappling with the being of the world. We are fortified through the ancestral inheritances of presence here, with protective deities always emergent in this place of protection and retreat; especially for the tricksters, it is a recourse.[4]

[1] Ann Daly, "Conversations about Race in the Language of Dance," *New York Times*, December 7, 1997, https://www.nytimes.com/1997/12/07/arts/conversations-about-race-in-the-language-of-dance.html.

[2] Markland Taylor, "Geography," *Variety*, November 2, 1997, https://variety.com/1997/film/reviews/geography-2-1200452037/amp.

[3] Adrienne Edwards, "Some Thoughts on a Constellation of Things Seen and Felt," *Brooklyn Rail*, November 2020, https://brooklynrail.org/2020/11/criticspage/Some-Thoughts-on-a-Constellation-of-Things-Seen-and-Felt.

[4] This paragraph adapted from Adrienne Edwards, "Pendants as Counterpoints/Sources of the 2022 Whitney Biennial: 'Quiet as It's Kept,'" in *Why I Do What I Do: Global Curators Speak*, ed. Steven Henry Madoff (London: Sternberg Press, 2024).

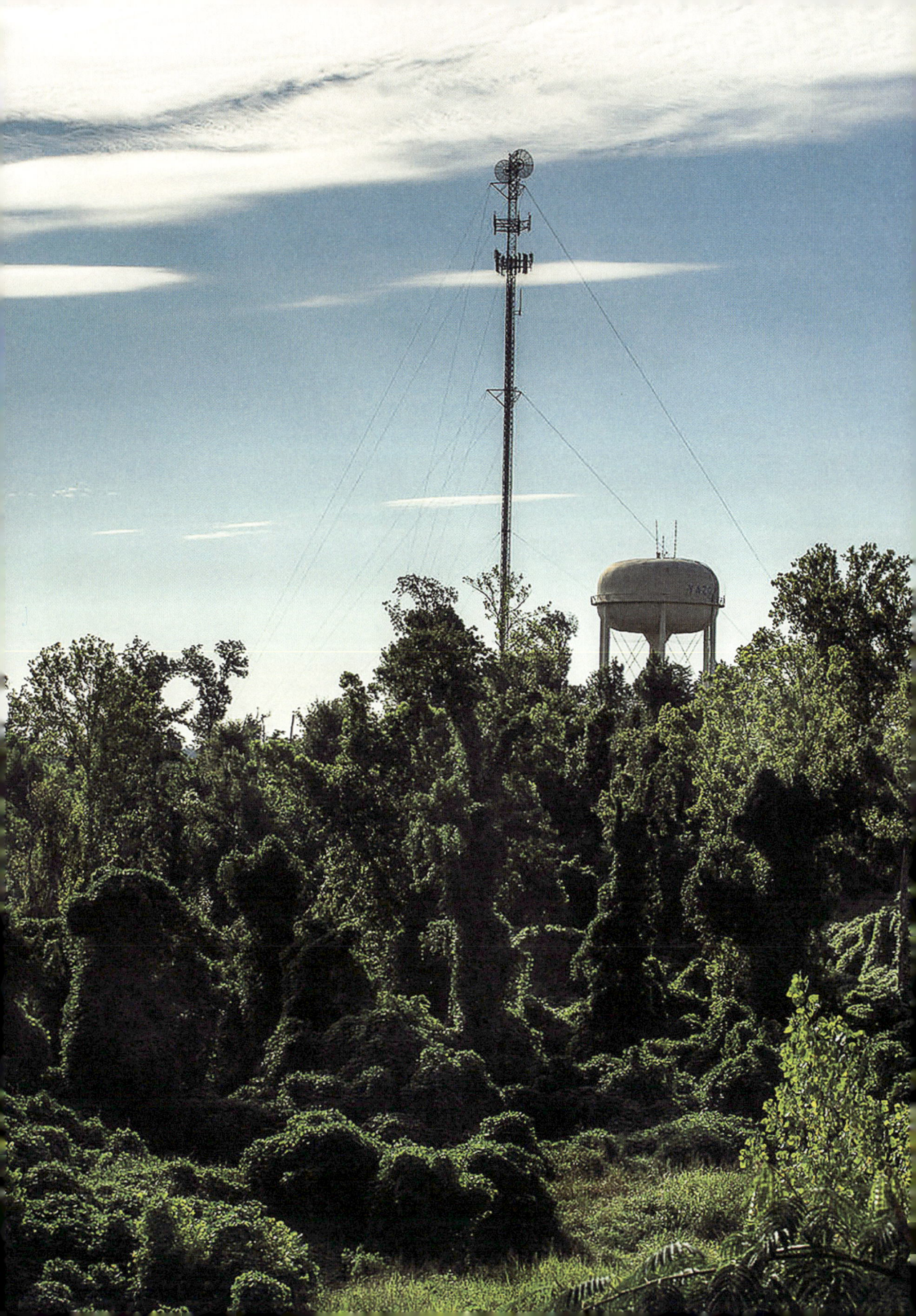

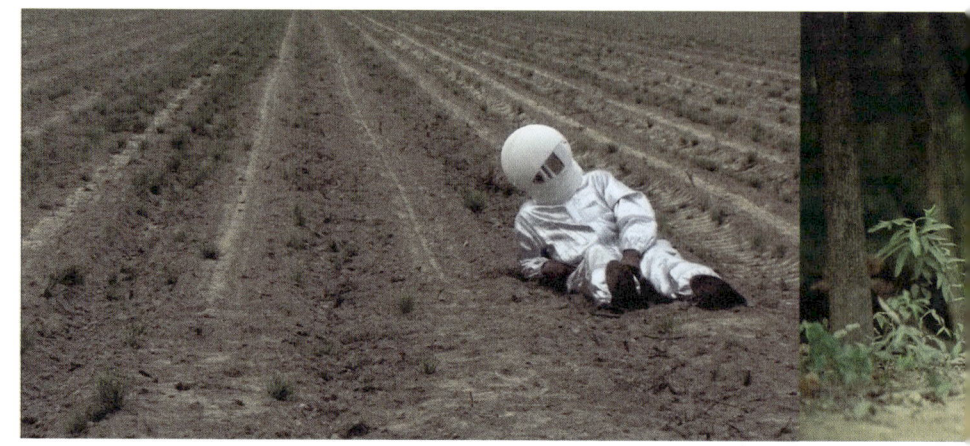

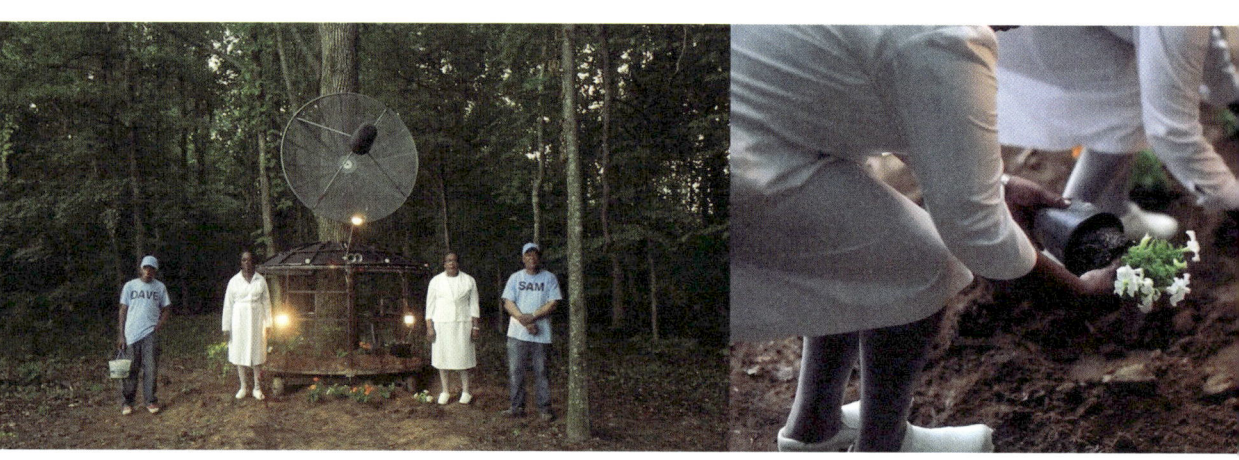

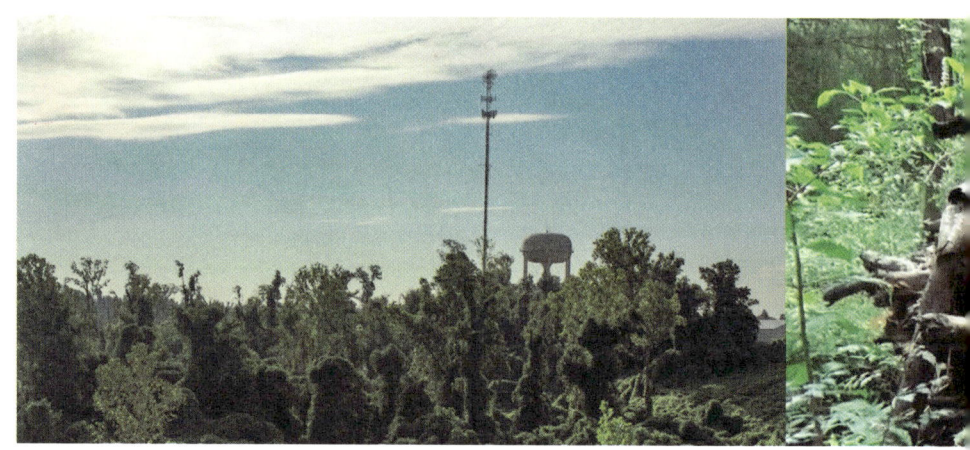

Walter Carter Suite, 2002—24

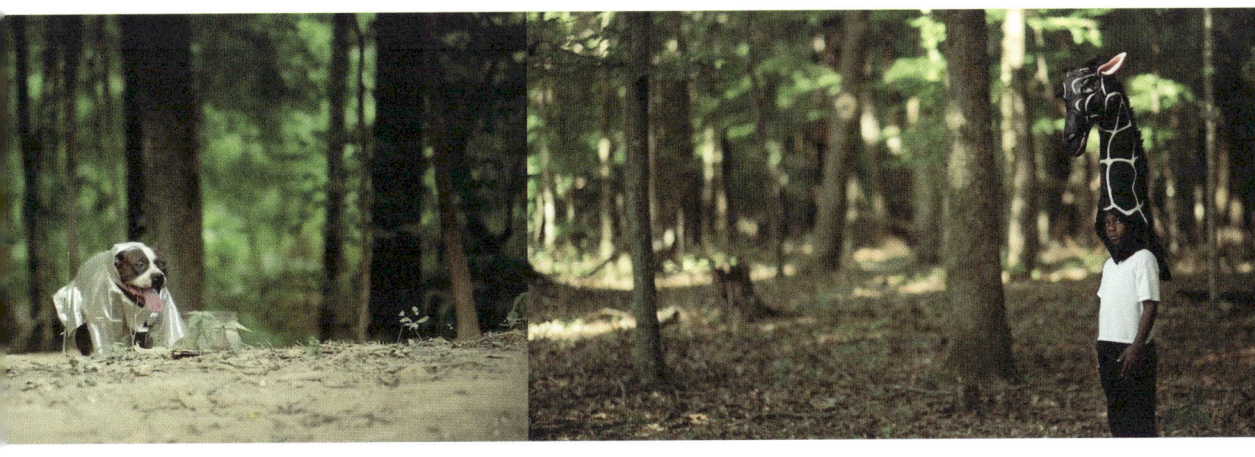

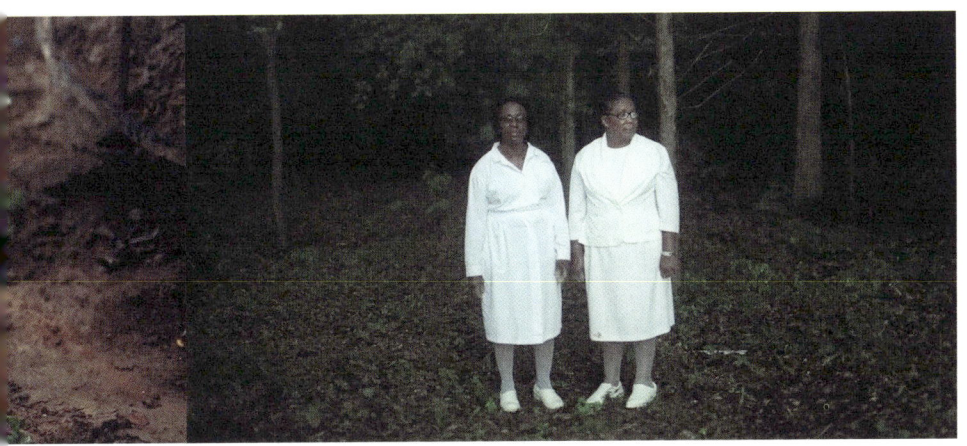

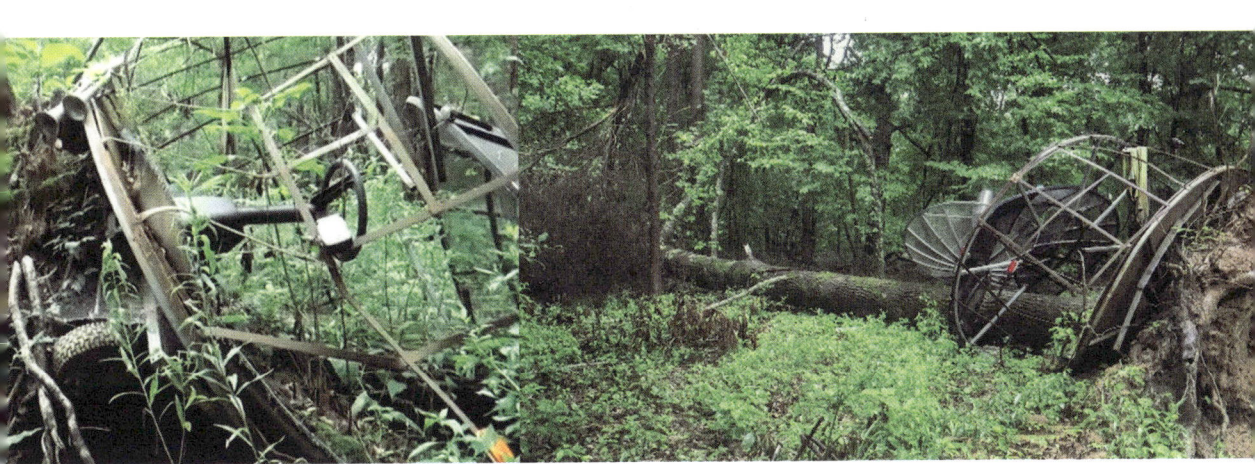

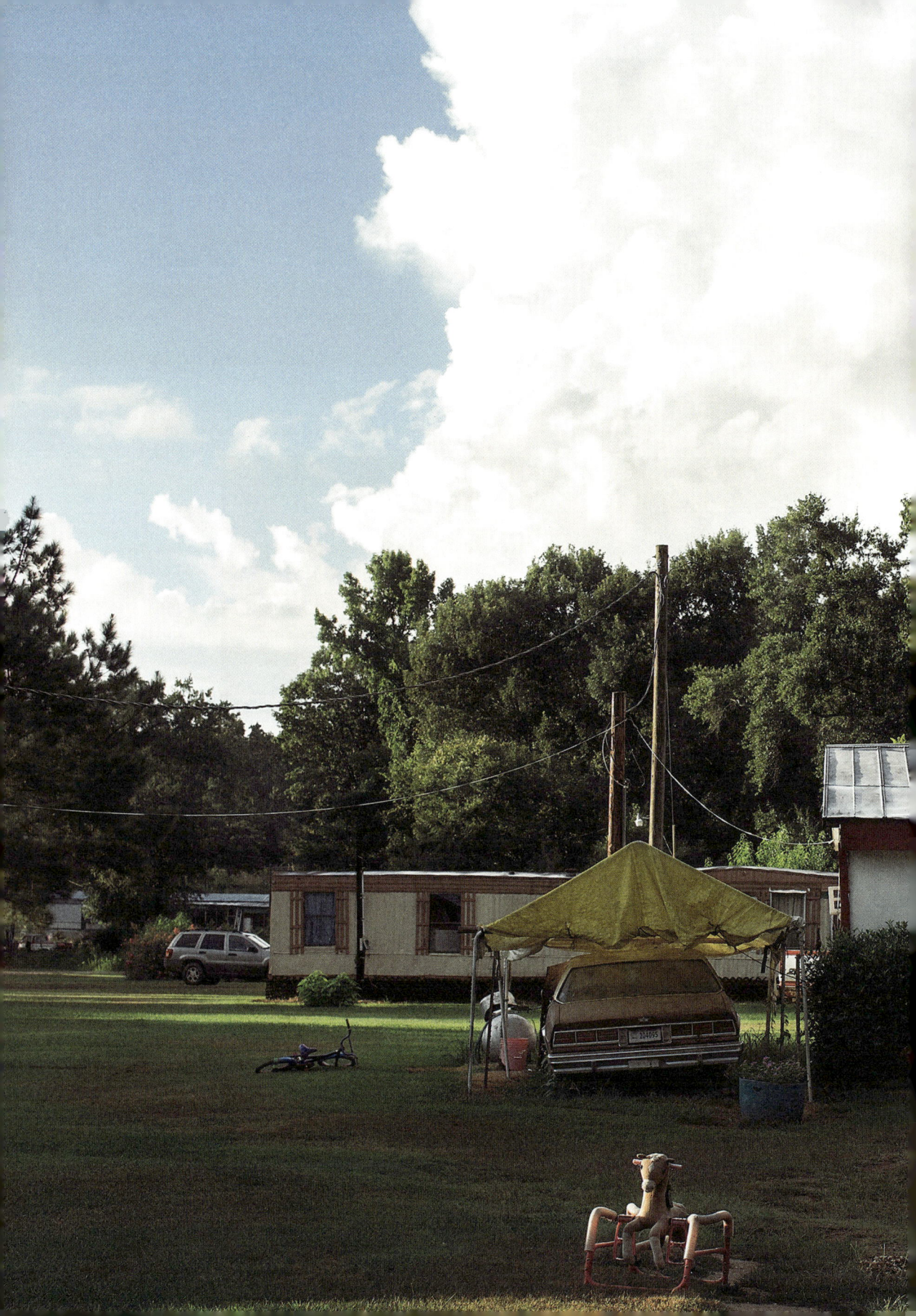

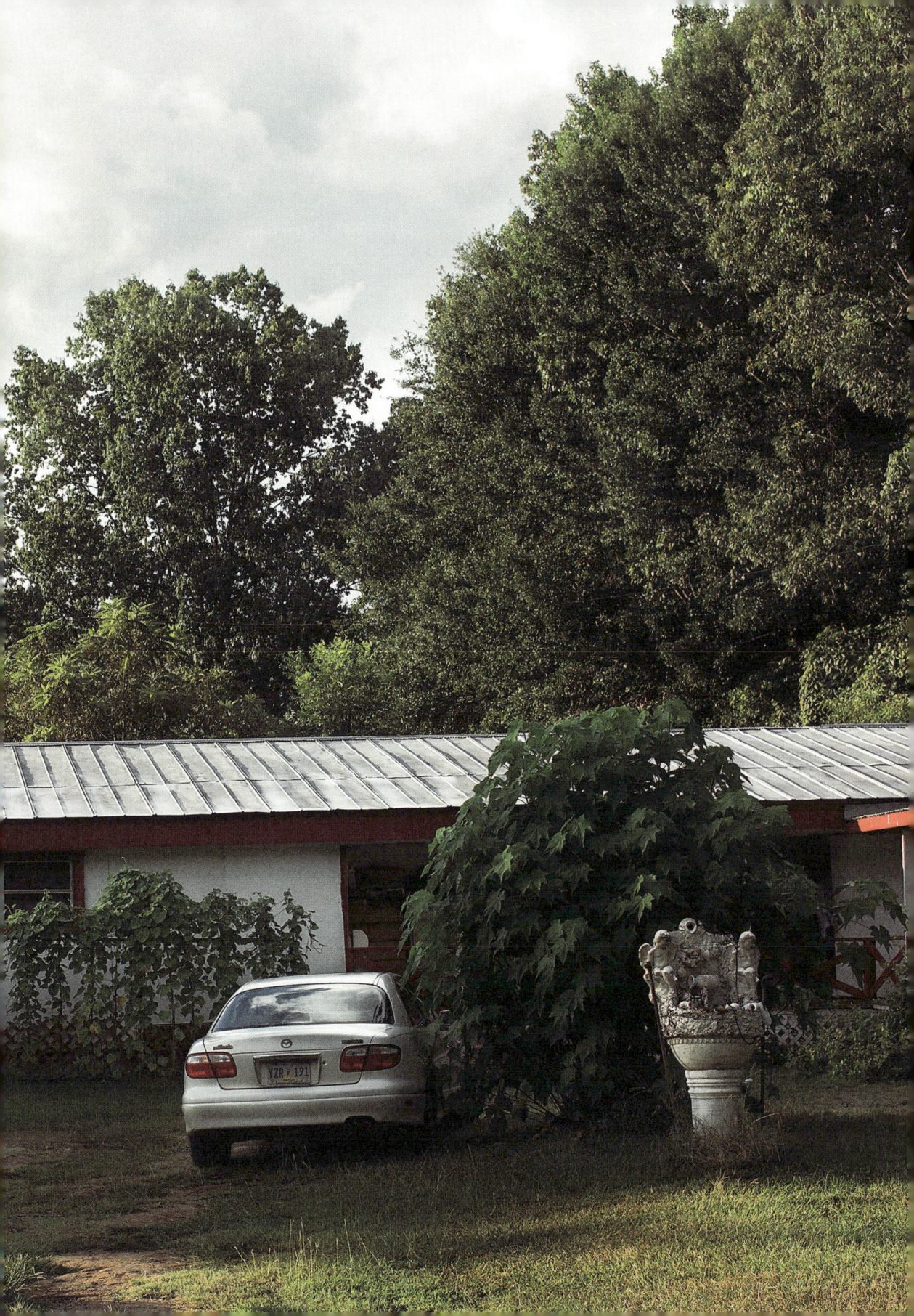

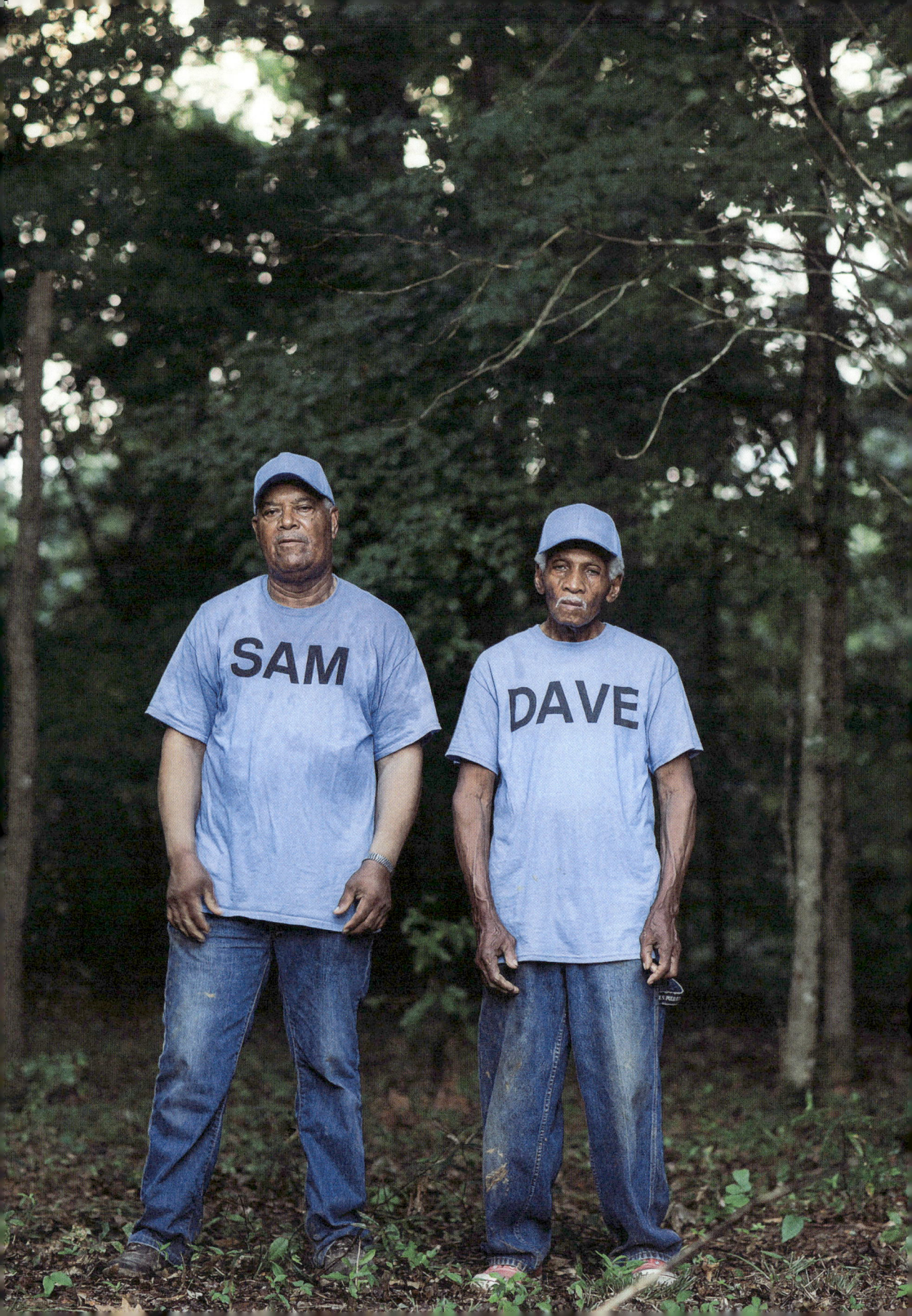

It could be a forest
Ralph Lemon

The following text was read by Lemon as voiceover in the video *It could be a forest* [Chapter 3] (2013). It recurs in *Ceremonies Out of the Air*, an artist talk to be performed at MoMA PS1 in 2025.

It could be a forest, if framed properly, the photo cropped just right. It sits a few yards away from Warren Carter's house, a fancy doublewide, almost a real country-rambler-style house, white, with a dark, blood-red trim. A series of cars surrounding the yards, front side, back, the field: a series of years to the models of the cars, 1970s to recent; white, maroon, and black; a Honda, a Dodge, an old Chevy. The cars and house and semi-manicured field surrounded by thick full green oaks and a few simple wooden utility poles with their overhead power lines. In the side right yard a small maze of forty to fifty young thin Carolina ash, with one thicker one, about three feet wide, that becomes the center.

There's a grassless (red) dirt dog yard a few yards from this center. Warren's son, Chester, is raising (fighter) pit bulls. Two at the moment, one a terrified runt. The runt won't ever fight, but they don't put it down, not sure why, maybe because it's weak. They are Christians, Southern Baptists, maybe that's why.

They dress the dogs in silver spacesuits; Lloyd Williams, Warren's good friend, and his wife, Emma, put them together. Patterned from pet-store-bought large-size camouflage dog jackets. The runt's costume becomes a silver cape; he/she is engulfed. Warren and his son did the actual dressing, put the silver suits on the dogs, because no one else wanted to get near them, not even near the cowering runt. Not me at least. The doghouses were painted the day before, three of them, a shade of purple (actually a purple closer to African violet). I thought this would be an interesting comment on Klein Blue, the color I was thinking about when I first saw the functional and quickly put-together plywood structures. I am not colorblind but actually prefer purple to Klein Blue. The structures badly needed a paint job, I thought. In my letter I asked Warren to find any purple, a convenient Home Depot purple. Now bright cartoon doghouses in a fifty-yard dirt perimeter, with a slight hill and tiny sink indentations, not quite actual holes but impending something more major.

This partially recreated landscape is also full of fleas or chiggers; both, I believe. Jumping off woody plants on anything unplanted and moving. A queer patience. Waiting for what? (Waiting for us, the work. How did they know? We just happened to be there.) I wear boots and thick jeans, am prepared, but it doesn't matter, am bitten up to my groin area. I go on the Internet investigating the marks and the pain and discover that I'm not really bitten if it is chiggers. I'm burrowed through the skin by something (and left with some kind of enzyme that makes a larger hole, a stylostome, I imagine, which causes red, pimple-like bumps). Whatever they are, they populate my body, for days. Starting at the ankles and climbing upward, it seems. Terrifying. Then they die, I suppose. Leaving larvae. The larvae drop, eventually becoming mites dropping to the ground, harmless to humans, laying eggs, and then the mites die, a second death.

This is the theater, our forest and reconstituted dog yard. Where Lloyd moved the flying saucer, from his garage, five miles away, still in Bentonia, Mississippi, though. Taking it apart after our celestial and countrified play three years before, when he first put it together and tried to make it work, actually fly. He said he would keep trying. He was able to get it rolling down a nearby freeway right away, an alternate lane. Three years later Lloyd took it apart, moving it in his truck the few miles to Warren's place, then repurposing it, circling it, mandala-like, around the three-foot-wide center tree in Warren's back side yard with his bare hands.

A voice off camera says, *Where is Walter?* Warren's father and the patriarch to this play. The story begins with him.

When we last saw Walter, he had flown off in his flying saucer. Lloyd got it to fly. Walter wanted to go to heaven, *where there aren't a lot of people. A chosen few*, he had said.

But Walter lands on what appears to be a futuristic barren cotton field. On another planet. The saucer falls around a treelike organism, maybe the same planet but maybe not. The inhabitants of this place (ghosts of the R&B singing duet Sam and Dave and their specter spouses, Emma and Lorraine, who on this day are elected Nurses of the Church, dressed in official Nurses of the Church white) find the saucer and plant an immaculate garden around it. They think it's a god.

Walter is never seen again.

At one point it began to rain, hard, and they had to pause.

Everyone soaking wet. Had to wait not only for the sun but also until their costumes were dry, to finish tending the garden, for the camera. Rain and sweat. The rain softening the earth, making the planting easier.

By sunset they were done. Lloyd turned on the flying saucer's headlights. Everything else in dark shadow. It sat that way through the night, hovering. Lloyd remarked that he was tired and limped back to Warren's house.

Silver-coated killer space dogs bark out high-frequency signals in the background.

A garden. A memorial. A sci-fi requiem—not one's expected (old) Black Southern rage, reactive violence. Also an escape; it is outer space after all, search for a kind world, forgiveness (or forgetting?). Imagined. Choreographed travels (death), which is also an escape. Down here, this South (like everywhere), funerals are theater.

Two years later I receive a text. *Here are pictures of the flying saucer. I'm sorry.* Emma texting and sending more photos to me from her cell phone, three, a close-up and two long shots, checking in after another great storm settled in the area, blew the tree down that held/centered the flying saucer. The only tree to fall in the little forest yard, completely uprooted. How strange. The saucer destroyed, a real wreck, sculpted by nature. Magnificent. Now a true (unfinished) masterpiece.

Lloyd and Warren used to work together, driving around collecting (good) junk and reselling it (until Warren got too tired). How the saucer got made. Yes, progress, what the storm wrought. Back to junk. Now broken to pieces in Warren's unkempt yard (uncollectable, because it's already there). Waiting for what? It's just waiting. In Emma's text she didn't mention how Lloyd felt about the damage, the obliteration. Not a word. The labor.

So I called Lloyd and said, *That was really good work, Lloyd. Thank you. I must get back down there, soon, we'll find another center, make something new, I'm sure. I am absolutely sure of it.* Though there is nothing idyllic about that place, where it is, what it represents, not even in my unreliable memory. There is the broad blue Mississippi sky. (Unless it's raining, or there's a great storm. Clouds hanging in clumps, like pre-Cubist snowmen, shapes more round).

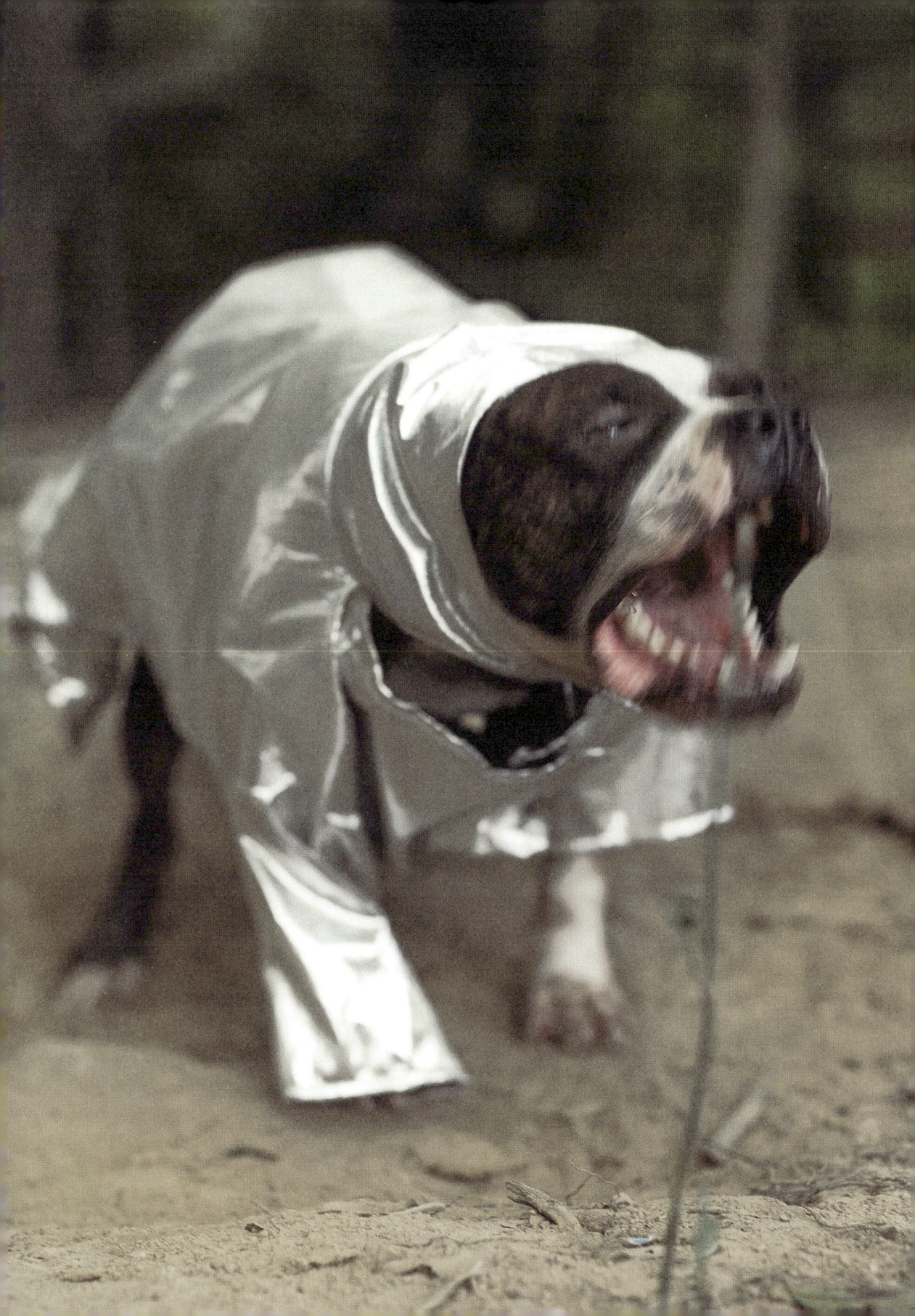

OUTER SPACE ROBBERY

NOT SO DEADLY AS IN

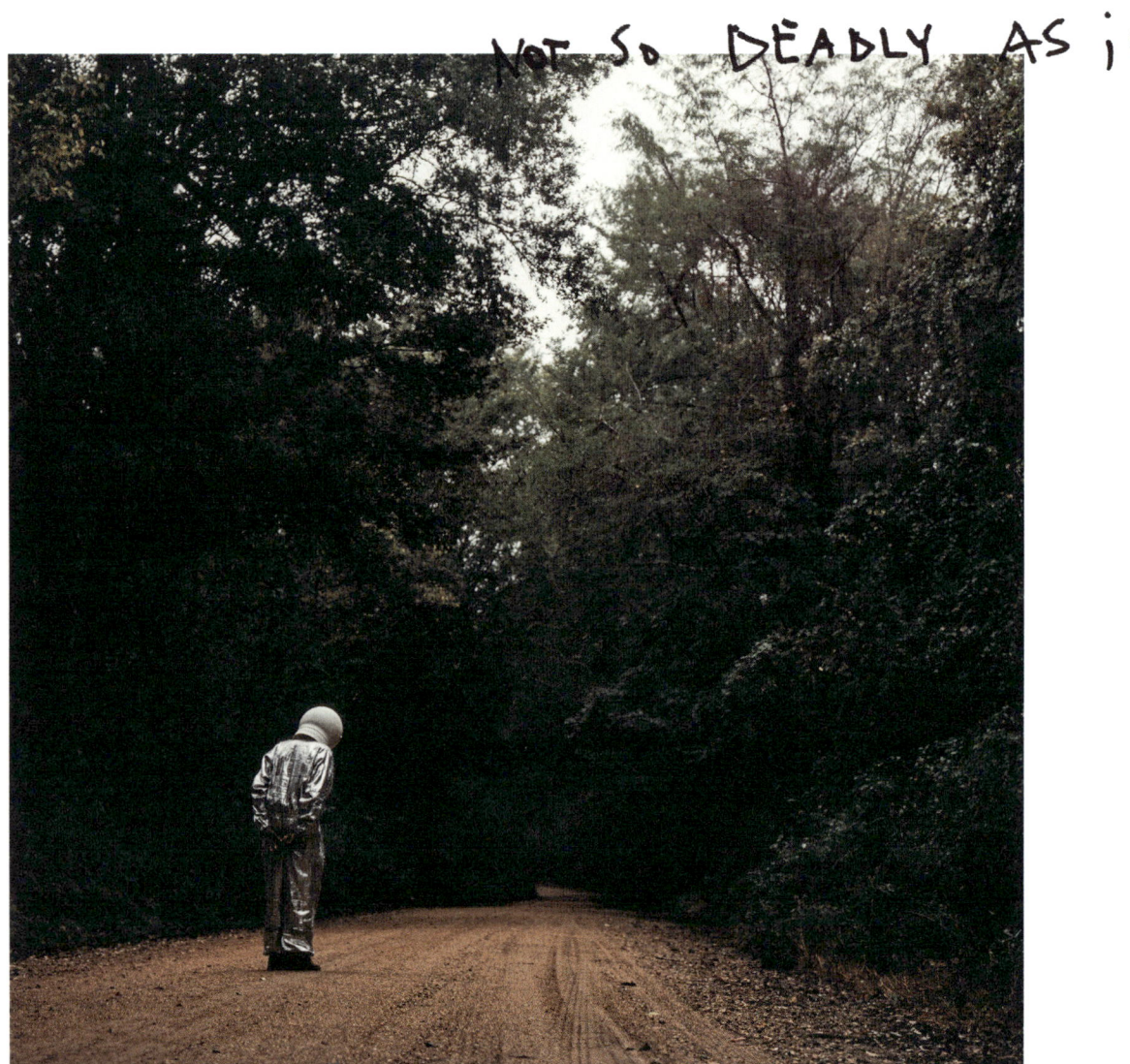

Walter Carter Suite, 2002—24

HE GHETTOS — NO GRAVITY

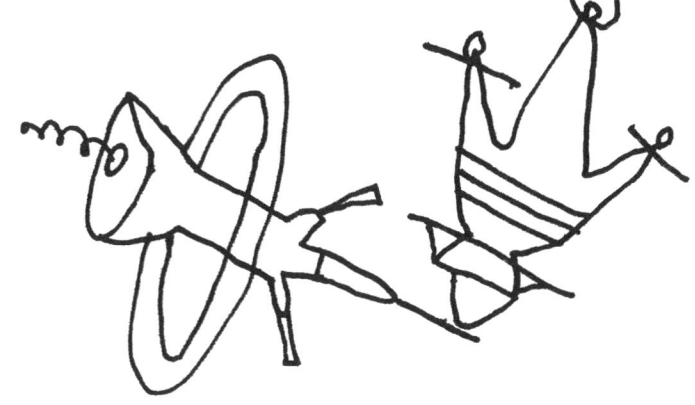

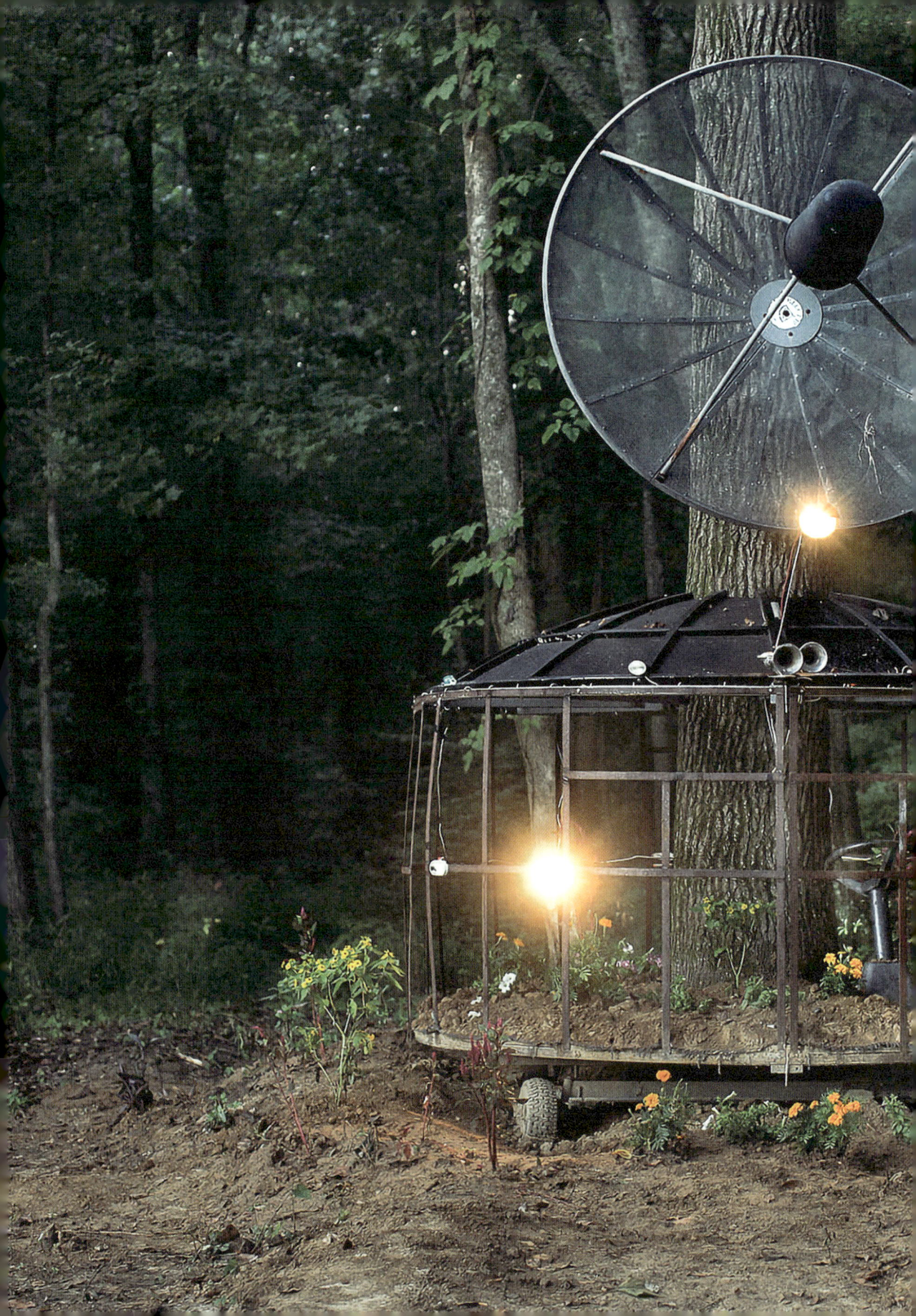

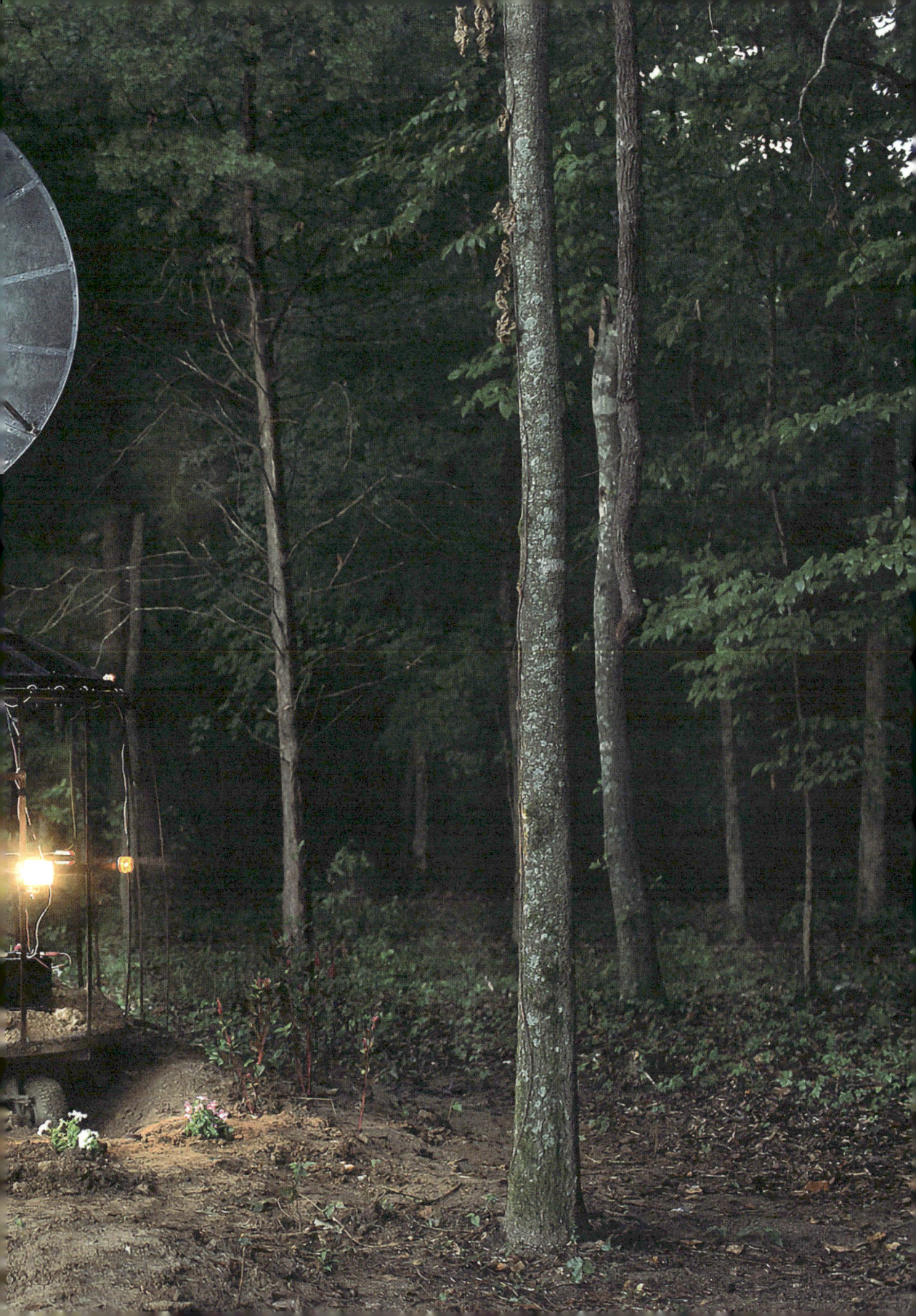

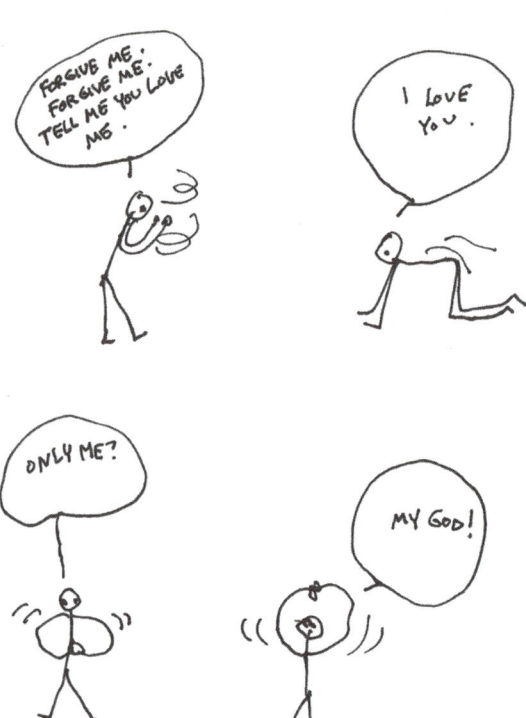

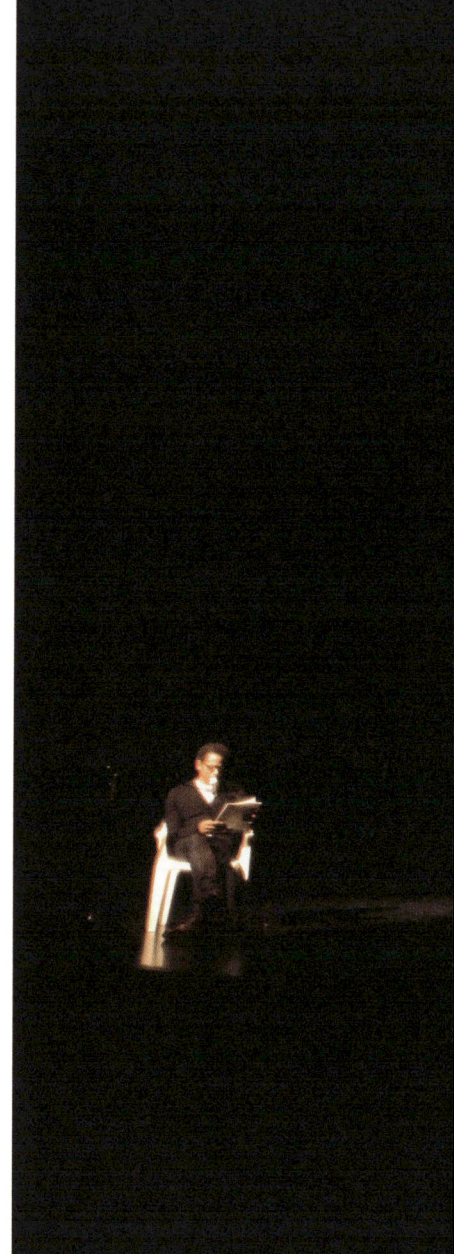

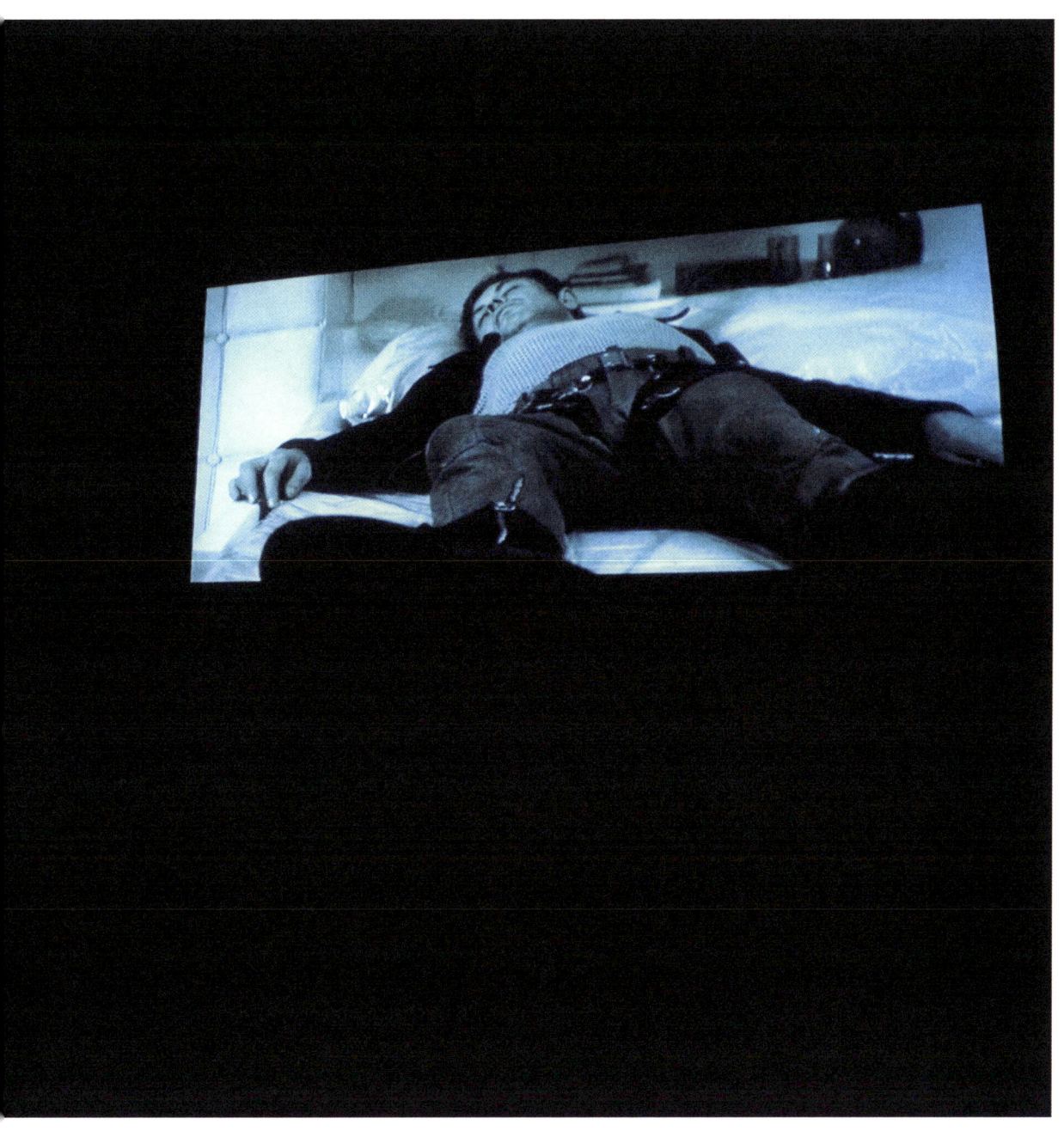

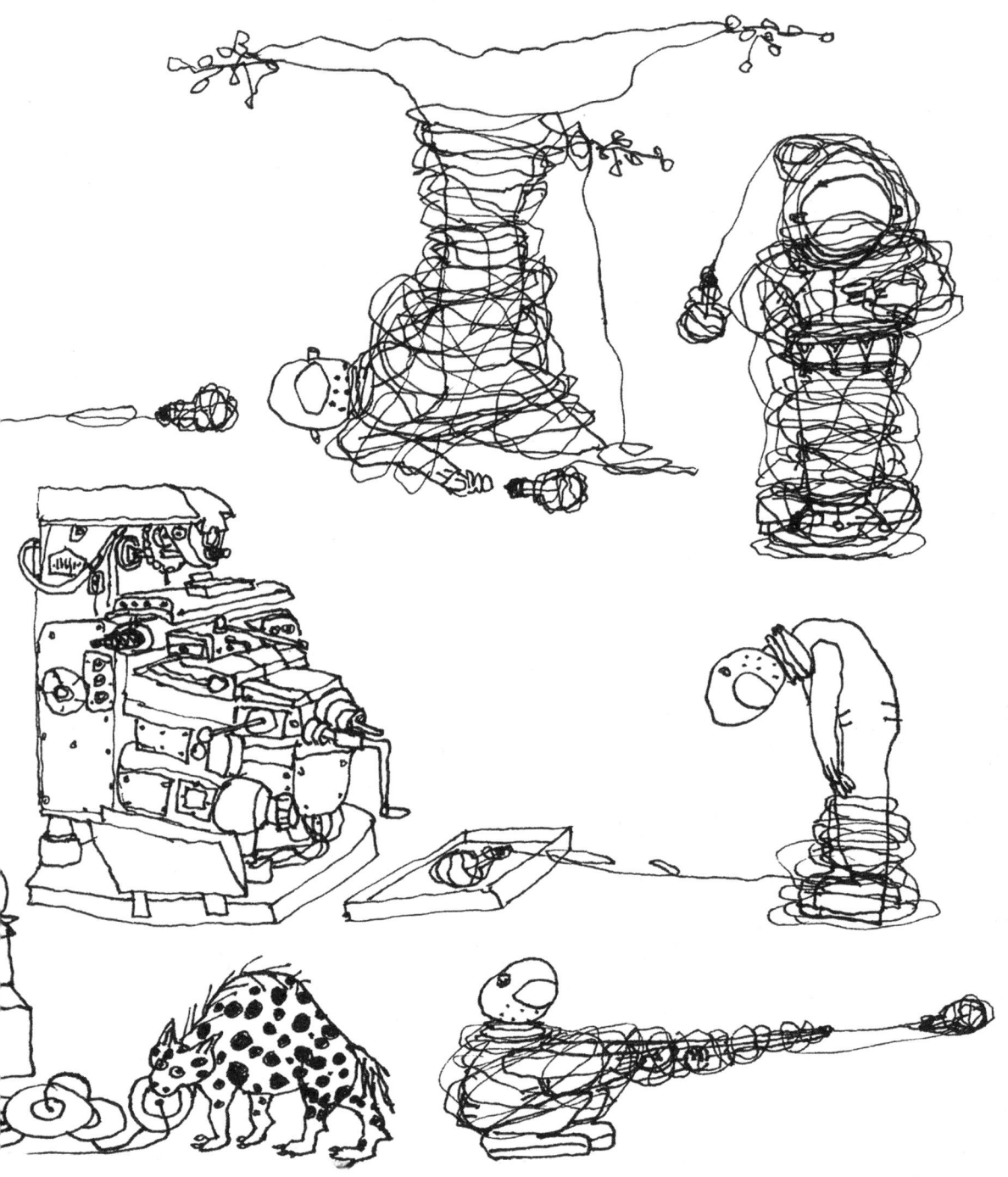

Preparations for Collective Departure
Thomas Lax

You know, they straightened out the Mississippi River in places, to make room for houses and livable acreage. Occasionally the river floods these places. "Floods" is the word they use, but in fact it is not flooding; it is remembering. Remembering where it used to be. All water has a perfect memory and is forever trying to get back to where it was. Writers are like that: remembering where we were, what valley we ran through, what the banks were like, the light that was there and the route back to our original place. It is emotional memory—what the nerves and the skin remember as well as how it appeared. And a rush of imagination is our "flooding."

—Toni Morrison, "The Site of Memory"[1]

Ralph Lemon has been preparing us to get out of here. Off the stage, out of the museum, away from this militarized campus. But is there any other landscape for us? No matter. For at least thirty years, he has been collaborating—plotting the end of one of these worlds, and then another.

In 1995, he closed his dance company, making the promise that his departure would allow for a different kind of return. "We'd have a good year touring, then the next year work would be cut in half. And I was one of the fortunate ones," he told the *New York Times*.[2] He would no longer make a new dance annually to take on the road for the same audience and hope he would be able to raise the $170,000 to pay the dancers' annual salaries and health insurance. Instead, he packed the group up and expressed the collective mourning of its devoted members—Brian Dawbin, Barbara Grubel, Alissa Hsu, Ted Johnson, Nicholas Leichter, Krista Miller, and Lisa Powers. "A grieving has been taking place," he said at the time. "There has been a sense of abandonment. There was anger." Some of the dancers went on to make their own work; others left dance. Ralph began performing with people in their homes or at unmarked historical sites—filming, photographing, writing, or drawing what came before and after.

I didn't see the Ralph Lemon Company's last performance, *Threestep (Shipwreck)*, a dance he made with Viola Farber in 1995, but its descriptions are animated by knowledge of the group's evanescence.[3] Farber was sixty-four and in fragile health. She and Lemon inhabited the same scene seemingly unaware of one another as cellist Michael Mermagen played Bach suites as accompaniment. At the very end, Farber locked her elbow under Ralph's outstretched arm. He weaved his arm around hers and they faced one another at *a tautly stretched distance*.[4] She would die three years later.

In 2006, Ralph left again, went further, tried harder to escape. He asked his friend and collaborator Walter Carter, then a ninety-eight-year-old former sharecropper from Little Yazoo, Mississippi, to build a spaceship with his friends and family. The group documented their process in a video cycle that begins with *1856 Cessna Road* [Chapter 1] (2008–9). With his son, Warren "Red" Carter, and a neighbor, Lloyd Williams, Carter used the junk available to them, attaching a wheel, antenna, and lights to an old fishing boat cut in half. They were preparing to send Carter out of the Earth's atmosphere. In the homemade flying saucer, he ascended to the sky—away from the land he had sharecropped and away from the lynching sites he had known in his youth—only to fall to a barren cotton field on the surface of an uncertain planet. The flight from the plantation returned him to ground zero.

~

Songs are either about falling in love or about heartache. The good
ones are about both. Gillian Welch's "I Dream a Highway,"
for example, has been playing in our apartment on repeat recently.
The folk song's six stanzas last fourteen minutes: a duration
you can almost convince yourself will outlast memory's lament.
Six times Welch sings, *I dream a highway back to you, love / I dream
a highway back to you / A winding ribbon with a band of gold /
A silver vision come and rest my soul / I dream a highway back to
you*. I am grieving, and Andrew, my boyfriend, sings along to these
lyrics of movement and migration. "Down into Memphis . . . I lie
and wait until the wagons come." He mouths each highway's *winding
ribbon* as Welch tries to get back to her lost love object, perhaps
dead and certainly gone. This ending is also a beginning, at least in
her dreams.

~

Fugitivity is one way the black radical tradition has termed the
coming and going of Welch's *silver vision*.

In his 2018 book *Stolen Life*, Fred Moten describes fugitivity as
"a desire for and a spirit of escape and transgression of the proper
and the proposed." A refusal of individualism and a transposition
of the given: fugitivity is a "desire for the outside, for a playing
or being outside."[5] Playing requires repetition, so Moten gives it to
us over and again in refrains that fall through language. For example, in an earlier poem titled "Fugitivity is immanent to the thing
but is manifest transversally," he offers up this ending: "some
stateless folks / spurn the pleasure they are driven // to be and
strive against. man, hit me again."[6] Desire and loss are part of the
same wheel of impossible return. Deferral—*pleasure spurned*—
is interrupted by the trample of violation, ironically, in the form
of a request: *hit me again*. (Some languages conjugate imperative
and subjunctive verbs the same way.)[7] And because it's something
we do with others, Moten joins his friend Stefano Harney in yet
a third text to indefinitely define fugitivity as "at home with the
homeless," "being separate from settling," and that which "escapes
even the fugitive."[8]

In a public conversation between Moten and Saidiya Hartman, Hartman historicized a late eighteenth-century version of fugitivity: *petit marronage*, in which enslaved people ran away from the plantation for a period of days or weeks, and then returned to its margins. They did not set up autonomous or sovereign communities; they did not set out to get free once and for all but rather practiced a version of freedom lived in intimate proximity to unfreedom. "Marronage on the border" was a form of fugitivity for "people who were close enough to the plantation to still be caught" and "who found a way to live in the trees but couldn't leave any marks of human habitation." She calls "this other mode of dwelling" "a certain dance."[9] Unclaimed, the land did not bear signs of use. Without a petition for nation or statehood, *petit marronage* made no declaration of culture—nationalist, multi-, or otherwise.

Culture—the word as well as the concept the word names—emerged linguistically in the sixteenth century but materialized historically four to three thousand years BCE when groups of people assembled to tend the soil and claim its future yield. What are the possibilities for activities made outside of this culture of civilization? For performances made with *ceremonies out of the air*? What returns await us when we leave without a trace?

~

After Ralph disbanded his company, he began to make more drawings. These images and texts recorded and reflected upon the travels he made through South, East, and Southeast Asia; West Africa; the Caribbean; and the Southeastern US—trips that led to collaborations over the ensuing three decades. After a flood in his storage space in the wake of Hurricane Sandy in 2012, he lost many of these works on paper.

Ralph wrote about the disaster in the performance *Scaffold Room* (2014–15) [pp. 18, 46]. April Matthis sang this story then and is scheduled to sing it again in the 2024 performance *Tell it anyway*, a new deformation of the older work. She will say:

> Underwater, they swam, tried to swim, sank. It took a month before we could get to them. The funeral went like this: [singing to Beyoncé's "Drunk in Love"] *We woke up in the kitchen sayin' how the hell did this shit happen / Aw baby.*

Last thing I remember is our beautiful bodies grindin' off in that club. [Singing acapella to a made-up nursery rhyme] *We waited till spring. Went to a nearby garden. Laid them out in the sun. Paper holds water well. In this case saltwater . . . piss shit water . . . water. Until it goes back to pulp . . . pulp . . . pulp. Until it goes back to water. Oh me, how sad. Water displaced. Loss. But most of the water returns home. Flows. Probably doesn't go the same way, ever.*

When a photograph gets wet, really wet, the image completely disappears. Emulsion is also water, two liquids in fact—colloids. An empty frame. One can't even remember what picture was taken: who, where, when.[10]

Feelings distort the facts, which were useless anyway. Waterlogged, the past resurfaces as emotion. Eventually, the feelings will disappear too.

Ralph's work is a preparation—a rehearsal for a teacher's return, an unlikely shot at love, a collaborator we didn't expect. (They all arrive as suddenly as they will depart. So we stretch, preparing to remember.) His work is also a way of commemorating those teachers, great loves, and collaborators who have come and gone. These are different names for the same thing: life, life's force.

~

When in 2010 Walter Carter died (or was never heard from again), his family buried the spaceship in the nearby woods: a ritualized mash-up of grief and love. Warren Carter and Lloyd Williams wore baby-blue T-shirts with the names of their characters from the video cycle, Sam and Dave, an old R&B singing duo [p. 110]. Their wives, Emma Williams and Lorraine Carter, played the Garden Ladies (aka Specter Spouses), dressed in Nurses of the Church white uniforms. Two Killer Space Dogs, costumed in silver space suits, Mylar heat-retention dog jackets bought at a local pet shop, joined the ensemble [p. 115].

In the funerary video *Garden* [Chapter 2] (2013), which immediately follows Carter's fall back to Earth, the family buries the vehicle around a tree trunk [pp. 106–7]. They shovel soil across the bottom of the ship; they plant yellow and orange and purple marigolds; they water them. A dog barks, and two kids in giraffe heads (Michael Sims and Jayden Williams, Emma and Lloyd's nephews) run around. Night descends. When Sam comes to turn off the spaceship's lights, the sounds of children yelling, birds chirping, cicadas squawking, and the dogs still barking can be made out in the background.

A year later, a great storm swept through the Delta and felled the tree, ripping the spaceship out of the ground. It's still there, deteriorating: *a perfect memory.*

1   Toni Morrison, "The Site of Memory," in *Inventing the Truth: The Art and Craft of Memory*, ed. William Zinsser (New York: Houghton Mifflin, 1995), 99.

2   All quotations this paragraph are from Ralph Lemon, quoted in Anna Kisselgoff, "Ralph Lemon Troupe Opens Its Final Season," *New York Times*, October 5, 1995, https://www.nytimes.com/1995/10/05/arts /dance-review-ralph-lemon-troupe-opens-its-final-season.html.

3   Farber had been a lead dancer in Merce Cunningham's company for more than a decade, from 1953 to 1965; Ralph met her when he was a dancer with Nancy Hauser's company in Minneapolis and Farber came to make two works with them.

4   This account, including the phrase "a tautly stretched distance," comes from Kisselgoff, "Ralph Lemon Troupe Opens Its Final Season."

5   Fred Moten, *Stolen Life*, vol. 2 of *consent not to be a single being* (Durham, NC: Duke University Press, 2018), 131. "Proper," like "property" and "propriety," is etymologically linked to having *one's own*, according to Oxford Languages, via Google's online English dictionary.

6   Fred Moten, "Fugitivity is immanent to the thing but is manifest transversally," in *hughson's tavern* (Providence, RI: Leon Works, 2008), 58.

7   One of these languages is black feminist thought. Saidiya Hartman describes a method that exploits "the capacities of the subjunctive (a grammatical mood that expresses doubts, wishes, and possibilities)," while Tina Campt gives language to her "prefigurative" use of the imperative as "a striving for the future you want to see, right now, in the present." See Saidiya Hartman, "Venus in Two Acts," *small axe* 25 (June 2008), 11; and Tina Campt, "Quiet Soundings: The Grammar of Black Futurity," in *Listening to Images* (Durham, NC: Duke University Press, 2017), 17. Another one of these languages is French; my grammar book offers *Vienne l'aube, les oiseaux chantant* (Come dawn, the birds sing) as an example in which the subjunctive is used as a wishful command.

8   Stefano Harney and Fred Moten, *The Undercommons: Fugitive Planning and Black Study* (New York: Minor Compositions, 2013), 97, 11, 50.

9   "Fred Moten and Saidiya Hartman at Duke University: The Black Outdoors," video of the panel discussion "The Black Outdoors: Humanities Futures after Property and Possession," Saidiya Hartman and Fred Moten in Conversation with J. Kameron Carter and Sarah Jane Cervenak, John Hope Franklin Humanities Institute at Duke University, posted October 5, 2016, video, 2:04:02, https://www.youtube.com /watch?v=t_tUZ6dybrc. For more information on *petit marronage*, see Marcus P. Nevius, *City of Refuge: Slavery and Petit Marronage in the Great Dismal Swamp, 1763–1856* (Athens: University of Georgia Press, 2020).

10   Ralph Lemon, "Ask a Friend to Give You a Sentence: An Evening with Joan Jonas and Friends," The Museum of Modern Art, New York, April 16, 2024.

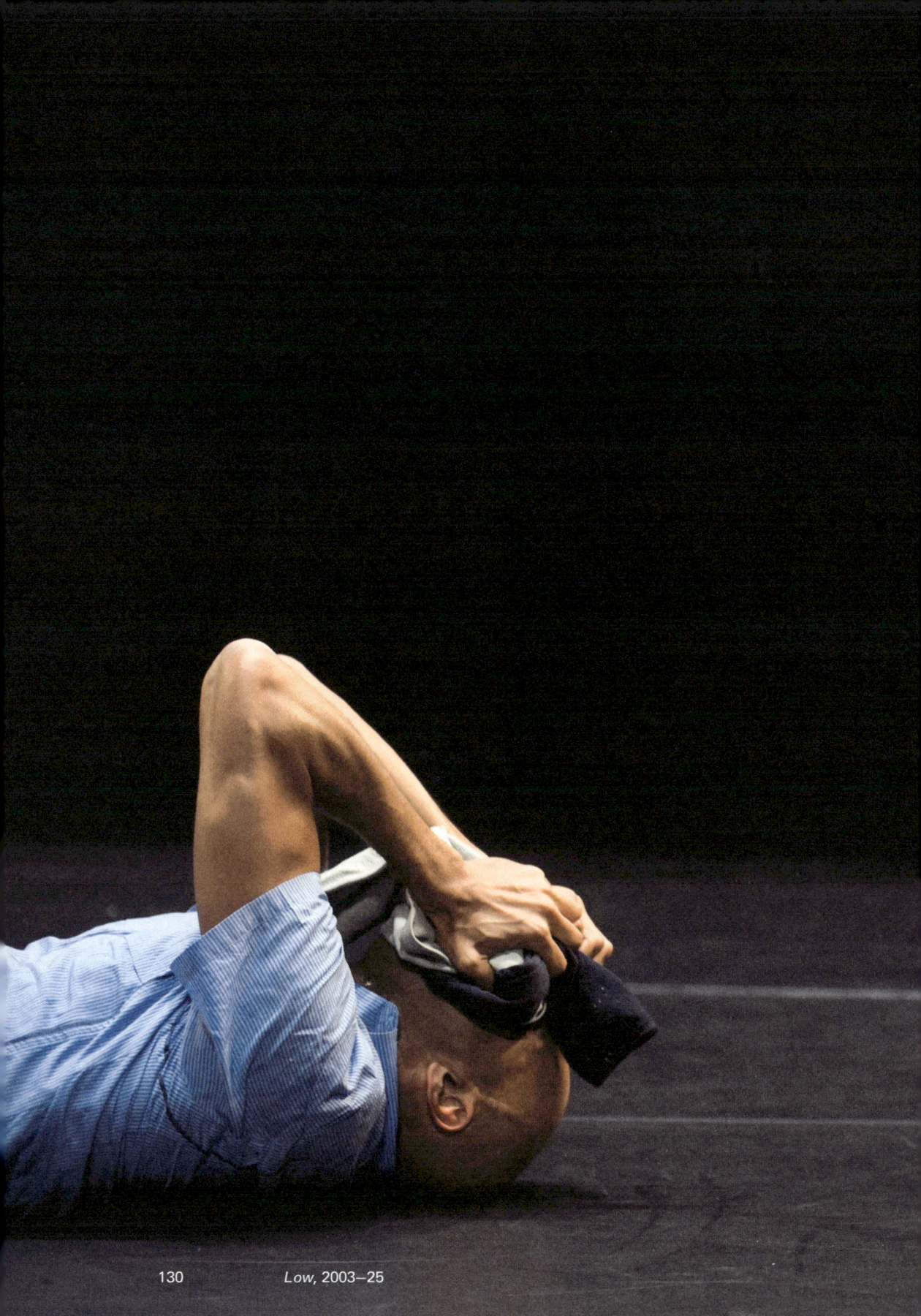

Low, 2003–25

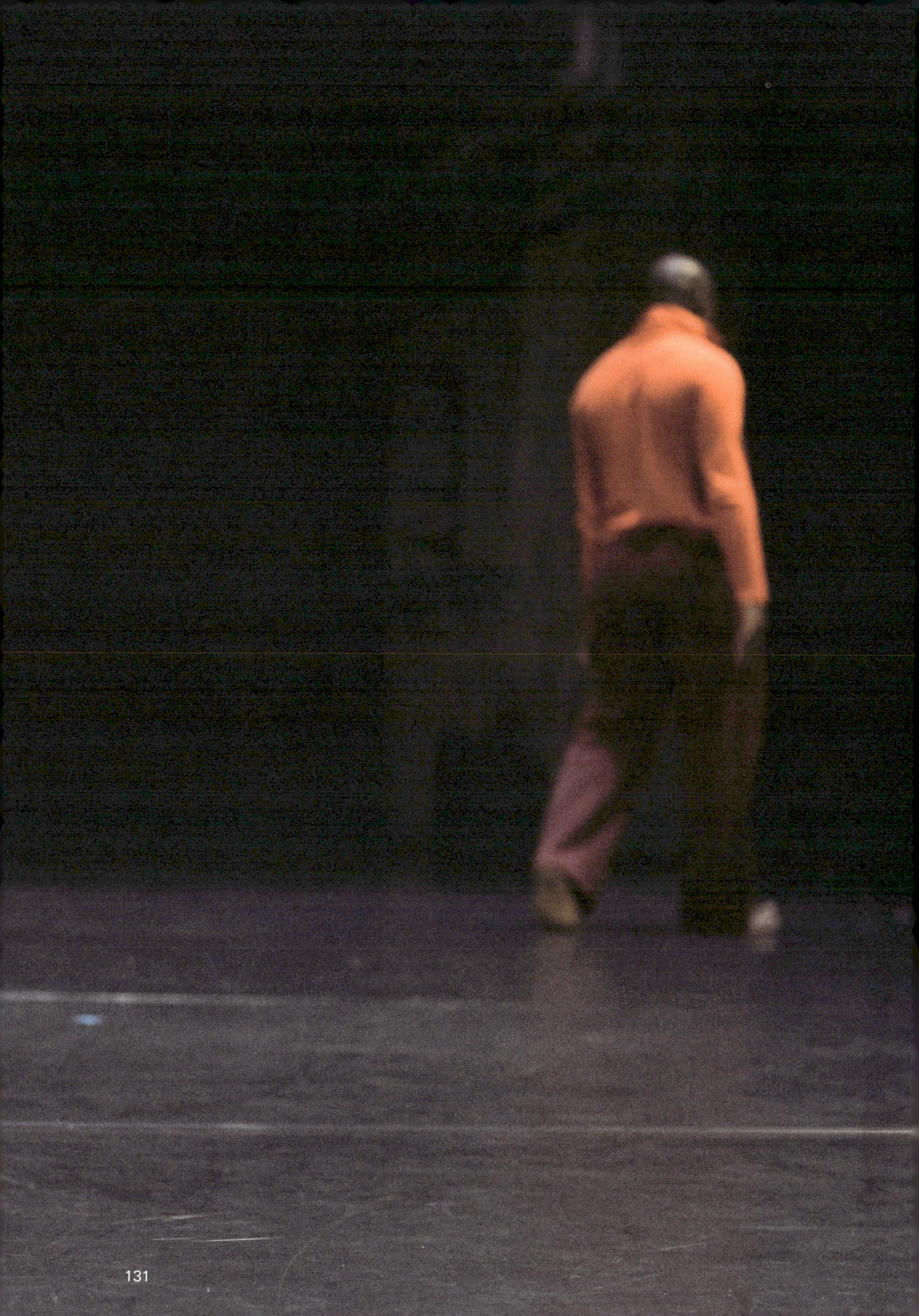

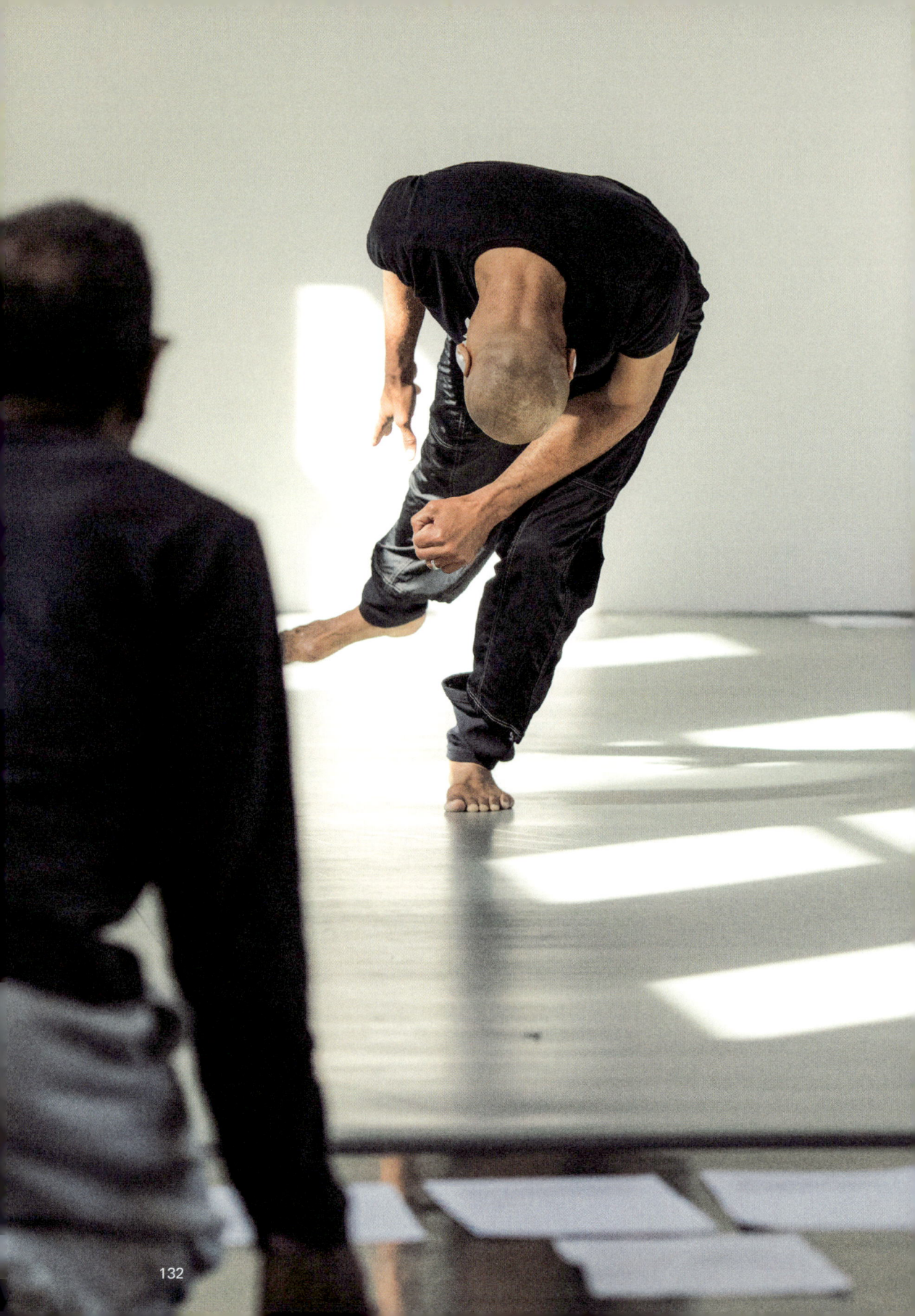

F-Words
Darrell Jones

This contribution comprises the "F-word" section from an in-progress annotated glossary detailing more than twenty years of collaboration between Darrell Jones and Ralph Lemon. Drawing from prompts for movement, notes, conversation, and reflections, the glossary traces the contours of a movement modality called Low within which Jones and Lemon have been working since 2003. Low is many things. It brings forward the energy that typically comes in the wake of performance, after exertion; it is the transition from fury and exhaustion to ecstasy.

4WALLS (2012)
The body is moving at a very high level for a long period of time, going in as many directions as it can, simultaneously.

There's never a still image—it's a moving blur.
—RL

FACE
Begin with the face, moving to the body.
Sitting with a partner, facing that partner, approx. 2 feet apart.
Allow your face to react to the face facing you.
Maybe replicating it (to begin).
It is impossible to match the other face, so there is no problem.
After a while (20 minutes?),

allow what's happening in the face to become the whole body.
A moving down and up, in and out.
The whole body expresses (something seen, not seen, heard, not heard).

30 minutes later move away (respectfully) from your focus on your partner's face/body.
—score for *The Godhead* (2010)

FAG-FAIRY

██████████████████
██████████████

FAILURE
Transcendence!
And failure is a (generative) mystery not a problem. :) xo
—RL

FAITH

████████████████████████

FALLING—NOT UP OR DOWN
This was a prompt, a koan,
an impossible puzzle given to
perpetuate enlightenment.

FAMILY
Insert picture of Chelsea, Ralph's
daughter. She was part of
the artistic process. Helping with
interviews and videotaping
during *Come home Charley
Patton*. Understanding his work
as a family operation. I asked
him why he disbanded the
Ralph Lemon Dance Company.
He said he couldn't bear to
have people leave.

FANTASTICAL
Descriptor for the "Jump" series

FASCIA
A body system particularly
important to the Low modality

FASHION
1. He made me shoes for the
Venice shows. An act of kindness
to counteract the marble
architecture of the floors.
2. Wearing a hard-soled '60s shoe,
I sprained my ankle in a photo
shoot for *Come home Charley
Patton*.
3. Transcribe the body trajectory
into the use of the jacket in
"Jacket Fury."

FAT
Life is FAT. And beautiful.
—RL

FATHER
dear friend

poems seem the proper thickness

to read lines
that shift the time

pausing space

in-betweens
of feel and think

for we
the body changed lightness

their weight is still
gaining fullness from their
living/lived-in volume
us

My loves go out to you and
your (large) family in this time
of transition.

FATIGUE
Put the gas on the accelerator,
we want to get to the edge of
fatigue as quickly as we can to
see what is on the other side.
—a description of getting from
FURY to ECSTASY

FAUNA
He had a little zoo in his small
East Village apartment . . . dog,
cat, bird, fish . . . excess.

FEAR
Something bad is going to
happen in that excess.
—notes from rehearsal, no name

FEET
He has massive strong feet and
hands for his size. My friend
used to call him Big Foot Ralph
Lemon.

FEMININE
The relationship to . . . the
cancel-culture conversation
was heated. It was almost
that he knows his particular
stance precludes or includes . . .
how to create a situation
beyond indictment.
Relationships with performers?

FERAL
His wild, as part of him, not only
attracted to but also trying to
stoke

FERVENT
High Passion + Low Logic

FETAL
As we went into rehearsal and
he talked about . . . he started
to sob uncontrollably . . .
we all came close to take care . . .
he collected himself and
then it happened again . . .
sobbing clenching up in the
fetal position . . . the 3rd, 4th,
5th times . . . no taking care . . .
noticing the time inside
the sobbing song and the form.

FETID

FETISH
I fell in love with this section
We called it "Mississippi/Duluth"
The Duluth of Dylan's
desolation row
A retreat from the breaking up
of our bodies back to a more
proscribed memory fetish of
movement and design
But one activated by keywords
from really bad things that
happened to known and
unknown black and white people
during the civil rights movement
of the 1960s
Watching this dance makes me
happy and sad at the same time
A goodbye dance before all
hell broke loose
—text from *HCYS*

FICTION/FICTITIOUS
The unreliable narrator, made-up
stories

FIGHT
Relationship with . . . past in
wrestling . . .

FIGURES
Drawings, sketches of people,
thin lines, character, caricature

FINAL
He told me that sometimes
when he's meditating that he's
practicing for his last breath.

FINANCES

FIND
Find 4 stations from Krannert
Low video.
Begin with standing/moving
Low. The physicality is
referencing Wall/Floor/Fury/
Ecstasy . . .
The wall is also your floor.
You have two floors and/or two
walls. Hold the proximity to
both. Find space within the wall
and floor. Creating a third space?
Plus Tabata
Plus your Father's lecture
recitation.
Find the alchemy of all
these things.
When you need to rest (after
20 minutes), go to the Krannert
Low stations. Improvise them.
—score, RL

FIRE TO FLAME
Watching the flame . . . *How
Can You Stay in the House
All Day and Not Go Anywhere*.
Fire kept coming from his
mouth as an image to orient
around. I understood the
potential of this element but how
to keep the force going for
20 minutes was the challenge.
Study a candle flame for five
minutes as preparation for
performance. How it ebbs
and flows, billows then burns,
invisible then explicit moments
right next to each other.

FIRST
I have a secret. I'm learning
from video a solo Ralph made in
1992. *Their Eyes Rolled Back in
Ecstasy*. He doesn't know I have
it. He doesn't know I've been
learning it. It's a period of work
that I'm not familiar with. Made
before I met him.

Someone asked me, "Ralph used
to make such beautiful work
and then it was a hard right turn.
What happened?"

Me: "I think beauty shifted."

FLY (2024)
Connected to a float quality,
Laban effort analysis, possibly
a way to mitigate the static
modality

FOCUS
the unseen, the thing you

can't necessarily focus
on constantly unending and
unfolding
I want to consider this
nonexistence
into nothingness, a language

FOLKTALES
Br'er Rabbit is a central figure
in an oral tradition passed
down by African Americans of
the Southern United States.

FOR EVER (2011/2020)
My mother went where she can
find to rest peaceful for ever.
—Djédjé Djédjé Gervais

FORMAT
My thought is to treat modalities,
like Jump or Fury, roman and
upper-case; sections, like
"Mississippi/Duluth," upper-
case in quotation marks;
and work titles, obviously in
italics—*4Walls*, etc. Does
that make sense?
—editorial note from Domenick

FRAME
(A common word to describe
the unwieldy)

DJ.
Some notes, thinking . . .
What is the ongoing research
to find YOUR Low? A
constellation of your practices
in conversation (argument?)
with my/our Ecstasy, Fury,
4Walls, Rant . . . flow obsession.
(Perpendicular to Ralph's

worldview)
The research of course is Low,
for now. But how do we
think about stations to share
the process? Finding something
interesting to witness outside
of our own patient questions?
A rigor that can be seen,
translates giftlike?
The stillness (exhaustion?) is the
biggest unknown it seems.
What is it beyond stillness? What
does that body, place, arrival
signal, speak to. Inside and out?
A new language. (A Hybrid
Language)
It should not have a name, or
sequence . . . But it should
be emphatic. Alive. (Present)
Some kind of score might be
useful. Something to do with
time. A narrative.
Volume is key. Volume and
how it's framed. Its arena.
And the stakes for you to be
wherever it is (whatever it
is) must be urgent. (Purposeful)
In the meantime, what is
the warm-up for that urgency?
(Purpose)
xxo
r

FRED MOTEN
Black and Blur

FRICTION, GENERATIVE
NO FORM
create a dance of "no form"
and "no style"—a "dance
that disappears"

FUCK RALPH (2005)
FUCK YOU RALPH
Ralph has always been full
of stories of rabbits throwing
themselves into the jaws
of generosity.
Vivid lessons to the bounty of
what might be perceived as acts
of overt violence.
During the last section, called
"Fury," each of the ten times
that I jumped and pummeled
the ground, "Fuck you, Ralph"
echoed in my head.

It was my beautiful mantra, a
way to align with the intense
physicality of what my body
didn't want to do and transcend
to the energy of its possibility.

FUCKING FANTASTIC AND
FINALLY!!!
Re: Ralph receives MacArthur
Foundation Fellowship!!!
—e-mail chain response

FULL
That first clip of you improvising
Fury has at least three things
(themes) i think would be nice to
explore. how round and soft
and full out deep Low it all is.
what would a 10/20 minute
version of one or two of those
concise themes be like?
xo
r

FUNERALS

FURNACE (2018)

This morning at 6 a.m. I drove to the crematorium. I had asked if I could be there for the last part of her journey. It was an atypically cold morning for Tallahassee. Very still. He was waiting (I can't remember his name) at the entryway. The glow of fire was behind him. Almost like a Vulcan god. As soon as I entered, she was there in the cardboard box sleeping. This was the third time I saw her, and each time I was surprised how present she felt. He gestured as if to say . . . It's ok. You can get closer . . . you can touch her. I did it as an obligatory response. I somehow sensed that it was in his hands now. He stepped back to give me space, and I stepped back to give home space. There was a series of steps: push toward the furnace, open the door, turn down the dial.

The warm felt good.

I immediately got on a plane back to Chicago. I remember my mom telling me when I was applying to colleges she wanted me to go as far as possible.

FURY (2011)

My father met Ralph Lemon when we were working on a grueling section of a piece called "Fury."

After seeing the work, my father spoke about an article the existential philosopher Camus had written called "The Myth of Sisyphus."

"One must imagine Sisyphus happy."
—Albert Camus

The idea being, although condemned to the arduous task of ceaselessly rolling a rock, Sisyphus was alive.

This "aliveness" was an aha moment, an alternative to just getting through the piece and a glimpse into the philosophical aspirations of what we do.

FUTURE

Questions?
How are you training?
How are you training your body?
How are you training your students?
What are you training for?
For the sustainable future?
AND
For the inevitable demise?
AND
For the potential of transformation?

Which is different than holding on.
—e-mail to Gesel Mason

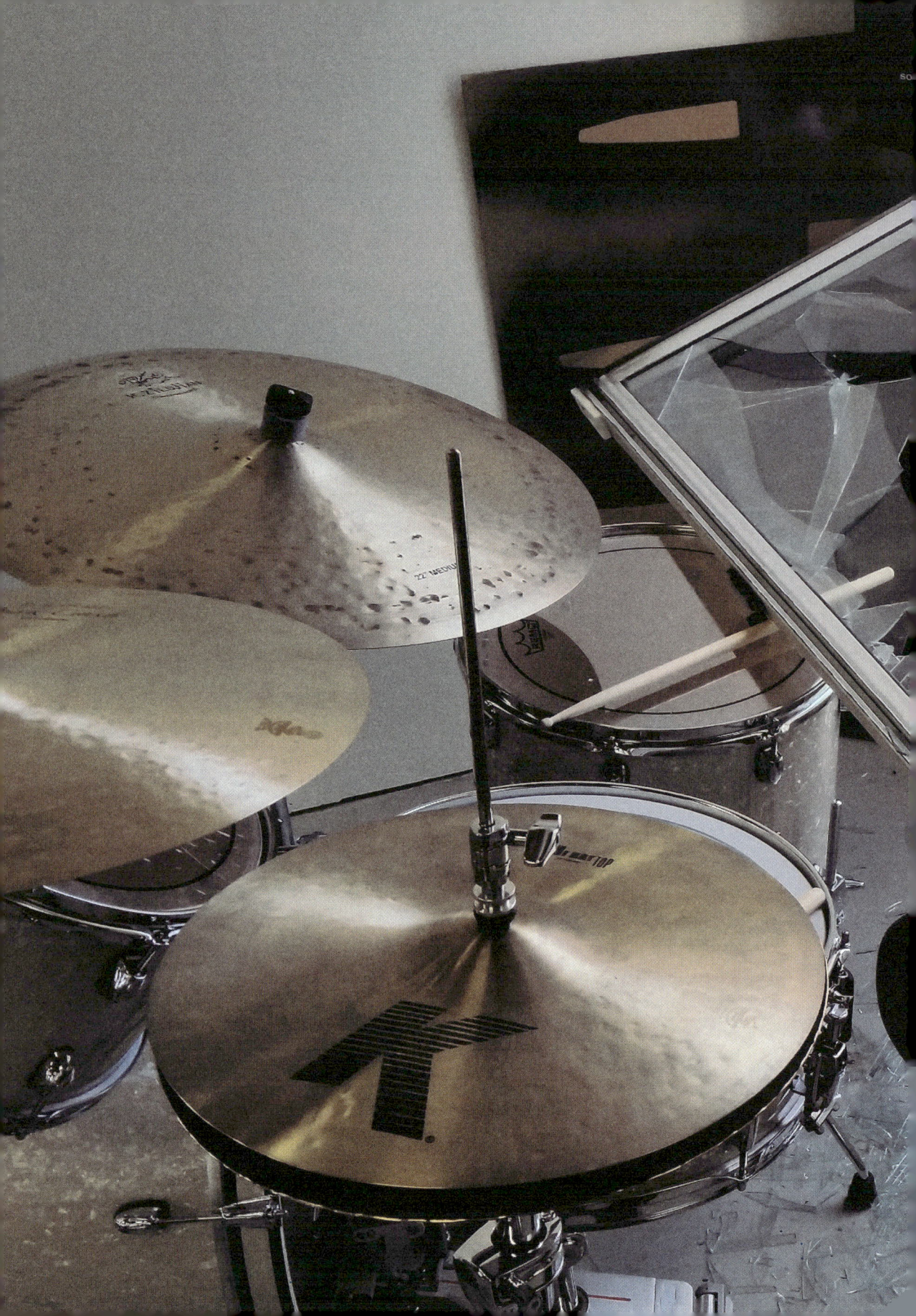

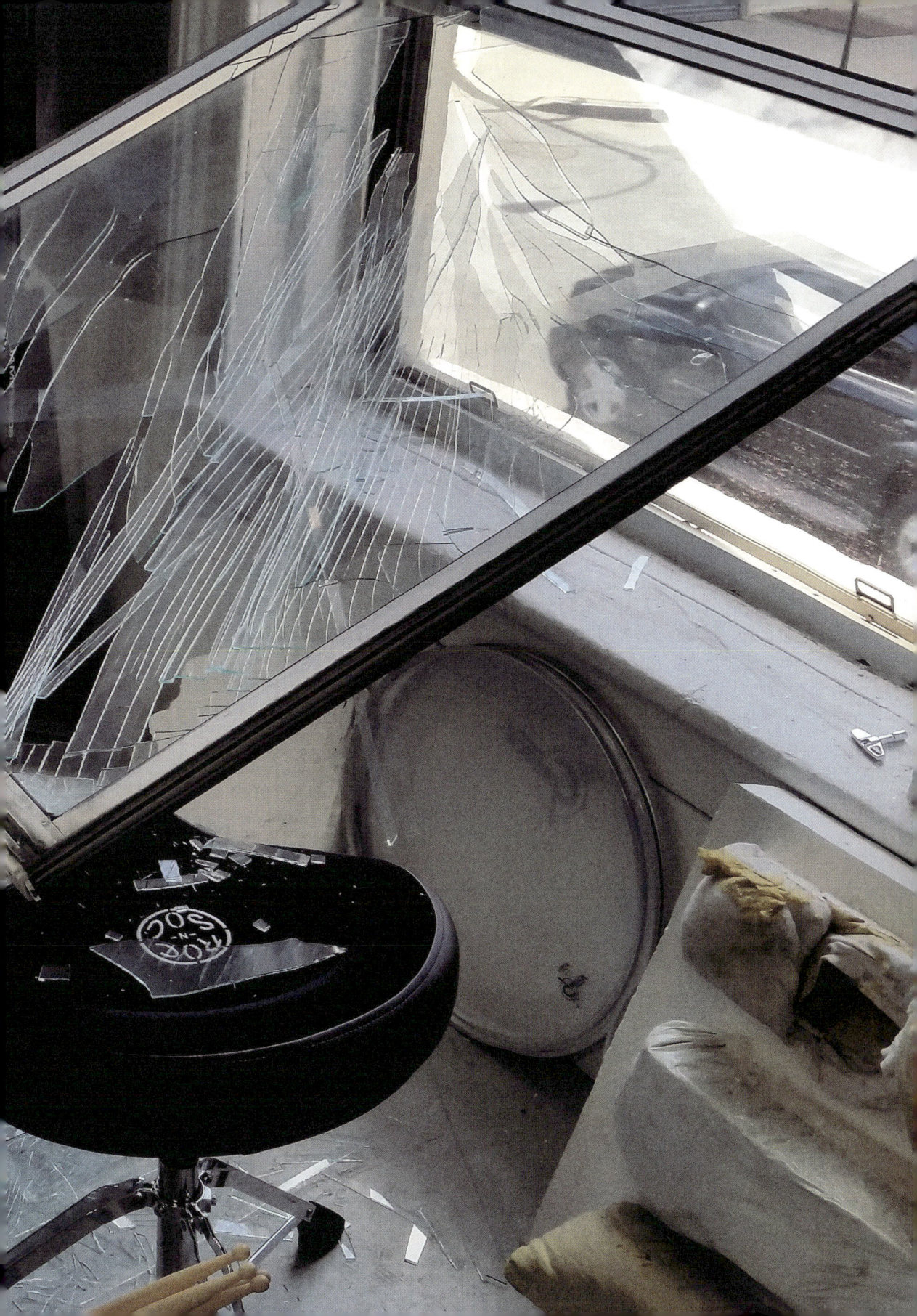

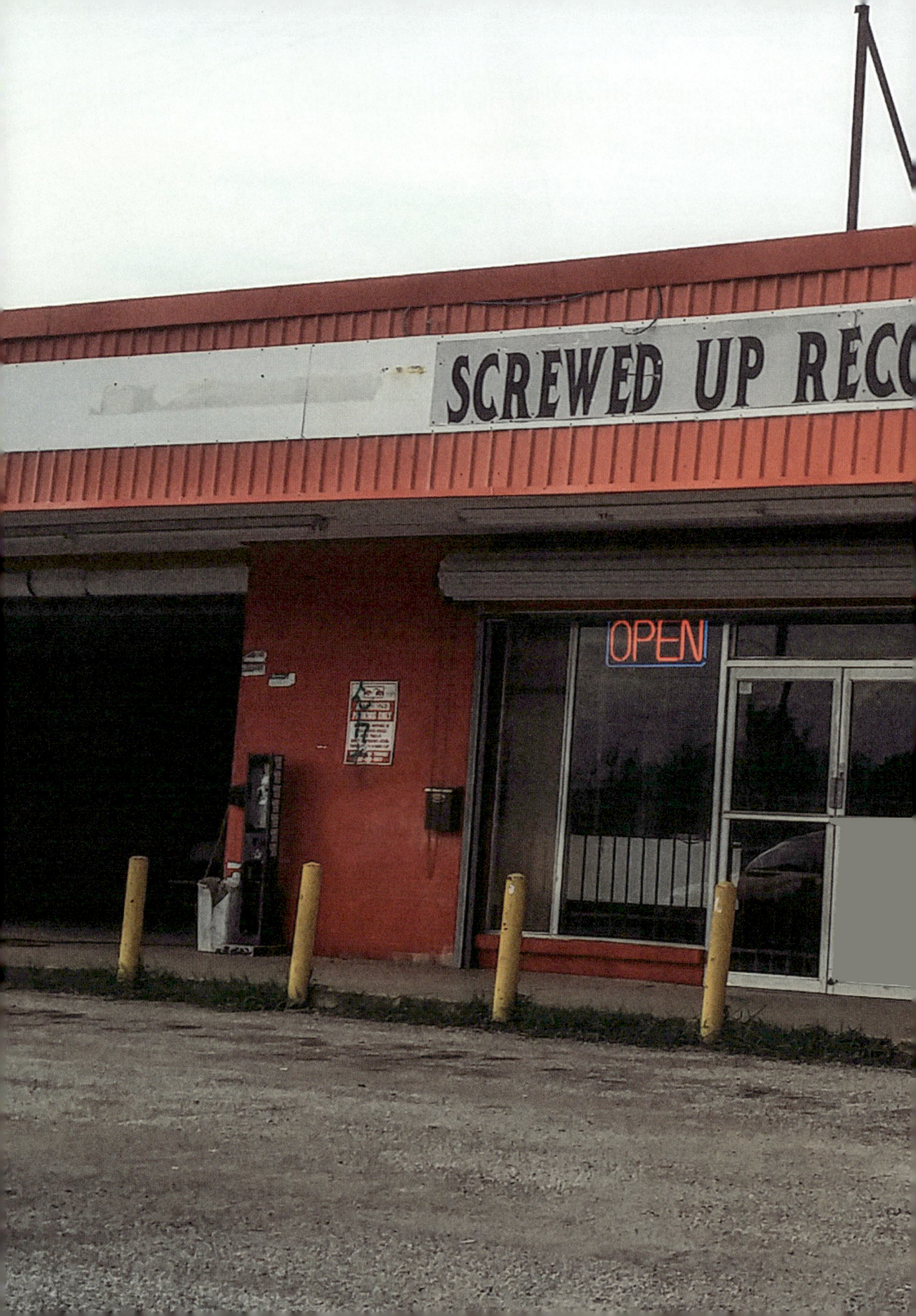

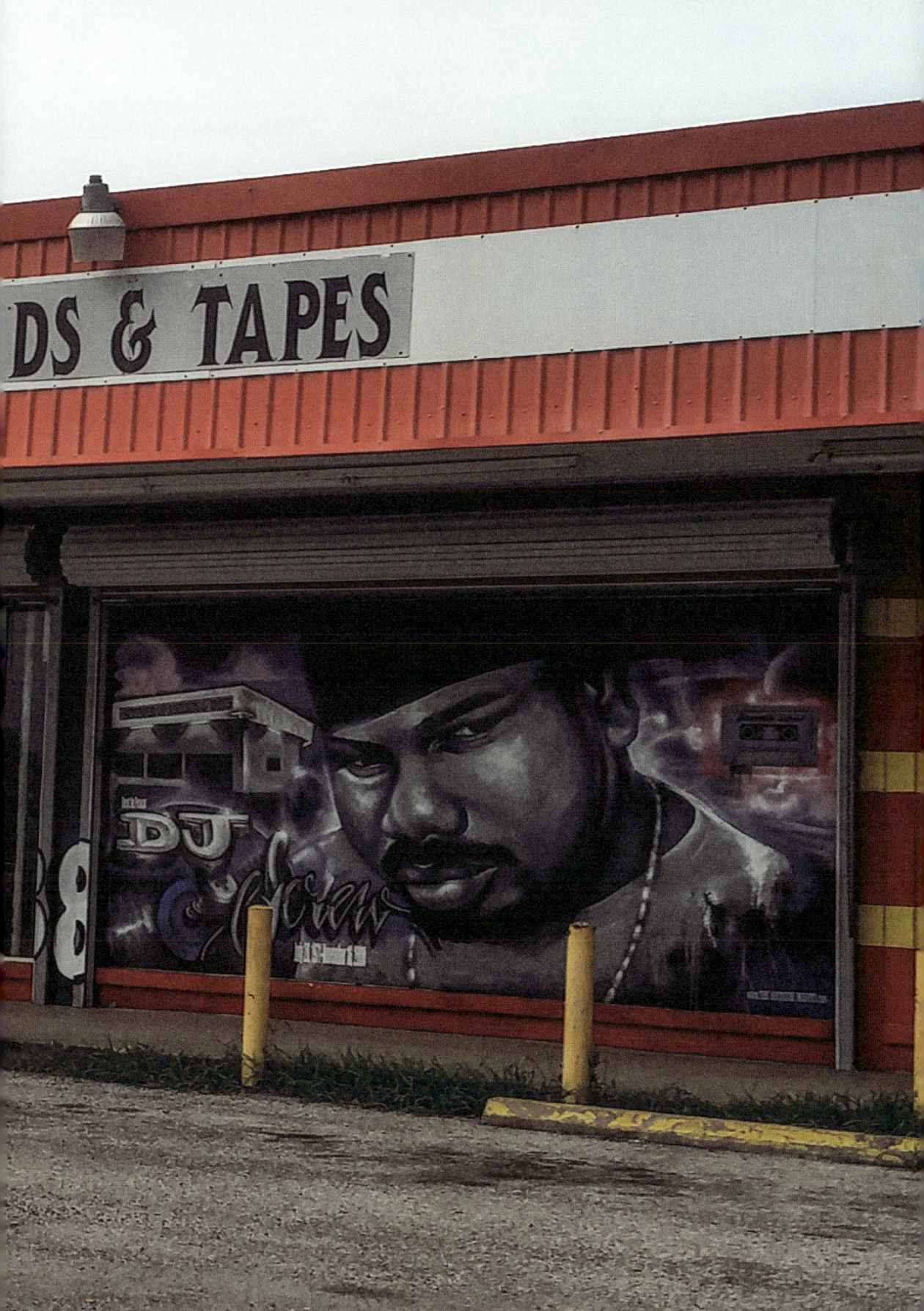

COMMENTS ABOUT - "I WANT MY SPOT BACK"
-THE TITLE COULD BE
" I WANT TO RUIN YOUR MUSEUM
EXPERIENCE " . . . .
AT LEAST THAT WOULD
GIVE THIS AURAL
DIARRHEAH SOME
PURPOSE—
STOP! NO MORE !
          NEEDS A MUTE BUTTON.

RALPH LEMON

jimena Paz 2016

VALENTINA RUTH

NICOLE LEGETTE
OCTOBER 2014   R-8

MAY 2016

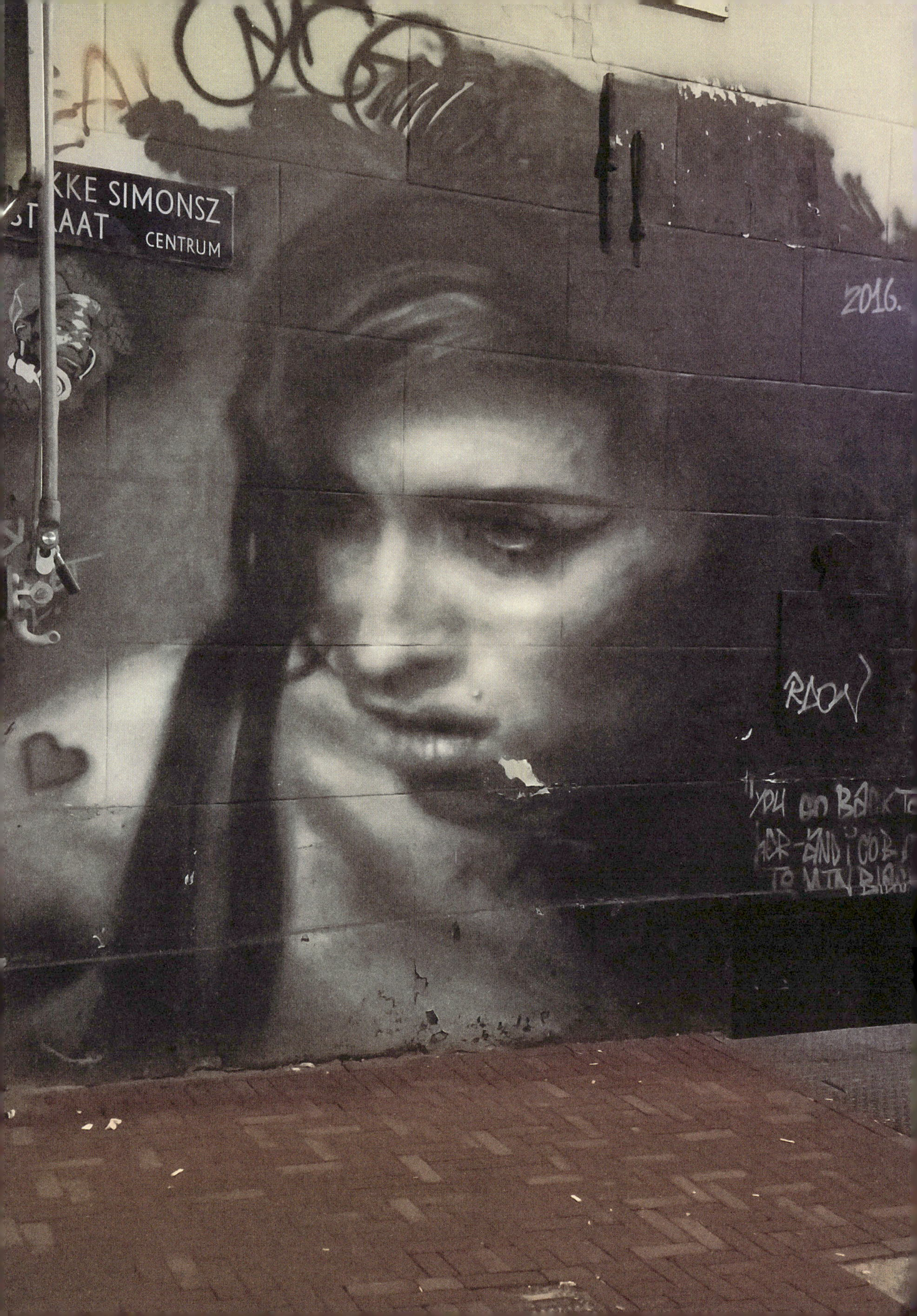
SIMONSZ
CENTRUM
2016.

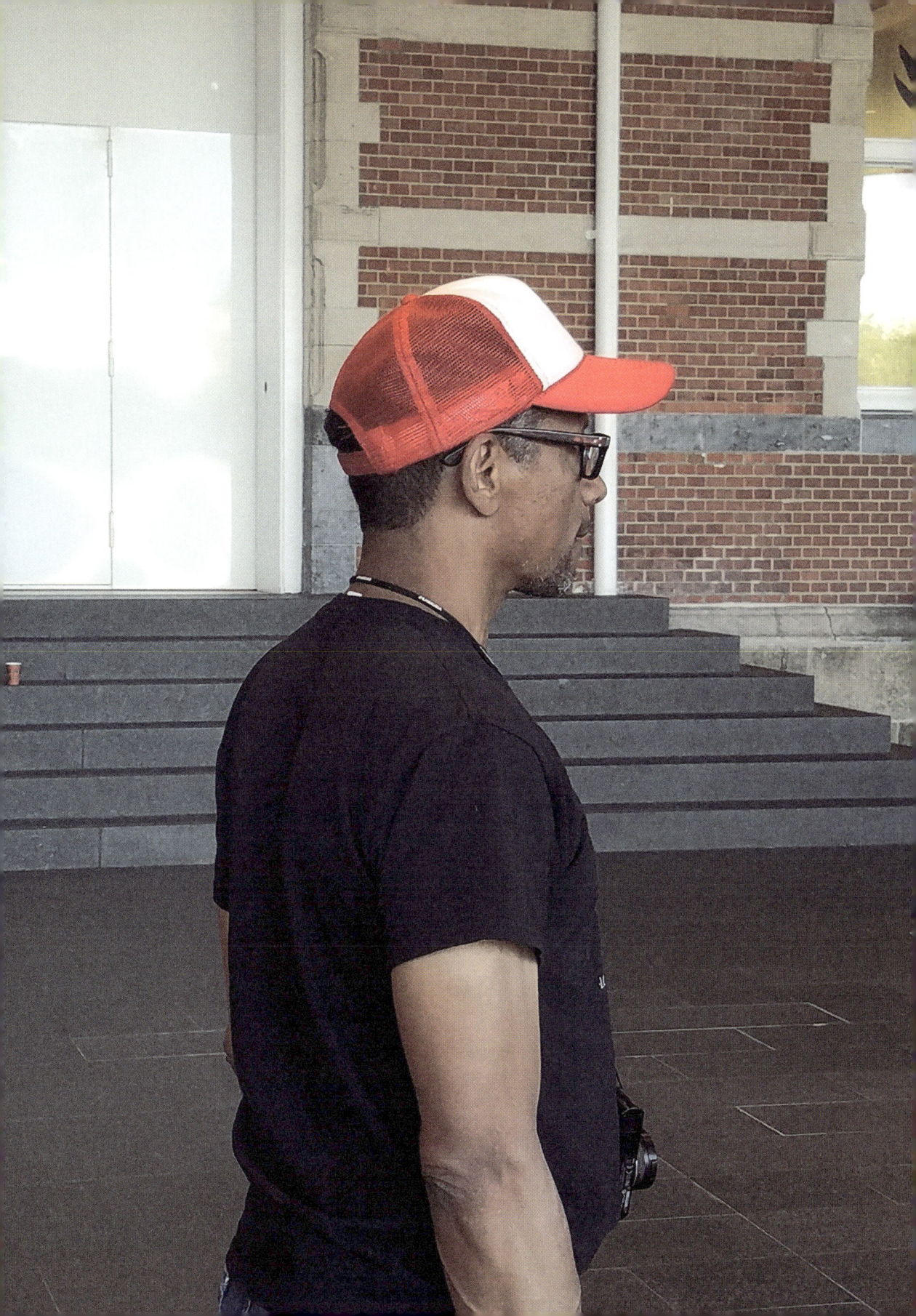

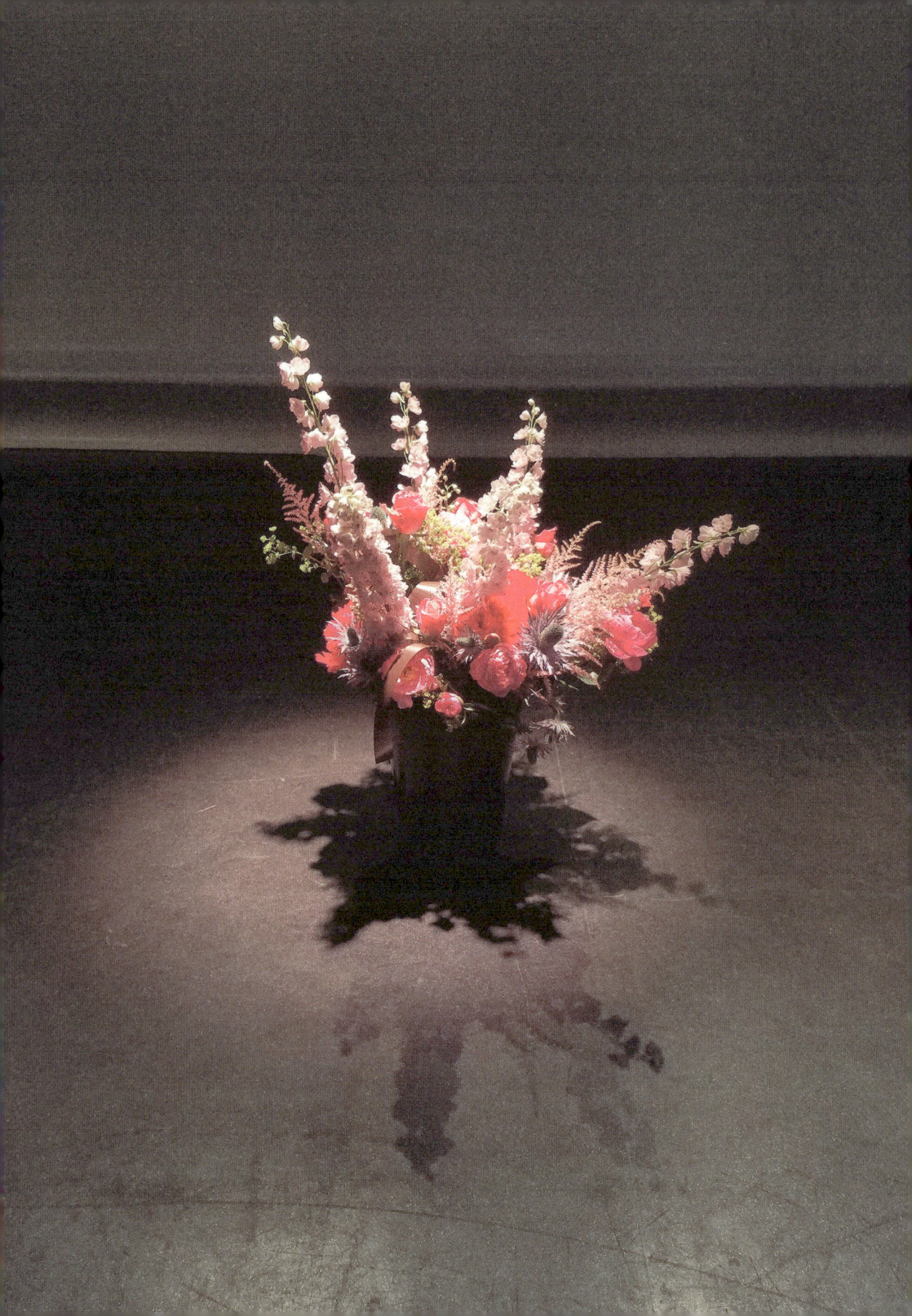

Acknowledgments

It takes the collaboration and steadfast efforts of many people to put together an exhibition of this magnitude, and we are profoundly grateful to the entire MoMA PS1 staff. Kari Rittenbach, Assistant Curator, was a key interlocutor and shepherded the exhibition to fruition. Lauren DiLoreto, Director of Program Production; Richard Wilson, Exhibition and Production Designer; Kate Robinson, Senior Registrar; Lilly Hern-Fondation, Senior Project Manager of Exhibitions and Commissions; Nick Scavo, Senior Project Manager of Music, Performance, and Events; Zachary Taube, Assistant Manager of Installation; Jetaime Pizarro, Assistant Registrar; Lauren Klenow, Program Production Coordinator; Anna Grofik, Preparator; and Dylan Newlon, Program Production Fellow, were each critical in managing the logistics of such an endeavor. Furthermore, we thank the installation team for skillfully mounting the exhibition, and the Administration, External Affairs, Operations, and Visitor Engagement teams for their support through all stages of this project. This publication would not have been possible without the dedicated work of Jody Graf, Assistant Curator, and Julia Schäfer, Graphic Designer, with additional assistance from Audrey Min, Curatorial Fellow. Domenick Ammirati's deft editing was crucial for shaping the commissioned texts. We are grateful to Stuart Comer, The Lonti Ebers Chief Curator of Media and Performance at MoMA, and Ruba Katrib, Curator and Director of Curatorial Affairs at MoMA PS1, as well as the rest of PS1's leadership team of Jose Ortiz, Deputy Director, and Molly Kurzius, Director of External Affairs, for their unwavering support of this project.

We also thank our colleagues in MoMA's Department of Drawings and Prints, including Christophe Cherix, The Robert Lehman Foundation Chief Curator of Drawings and Prints; Lanka Tattersall, Laurenz Foundation Curator; John Prochilo, Manager; and Kunbi Oni, Collection Specialist, for bringing Lemon's fabulous series of drawings *Untitled (The greatest [Black] art history story ever told. Unfinished)* (2015–) into the Museum's collection and allowing us to include them in this exhibition. Robert Wilson and Noah Khoshbin, Curator, graciously agreed to lend four African figures from the Watermill Center Collection, and we are grateful for their openness to collaboration around these works. Our thanks go to Scott Rothkopf, Alice Pratt Brown Director; Adrienne Edwards, Engell Speyer Family Senior Curator and Associate Director of Curatorial Programs; and Kim Conaty, Nancy and Steve Crown Family Chief Curator, at the Whitney Museum for their enthusiasm in lending *FBN* (2009—19) and to Beth Huseman, Director of Publications, for additional support. The Kitchen has long been an important venue for Lemon's work, and we are grateful to Legacy Russell, Executive Director and Chief Curator; Matthew Lyons, Curator; and Angelique Rosales Salgado, Curatorial Assistant, for their assistance in accessing materials on past projects. We also thank Isabelle Hogenkamp at Mitchell-Innes & Nash and the Estate of Pope.L for facilitating the publication of his wonderful text. Our gratitude goes out to the photographers who have allowed us to reproduce their work in this book—especially Paula Court, who has documented Lemon's dances for decades—and the many people who helped us gather these images. In particular, we thank Linda Court Salisbury and Esa Nickle, Managing Director and Executive Producer, Performa, for their care of Court's archive.

Ralph works with an extraordinary group of dancers and collaborators. We extend our deepest thanks to all those without whom this exhibition would not have happened: Kevin Beasley, Daphne Brooks, Dwayne Brown, Paul Hamilton, Saidiya Hartman, Bob Hoffnar, Darrell Jones, Lysis (Ley), April Matthis, Roderick Murray, Naoko Nagata, Mariama Noguera-Devers, Okwui Okpokwasili, Jimena Paz, Angie Pittman, Will Rawls, Samita Sinha, Mike Taylor, Philip White, and all of the musicians in the brass band.

Finally, we want to thank Ralph. As a teacher (aka guru), friend (aka family), and interlocutor (aka trickster), he has had a profound impact on both of us, reimagining our sense of what is possible in and beyond our work and reinspiring our engagement with art and the places it takes us. We realize that inviting an artist to organize a show of their work is no small ask, and Ralph has been gracious, humble, and generous from the first. It has been an unalloyed privilege to engage with him and his community of collaborators over time, including in bringing this exhibition into the world.

Connie Butler
The Agnes Gund Director,
MoMA PS1

Thomas Lax
Curator, Department of Media
and Performance, MoMA

Artist's Acknowledgments

Ralph Lemon would like to thank, at MoMA PS1:
Connie Butler (for asking, yet again), Lauren DiLoreto, Jody Graf,
Anna Grofik, Lilly Hern-Fondation, Molly Kurzius, Dylan Newlon,
Kari Rittenbach, Kate Robinson, Nick Scavo, Julia Schäfer,
Daniel Schaeffer, Zachary Taube, and Richard Wilson

MoMA:
Thomas Lax (for the long ongoing partnership, experiment),
Christophe Cherix, Glenn Lowry, and Lanka Tattersall

The collaborators:
Kevin Beasley, Brass Band, Daphne Brooks, Dwayne Brown,
Ariel Derris (618 Design), Jim Findlay, Carol Fonde (for the perfect
prints), Paul Hamilton, Saidiya Hartman, Bob Hoffnar, Darrell Jones,
KB Studio, Chelsea Lemon Fetzer, Lysis (Ley), April Matthis, Gina
Michaels (and Legacy Atelier), Victor Morales, Roderick Murray,
Naoko Nagata, Mariama Noguera-Devers, Okwui Okpokwasili,
Jimena Paz, Valentina Paz-Lemon, Angie Pittman, Katherine Profeta,
Will Rawls, Ann Rosenthal, Tim Rusterholz, Melanie Silva, Samita
Sinha, Louis Sparre, Mike Taylor, Philip White, Cameron Wittig,
Paul Ziemer, and all of the musicians.

To all those in Little Yazoo and Bentonia, Mississippi:
Edna Carter, Lorraine Carter, Walter Carter, Warren (Red) Carter,
Betty Clifton, Albert Johnson, Christy Johnson, Geneva Johnson,
Michael Sims, Emma Williams, Jayden Williams, and Lloyd Williams

The writers:
Connie Butler, Adrienne Edwards, Darrell Jones, Thomas Lax,
Okwui Okpokwasili, Pope.L, Kevin Quashie, and Kari Rittenbach

For all the past and ongoing support:
Anthony Allen, Carlos Basualdo, Philip Bither and Pavel Pyś
(Walker Art Center), Paula Court, Linda Court Salisbury, Adrienne
Edwards, Hendrik Folkerts, Djédjé Djédjé Gervais, Gina Gibney,
Tim Griffin, Kathy Halbreich, Judy Hussie-Taylor, Jack Kupferman,
Malcolm Low, Gesel Mason, Sarah Michelson, Esa Nickle, Omagbitse
Omagbemi, yon Tande, David Thomson, Triple Canopy, Watermill
Center, Marcus Williams, and Robert Wilson

Contributors

Kevin Beasley received his BFA from the College for Creative Studies, Detroit, in 2007 and his MFA from Yale University School of Art in 2012. Beasley's practice spans sculpture, photography, sound, and performance, while centering on materials of cultural and personal significance, from raw cotton harvested from his family's property in Virginia to sounds gathered using contact microphones. Beasley alters, casts, and molds these diverse materials to form a body of works that acknowledge the complex, shared histories of the broader American experience, steeped in generational memories. Beasley lives and works in New York.

Connie Butler is The Agnes Gund Director of MoMA PS1 in Long Island City, New York. Prior to her arrival in fall 2023, she was Chief Curator at the Hammer Museum in Los Angeles, where she organized exhibitions including *Made in LA* (2014), *Mark Bradford: Scorched Earth* (2015), *Marisa Merz: The Sky Is a Great Space* (2017), *Lari Pittman: Declaration of Independence* (2019), and *Witch Hunt* (2021). She also co-organized *Adrian Piper: A Synthesis of Intuitions, 1965–2016* with The Museum of Modern Art, which opened at the Hammer in October 2018. From 2006 to 2013, she was the Robert Lehman Foundation Chief Curator of Drawings at MoMA, where she cocurated the first major Lygia Clark retrospective in the United States (2014) and *On Line: Drawing Through the Twentieth Century* (2010–11) in addition to *Greater New York* (2010) and *Mike Kelley* (2013) at MoMA PS1. Butler organized the groundbreaking survey *WACK! Art and the Feminist Revolution* (2007) at the Museum of Contemporary Art, Los Angeles, where she was curator from 1996 to 2006. In 2020, Butler received the Bard College Audrey Irmas Award for Curatorial Excellence.

Dr. Adrienne Edwards is Engell Speyer Family Senior Curator and Associate Director of Curatorial Programs at the Whitney Museum of American Art in New York. She cocurated the 2022 Whitney Biennial and was president of the International Jury of the 59th Venice Biennale. She organized an exhibition and performances on the choreographer Alvin Ailey that opened at the Whitney in September 2024. Previously, she served as curator of Performa in New York and as curator-at-large for the Walker Art Center in Minneapolis. In addition to over fifty interdisciplinary performance and moving-image commissions, Edwards's curatorial projects include *Jason Moran* at the Walker Art Center, ICA Boston, and Wexner Center for the Arts (2018–19) as well as *Moved by the Motion: Sudden Rise* (2019), *Dave McKenzie: The Story I Tell Myself* (2021), *My Barbarian* (2021–22), and *Every Ocean Hughes: Alive Side* (2023) at the Whitney. She was part of the Whitney's core team for David Hammons's public art monument *Day's End*. Edwards has taught at New York University, the New School, and the CUNY Graduate Center.

Darrell Jones is a performer, educator, researcher, and choreographer. He has performed across the United States and globally, at venues including Links Hall, Chicago; Danspace Project, New York; ArtTheater dB KOBE, Japan; and the Venice Biennale. He maintains long-term collaborative relationships with Bebe Miller Company and Ralph Lemon. Additional foundational experiences have included working with Min Tanaka, Ronald K. Brown, Kokuma Dance Theatre, and Urban Bush Women. Jones is a two-time Bessie Award recipient and has received grants and awards from organizations including 3Arts, Chicago Dancemakers Forum Lab, Foundation for Contemporary Arts, and the MAP Fund. He is a tenured faculty member at the Dance Center of Columbia College Chicago and holds an MFA in dance from Florida State University.

Thomas Lax is Curator of Media and Performance at the Museum of Modern Art in New York. They co-organized the exhibition *Just Above Midtown: Changing Spaces* (2022) at MoMA with Lilia Rocio Taboada in collaboration with JAM's founder, Linda Goode Bryant. They worked with colleagues across the Museum on a major collection rehang (2019) and co-organized *Judson Dance Theater: The Work Is Never Done* (2018) with Ana Janevski and Martha Joseph. Other collaboratively organized exhibitions include the Projects Series with Lanka Tattersall; *Unfinished Conversations*, inspired by the cultural theorist Stuart Hall (2017); *Greater New York* at MoMA PS1 (2015); and commissions by artists including Neïl Beloufa, Maria Hassabi, and Steffani Jemison. Previously, they worked at the Studio Museum in Harlem, where they organized *When the Stars Begin to Fall: Imagination and the American South* (2014) and participated in the landmark "f show" contemporary art series.

Ralph Lemon is a choreographer, writer, and visual artist based in Philadelphia. His work has been the subject of exhibitions at The Kitchen (2007/2015); Contemporary Art Center, New Orleans (2008); the Studio Museum in Harlem (2012); and the Walker Art Center (2014). At The Museum of Modern Art, New York, he performed in the Museum's Donald B. and Catherine C. Marron Atrium for *On Line: Drawing Through the Twentieth Century* (2010–11), organized the performance series *Some sweet day* (2012), and led the discursive project *Value Talks* as an Annenberg Fellow (2013–14). MoMA published the first monograph on his oeuvre, *Ralph Lemon* (2016) as part of the Modern Dance series. Lemon is a recipient of a Bucksbaum Award (2022), a MacArthur Fellowship (2020), a Heinz Family Foundation Award (2018), three Bessie Awards (1986, 2005, 2016), two Foundation for Contemporary Arts Awards (1986, 2012), a Doris Duke Performing Artist Award (2012), and a Guggenheim Fellowship (2009). In 2015, he received a National Medal of Arts from President Barack Obama. His works are in the permanent collections of institutions including MoMA, the Walker Art Center, the Studio Museum in Harlem, and the Whitney Museum of American Art.

Okwui Okpokwasili is a Brooklyn-based performer, choreographer, and writer creating multidisciplinary performance pieces. The child of immigrants from Nigeria, Okpokwasili was born and raised in the Bronx, and the histories of these places and the girls and women who inhabit them feature prominently in much of her work. Her productions include the Bessie Award–winning *pent-up: a revenge dance* (2008), and the Bessie Award–winning *Bronx Gothic* (2014), as well as *poor people's TV room* (2017), *poor people's TV room (SOLO)* (2014), *when I return who will receive me* (2019), *Adaku's revolt* (2019), and *Sitting on a Man's Head* (2018). In 2022, she was the first artist-in-residence at the Marie-Josée and Henry Kravis Studio at The Museum of Modern Art. She is the recipient of awards and fellowships including a Princeton University Hodder Fellowship, a Herb Alpert Award in Dance, a Doris Duke Artist Award, and a MacArthur Fellowship (all 2018).

Pope.L was a visual artist and educator whose multidisciplinary practice used binaries, contraries, and preconceived notions embedded within contemporary culture to create artworks in various formats, for example, writing, painting, performance, installation, video, and sculpture. Building upon his long history of enacting arduous, provocative, absurdist performances and interventions in public spaces, Pope.L applied some of the same social, formal, and performative strategies to his interests in language, system, gender, race, and community. The goals for his work were several: joy, money, and uncertainty—not necessarily in that order.

Kevin Quashie is Royce Family Professor of Teaching Excellence in the department of English at Brown University. He is the author or editor of four books, most notably *The Sovereignty of Quiet: Beyond Resistance in Black Culture* (2012) and *Black Aliveness, or A Poetics of Being* (2021). In 2022, *Black Aliveness* was awarded the James Russell Lowell Prize for best overall book from the Modern Language Association and the Pegasus Award for Poetry Criticism from the Poetry Foundation.

Kari Rittenbach is an Assistant Curator at MoMA PS1, where she has organized the exhibitions *Reynaldo Rivera: Fistful of Love / También la belleza* (with Lauren Mackler, 2024) and *Onyeka Igwe: A Repertoire of Protest (No Dance, No Palaver)* (2023), as well as commissions by Stewart Uoo, Raque Ford, Alex Tatarsky, and Poncili Creación. At PS1, she has curated the music series Warm Up and worked on the mid-career survey *Rirkrit Tiravanija: A LOT OF PEOPLE* (2023). She previously organized numerous projects independently, including *You've Come a Long Way, Baby: The Sapphire Show*, Ortuzar Projects, New York (2021); *Silvia Kolbowski: That Monster, An Allegory*, Institute of Contemporary Arts, London (2019); *Coming Soon* (with Mira Asriningtyas and Nora Heidorn), Fondazione Sandretto Re Rebaudengo, Turin (2018); and *Trees in the Forest*, Yale Union, Portland, Oregon (2016). She is a visiting critic at the Yale School of Art.

Checklist of the Exhibition

All works courtesy the artist unless
otherwise noted.

James Baldwin Dharma Talk, 2004
Video animation (color, sound)
15 min., 6 sec.

(The efflorescence of) Walter, 2005
Video (color, sound)
19 min., 30 sec.

Instruction Drawing (Spaceship), 2006
Ink on paper
5 × 3 ½ in. (12.7 × 8.9 cm)

Walter Harvesting Orange String, 2006
Video (color, sound)
20 min.

Ralph Lemon in collaboration with
Lloyd Williams, Warren Carter, and
Walter Carter
Spaceship #1, 2007
Mixed media
75 × 66 × 84 in. (190.5 × 167.6 ×
213.4 cm)

(Solaris no people), 2008
Video (color, sound)
22 min., 45 sec.

1856 Cessna Road [Chapter 1],
2008–9
Video (color, sound)
35 min., 10 sec.

Spaceman Drawings, 2008–10
Ink on paper
18 drawings, each 4 ½ × 6 ¾ in.
(11.4 × 17.1 cm)

Untitled, 2009
Archival pigment print
30 × 20 in. (76.2 × 50.8 cm)

Untitled, 2009
Archival pigment print
40 × 40 in. (101.6 × 101.6 cm)

Untitled, 2009
Archival pigment print
40 × 40 in. (101.6 × 101.6 cm)

Untitled, 2009
Archival pigment print
40 × 40 in. (101.6 × 101.6 cm)

FBN, 2009–19
Single-channel video installation with
neon and aluminum platform
Overall dimensions variable
Video (color, sound): 4 min., 2 sec.
Whitney Museum of American Art, New
York. Purchase, with funds from the
Painting and Sculpture Committee

Albert & Betty, 2013
Video (color, silent)
4 min., 44 sec.

Garden [Chapter 2], 2013
Video (color, sound)
13 min., 15 sec.

It could be a forest [Chapter 3], 2013
Video (color, sound)
11 min., 30 sec.

Untitled, 2013
Archival pigment print
15 × 20 in. (38.1 × 50.8 cm)

Untitled, 2013
Archival pigment print
40 × 40 in. (101.6 × 101.6 cm)

Consecration of Ancestor Figures #3,
2015
Carved wood and textile
6 × 2 ¼ × 2 in. (15.2 x 5.7 × 5.1 cm)

Consecration of Ancestor Figures #4,
2015
Carved wood and textile
12 × 2 ¼ × 2 in. (30.5 x 5.7 × 5.1 cm)

Consecration of Ancestor Figures #7,
2015
Carved wood and textile
13 × 4 × 3 in. (33 × 10.2 × 7.6 cm)

Consecration of Ancestor Figures #8,
2015
Carved wood and textile
13 × 3 ½ × 3 ¼ in. (33 × 8.9 × 8.3 cm)

Ralph Lemon in collaboration with
Jim Findlay
The (Killer Space)Doghouse, 2015
Maple and video (black-and-white, silent)
28 × 37 × 27 in. (71.1 × 94 × 68.6 cm)
Video: 2 min.

Untitled 1, 2016
From the series *Untitled (The greatest
[Black] art history story ever told.
Unfinished)*, 2015—
Ink, acrylic, pencil, watercolor, gansai
tambi, and sumi ink on paper
22 ¼ × 30 × in. (56.5 × 76.5 cm)
The Museum of Modern Art, New York.
Acquired through the generosity of
The Judith Rothschild Contemporary
Drawings Collection Gift (by exchange)
and Linda Goldstein

Untitled 2, 2016—17
From the series *Untitled (The greatest
[Black] art history story ever told.
Unfinished)*, 2015—
Ink, acrylic, pencil, watercolor, gansai
tambi, and sumi ink on paper
22 ⅜ × 30 ³⁄₁₆ in. (56.8 × 76.7 cm)
The Museum of Modern Art, New York.
Acquired through the generosity of
The Judith Rothschild Contemporary
Drawings Collection Gift (by exchange)

Untitled 3, 2017
From the series *Untitled (The greatest
[Black] art history story ever told.
Unfinished)*, 2015—
Ink, acrylic, pencil, watercolor, gansai
tambi, and sumi ink on paper
22 ⁵⁄₁₆ × 30 ³⁄₁₆ in. (56.7 × 76.7 cm)
The Museum of Modern Art, New York.
Acquired through the generosity of
The Judith Rothschild Contemporary
Drawings Collection Gift (by exchange)

I am the light (Sam and Dave)
[Chapter 4], 2018
Video (color, sound)
15 min., 35 sec.

Saturnalia [Coda], 2018
Video (color, sound)
17 min., 29 sec.

Untitled, 2018
Archival pigment print
11 × 8 ½ in. (27.9 × 21.6 cm)

Untitled, 2018
Archival pigment print
20 × 30 in. (50.8 × 76.2 cm)

Untitled 4, 2018
From the series *Untitled (The greatest
[Black] art history story ever told.
Unfinished)*, 2015—
Ink, acrylic, pencil, watercolor, gansai
tambi, and sumi ink on paper
22 ⁷⁄₁₆ × 30 ⅛ in. (57 × 76.5 cm)
The Museum of Modern Art, New York.
Acquired through the generosity of
The Judith Rothschild Contemporary
Drawings Collection Gift (by exchange)

Untitled 5, 2018
From the series *Untitled (The greatest [Black] art history story ever told. Unfinished)*, 2015–
Ink, acrylic, pencil, watercolor, gansai tambi, and sumi ink on paper
22 ¼ × 30 ⅛ in. (56.5 × 76.5 cm)
The Museum of Modern Art, New York. Acquired through the generosity of the Contemporary Arts Council of The Museum of Modern Art's 75th Anniversary Acquisition Fund

Untitled 6, 2018
From the series *Untitled (The greatest [Black] art history story ever told. Unfinished)*, 2015–
Ink, acrylic, pencil, watercolor, gansai tambi, and sumi ink on paper
22 ⅜ × 30 ³⁄₁₆ in. (56.8 × 76.7 cm)
The Museum of Modern Art, New York. Acquired through the generosity of The Judith Rothschild Contemporary Drawings Collection Gift (by exchange)

Untitled 7, 2019
From the series *Untitled (The greatest [Black] art history story ever told. Unfinished)*, 2015–
Ink, acrylic, pencil, watercolor, gansai tambi, and sumi ink on paper
22 ⁵⁄₁₆ × 30 ³⁄₁₆ in. (56.7 × 76.7 cm)
The Museum of Modern Art, New York. Acquired through the generosity of The Judith Rothschild Contemporary Drawings Collection Gift (by exchange)

Untitled 8, 2020
From the series *Untitled (The greatest [Black] art history story ever told. Unfinished)*, 2015–
Ink, acrylic, pencil, watercolor, gansai tambi, and sumi ink on paper
22 ⁵⁄₁₆ × 30 ⅛ in. (56.7 × 76.5 cm)
The Museum of Modern Art, New York. Acquired through the generosity of The Judith Rothschild Contemporary Drawings Collection Gift (by exchange)

Untitled 9, 2020
From the series *Untitled (The greatest [Black] art history story ever told. Unfinished)*, 2015–
Ink, acrylic, pencil, watercolor, gansai tambi, and sumi ink on paper
22 ⁵⁄₁₆ × 30 ⅛ in. (56.7 × 76.5 cm)
The Museum of Modern Art, New York. Acquired through the generosity of The Judith Rothschild Contemporary Drawings Collection Gift (by exchange)

Ralph Lemon and Kevin Beasley
Rant Residuum, 2020–24
Mixed media installation
Dimensions variable

Ralph Lemon and Kevin Beasley
Rant (redux), 2020–24
Four-channel video installation with eight-channel sound
14 min.

Untitled 4, 2020–24
Untitled 5–7, 2022
Untitled 9–14, 2022–24
From the series *Untitled (Rapture weft)*, 2020–
Acrylic and oil on paper
Each 30 × 50 in. (76.2 × 127 cm)

Untitled 10, 2021
From the series *Untitled (The greatest [Black] art history story ever told. Unfinished)*, 2015–
Ink, acrylic, pencil, watercolor, gansai tambi, and sumi ink on paper
38 ⅜ × 50 in. (97.5 × 127 cm)
The Museum of Modern Art, New York. Acquired through the generosity of Erin and Peter Hess Friedland

Untitled 11, 2022
From the series *Untitled (The greatest [Black] art history story ever told. Unfinished)*, 2015—
Ink, acrylic, pencil, watercolor, gansai tambi, and sumi ink on paper
38 ⅜ × 50 in. (97.5 × 127 cm)
The Museum of Modern Art, New York. Acquired through the generosity of the Contemporary Arts Council of The Museum of Modern Art's 75th Anniversary Acquisition Fund

Untitled 12, 2023
From the series *Untitled (The greatest [Black] art history story ever told. Unfinished)*, 2015—
Ink, acrylic, pencil, watercolor, gansai tambi, and sumi ink on paper
38 ⅜ × 50 in. (97.5 × 127 cm)
The Museum of Modern Art, New York. Acquired through the generosity of Erin and Peter Hess Friedland

Untitled 13, 2023
From the series *Untitled (The greatest [Black] art history story ever told. Unfinished)*, 2015—
Ink, acrylic, pencil, watercolor, gansai tambi, and sumi ink on paper
38 ¼ × 50 in. (97.2 × 127 cm)
The Museum of Modern Art, New York. Acquired through the generosity of the Contemporary Arts Council of The Museum of Modern Art's 75th Anniversary Acquisition Fund

(Solaris water), 2024
Video (color, silent)
8 min., 13 sec.

Consecration of Ancestor Figures #13, 2024
Carved wood (Bette female figure, Côte d'Ivoire, c. 1940) and textile
28 × 9 × 5 in. (71.1 × 22.9 × 12.7 cm)
Figure on loan from Watermill Center Collection, Watermill, New York

Consecration of Ancestor Figures #14, 2024
Carved wood (Mende male figure, Sierra Leone, c. 1940) and textile
30 × 7 × 7 in. (76.2 × 17.8 × 17.8 cm)
Figure on loan from Watermill Center Collection, Watermill, New York

Consecration of Ancestor Figures #15, 2024
Carved wood (Attie female figure, Côte d'Ivoire, c. 1940) and textile
24 × 5 × 5 in. (61.0 × 12.7 × 12.7 cm)
Figure on loan from Watermill Center Collection, Watermill, New York

Consecration of Ancestor Figures #16, 2024
Carved wood (Mende male figure, Sierra Leone, c. 1950) and textile
36 × 6 × 6 in. (91.4 × 15.2 × 15.2 cm)
Figure on loan from Watermill Center Collection, Watermill, New York

Godhead under the kitchen table, 2024
Aluminum, LEDs, cast bronze, and cables
Approx. 30 × 90 × 30 in. (76.2 × 228.6 × 76.2 cm) overall

Installation sketch for *Spaceship #1*, 2024
Ink and watercolor on paper
6 × 3 ¼ in. (15.2 × 8.3 cm)

Untitled (Black music) #1, 2024
Audio (looped)
360 min.

Untitled (Black music) #2, 2024
Audio (looped)
360 min.

Program of Performances

Tell it anyway, 2024

PERFORMERS Kevin Beasley, Dwayne Brown, Paul Hamilton, Darrell Jones, Ralph Lemon, Lysis (Ley), April Matthis, Mariama Noguera-Devers, Okwui Okpokwasili, Angie Pittman, Samita Sinha

November 14, 2024 (NYC PREMIERE)
November 16, 2024

Untitled (The greatest [Black] art history story ever told. Unfinished), Interpreted, 2024–25

READER Daphne Brooks

December 14, 2024

Untitled (The greatest [Black] art history story ever told. Unfinished), Interpreted, 2024–25

READER Bob Hoffnar

January 11, 2025

In Proximity, 2022–25

PERFORMERS Brass Band, Darrell Jones, Lysis (Ley), Jimena Paz, Samita Sinha

January 16, 2025 (US PREMIERE)
January 18, 2025
January 19, 2025*
*Brass Band only

Untitled (The greatest [Black] art history story ever told. Unfinished), Interpreted, 2024–25

READER Will Rawls

February 15, 2025

Low, 2003–25

PERFORMERS Darrell Jones, Ralph Lemon

February 20, 2025 (WORLD PREMIERE)
February 22, 2025

Ceremonies Out of the Air, 2025

PERFORMERS Darrell Jones, Ralph Lemon

March 1, 2025 (WORLD PREMIERE)

Untitled (The greatest [Black] art history story ever told. Unfinished), Interpreted, 2024–25

READER Saidiya Hartman

March 8, 2025

Rant #6, 2025

PERFORMERS Kevin Beasley, Dwayne Brown, Paul Hamilton, Darrell Jones, Ralph Lemon, Lysis (Ley), Mariama Noguera-Devers, Okwui Okpokwasili, Angie Pittman, Samita Sinha

March 22, 2025

Image Captions and Credits

All artworks and performances by Ralph Lemon unless otherwise noted. All images of artworks by Ralph Lemon courtesy and copyright the artist unless otherwise noted.

p. 9: Darrell Jones in *Dust*, 2023. Performance view, site near Josephine Baker's childhood home, *Counterpublic*, St. Louis, 2023. Courtesy Counterpublic. Photo: Nyara Williams. Performance research from *Dust* was eventually worked into the ensemble piece *Tell it anyway*, which premiered at the Walker Art Center, Minneapolis, in October 2024.

pp. 10—11, top: *Dust*, 2023. Performance view, *Counterpublic*, St. Louis, 2023. Photo: Ralph Lemon

pp. 10—11, bottom: *Dust*, 2023. Performance view, *Counterpublic*, St. Louis, 2023. Courtesy Counterpublic. Photos: Nyara Williams

pp. 12—13: *Untitled 13*, 2023 (detail). From the series *Untitled (The greatest [Black] art history story ever told. Unfinished)*, 2015—

p. 14: Kevin Beasley's sound equipment from *Rant #3*, The Kitchen, New York, 2020. Presented by Danspace Project and The Kitchen. Photo © 2020 Paula Court

p. 16: *Untitled 12*, 2023 (detail). From the series *Untitled (GBAHSET)*, 2015—

pp. 16—17: Kevin Beasley, Darrell Jones, Ralph Lemon, and Okwui Okpokwasili in *Dust*, 2023. Performance views, Gene's Bar and Grill, *Counterpublic*, St. Louis, 2023. Courtesy Counterpublic. Photos: Katherine Reynolds

p. 18: April Matthis in *Scaffold Room*, 2014—15. Performance view, The Kitchen, New York, 2015. Photo © 2015 Paula Court

p. 23: Ralph Lemon and Okwui Okpokwasili in *Untitled* [2008]. Performance views, *On Line: Drawing Through the Twentieth Century*, The Museum of Modern Art, New York, 2011. Courtesy The Museum of Modern Art, New York. Photos: Yi-Chun Wu

pp. 27—28: Darrell Jones and Jimena Paz in *In Proximity*, 2022—25. Performance view, *Dancing Studies*, COSMO, Campo San Cosmo, Venice, 2022. © Palazzo Grassi, Pinault Collection. Photo: Matteo De Fina

pp. 28—29: *Untitled 11*, 2022 (detail). From the series *Untitled (GBAHSET)*, 2015—

pp. 28—29: Brass Band in *In Proximity*, 2022—25. Performance view, *Dancing Studies*, Venice, 2022. © Palazzo Grassi, Pinault Collection. Photo: Matteo De Fina

p. 30: Darrell Jones and Lysis (Ley) in *In Proximity*, 2022—25. Performance views, *Dancing Studies*, Venice, 2022. © Palazzo Grassi, Pinault Collection. Photos: Matteo De Fina

pp. 30—31: Jimena Paz in *In Proximity*, 2022—25. Performance view, *Dancing Studies*, Venice, 2022. © Palazzo Grassi, Pinault Collection. Photo: Matteo De Fina

pp. 32, 66—67, 87, 122, 168: Details from *Spaceman Drawings*, 2008—10

p. 32: Samita Sinha in *In Proximity*, 2022—25. Performance view, *Dancing*

Studies, Venice, 2022. © Palazzo Grassi, Pinault Collection. Photo: Matteo De Fina

p. 40: Rant #5, 2022. Performance view, Lifes, Hammer Museum, Los Angeles, 2022. Photo: Ralph Lemon

pp. 40–41: Lysis (Ley), Mariama Noguera-Devers, and Dwayne Brown in Rant #3, 2020. Performance views, The Kitchen, New York, 2020. Presented by Danspace Project and The Kitchen. Photos © 2020 Paula Court

p. 41: Ralph Lemon and Kevin Beasley, Rant Residuum, 2020–24. Installation view, Ice and Fire, The Kitchen, New York, 2020–21. Photo: Phoebe d'Heurle

p. 42, top: Okwui Okpokwasili and Ralph Lemon in Rant #3, 2020. Performance view, The Kitchen, New York, 2020. Presented by Danspace Project and The Kitchen. Photo © 2020 Paula Court

p. 42, bottom: Ralph Lemon and Kevin Beasley in Rant #3, 2020. Performance view, The Kitchen, New York, 2020. Presented by Danspace Project and The Kitchen. Photo © 2020 Paula Court

p. 43: Rant #3, 2020. Performance view, The Kitchen, New York, 2020. Presented by Danspace Project and The Kitchen. Photo © 2020 Paula Court

pp. 44–45: Lysis (Ley), Mariama Noguera-Devers, Dwayne Brown, and Paul Hamilton in Rant #3, 2020. Performance view, The Kitchen, New York, 2020. Presented by Danspace Project and The Kitchen. Photo © 2020 Paula Court

p. 46, top: Okwui Okpokwasili as Adele as Amy Winehouse as Biggie Smalls as Bob Dylan in Scaffold Room, 2014–15. Rehearsal view, Maggie Allsee National Center for Choreography, Tallahassee, Florida, 2014. Courtesy MANCC. Photo: Chris Cameron

p. 46, bottom: Ralph Lemon in Rant #2, 2019. Performance view, Forum do Futuro, Porto, Portugal, 2019. Photo: Jose Caldeira

pp. 50–51: Untitled 14, 2024. From the series Untitled (Rapture weft), 2020–. Photo: Brent Wahl

pp. 52–53: Untitled 9, 2022. From the series Untitled (RW), 2020–. Photo: Brent Wahl

pp. 54–56: Untitled 12, 2023 (detail). From the series Untitled (RW), 2020–. Photo: Brent Wahl

p. 56: Fitting for Consecration of Ancestor Figures #13, 2024. Photo: Naoko Nagata

p. 57, left to right: Consecration of Ancestor Figures #7, 2015; Consecration of Ancestor Figures #8, 2015. Photo: Brent Wahl

pp. 58–59: Untitled 11, 2022 (detail). From the series Untitled (GBAHSET), 2015–

pp. 60–61: Untitled 1, 2016 (detail). From the series Untitled (GBAHSET), 2015–. Image courtesy The Museum of Modern Art, New York. Photo: Martin Parsekian

pp. 62–63: Untitled 2, 2016. From the series Untitled (GBAHSET), 2015–. Image courtesy The Museum of Modern Art, New York. Photo: Martin Parsekian

pp. 64–65: Untitled 3, 2017. From the series Untitled (GBAHSET), 2015–. Image courtesy The Museum of Modern Art, New York. Photo: Martin Parsekian pp. 77–79: *FBN*, 2009–19 (video stills)

p. 80: *Untitled 6*, 2018 (detail). From the series *Untitled (GBAHSET)*, 2015–

pp. 88–89: *James Baldwin Dharma Talk*, 2004 (video stills)

pp. 90–91: *Untitled*, 2013–14. Digital photograph

pp. 92–93: *Saturnalia*, 2018 (video stills)

p. 94: *Untitled*, 2018. Digital photograph

p. 95: *Untitled*, 2018. Digital photograph

p. 96: *Untitled*, 2009

p. 97, top: Installation sketch for *Spaceship #1* (2007) and *(Solaris water)* (2024), 2024

p. 97, bottom: *Untitled*, 2018. Digital photograph

p. 98, top: Ralph Lemon in *Rant #3*, 2020. Performance view, The Kitchen, New York, 2020. Presented by Danspace Project and The Kitchen. Photo: Ralph Lemon

p. 98, bottom: Study for spaceship animation, 2006

p. 105: *Untitled*, 2013. Digital photograph

pp. 106–7, top and middle: *Garden* [Chapter 2], 2013 (video stills)

pp. 106–7, bottom: *It could be a forest* [Chapter 3], 2013 (video stills)

pp. 108–9: *Untitled*, 2013. Digital photograph

p. 110: *Untitled*, 2013. Digital photograph

p. 115: *Untitled*, 2010. Digital photograph

p. 116: *Untitled*, 2009

pp. 116–17: *Untitled (wall drawing)*, 2008 (detail). Originally installed at Contemporary Arts Center, New Orleans

pp. 117–19: *Untitled*, 2013. Digital photograph

p. 120: Score for an unfinished dance (detail), Paris, 2008

pp. 120–21: Ralph Lemon performing "Sunshine Room" in *How Can You Stay in the House All Day and Not Go Anywhere?*, 2010. Performance view, Krannert Center for the Performing Arts, University of Illinois at Urbana-Champaign, 2010. On-screen: Kris Kelvin (Donatas Banionis) in Andrei Tarkovsky's *Solaris* (1972). Photo: Dan Merlo

pp. 130–31: Darrell Jones and Djédjé Djédjé Gervais performing "Wall/Hole" in *How Can You Stay in the House All Day and Not Go Anywhere?*, 2010. Performance view, Krannert Center for the Performing Arts, University of Illinois at Urbana-Champaign, 2010. Photo: Dan Merlo. This twenty-minute extended improvisation, which developed from the search for a certain kind of formlessness in *Come home Charley Patton's* "Ecstasy" (2004), was a key movement threshold for establishing the modality of Low.

p. 132: Ralph Lemon and Darrell Jones, research for Low, Watermill Center, Watermill, NY, 2023. Courtesy Watermill Center. Photo: Phillip Lehans

pp. 140–48: Kevin Beasley, *For Ralph*, 2024. Courtesy Kevin Beasley.
© Kevin Beasley

MoMA PS1 Staff

Andrea Achelis
Visitor Engagement Associate

Kara Aghabekian
Director of Building Operations

Herb Armstrong
Maintenance Technician

Arnold Ayala
Maintainer

Philip Brand
Manager of Institutional Giving

Connie Butler
The Agnes Gund Director

Juan Pablo Caicedo Torres
Program Production Coordinator

Megan Carlo
*Director of Human Resources and
Inclusion*

Marshia Chambers
*Payroll Manager / Human Resources
Generalist*

Natalie Cheney
*Assistant Manager of Visitor
Engagement*

Sunny Chu
Senior Accountant

Sarita Cornell
Visitor Engagement Associate

Stephanie Dias
External Affairs Assistant

Lauren DiLoreto
Director of Program Production

Basel Elmalla
Staff Accountant

Julia Fesser
*Communications and Publicity
Coordinator*

Jody Graf
Assistant Curator

Sheldon Gooch
Curatorial Assistant

Anna Grofik
Preparator

Odean Groves
Maintainer

Maria Hernandez
Maintainer

Lilly Hern-Fondation
*Senior Project Manager, Exhibitions
and Commissions*

Sarah Isenberg
Digital Marketing Coordinator

David Jamie
Maintainer

Ruba Katrib
*Curator and Director of
Curatorial Affairs*

Elena Ketelsen González
Assistant Curator

Lauren Klenow
Program Production Coordinator

Molly Kurzius
Director of External Affairs

Erin Lee
Executive Assistant of Administration

Teresa Lillis
Manager of Individual Giving

Janggo Mahmud
*Public Programs and Community
Engagement Fellow*

Audrey Min
Curatorial Fellow

Annie Moretto
*Executive Assistant and Special
Projects Coordinator*

Randy Navarro
Manager of Building Operations

Dylan Newlon
Program Production Fellow

Amy Ni
Visitor Engagement Associate

Jose Ortiz
Deputy Director

Dante Osei
Director of Finance / CFO

Jose Paz
Maintenance Technician

Jetaime Pizarro
Assistant Registrar

Jack Radley
Editor

Kari Rittenbach
Assistant Curator

Kate Robinson
Senior Registrar

Nora Rodriguez
*Assistant Director of Digital Strategy
and Content*

Andrea Sánchez
Coordinator of Curatorial Affairs

Nick Scavo
*Senior Project Manager, Music,
Performance, and Events*

Daniel Schaeffer
Director of Development

Julia Schäfer
Graphic Designer

Catherine Schreiber
Major Gifts Officer

Princess Somefun
Human Resources Fellow

Zachary Taube
Assistant Manager of Installation

Tony Tirador
Production Assistant

Andley Tyson
Visitor Engagement Coordinator

Richard Wilson
Exhibition and Production Designer

Laura Zapp
*Assistant Director of Visitor
Engagement*

Published on the occasion of the exhibition *Ceremonies Out of the Air: Ralph Lemon* at MoMA PS1, Long Island City, NY, November 14, 2024–March 24, 2025. Organized by Connie Butler, The Agnes Gund Director, MoMA PS1, and Thomas Lax, Curator, Department of Media and Performance, MoMA, with Kari Rittenbach, Assistant Curator, MoMA PS1.

Major support for *Ceremonies Out of the Air: Ralph Lemon* is provided by Sarah Arison and the Ford Foundation.

Ford Foundation

Generous support is provided by the Doris Duke Foundation, the Lise M. Stolt-Nielsen Family, and the Wallis Annenberg Director's Fund for Innovation in Contemporary Art.

Significant support is provided by A4 Arts Foundation and the Black Arts Council of The Museum of Modern Art.

Additional support is provided by anonymous, James Keith (JK) Brown and Eric Diefenbach, and Zenas Hutcheson. Funding is also provided by the Harkness Foundation for Dance, Katherine Sachs, and Catharine and Jeffrey Soros.

The exhibition is made possible through Mellon Foundation's generous institutional support.

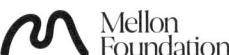
Mellon
Foundation

LCCN: 2024943898
ISBN: 9780984177691

Published by MoMA PS1
22-25 Jackson Avenue
Long Island City, NY 11101
www.momaps1.org

Available through D.A.P./Distributed Art Publishers
75 Broad Street, Suite 630
New York, NY 10004
www.artbook.com

Editors: Connie Butler, Thomas Lax, Kari Rittenbach, and Jody Graf
Managing Editors: Jody Graf and Kari Rittenbach
Design: Julia Schäfer and Asel Tambay
Copy Editor: Domenick Ammirati
Proofreader: Dana Kopel

This publication is typeset in Selectric UN and printed on Munken Polar. Printed and bound in Italy by Grafiche Veneziane.

Front and back cover: Ralph Lemon, *Untitled 7*, 2019, from the series *Untitled (The greatest [Black] art history story ever told. Unfinished)*, 2015–, with overlaid title design by the artist. Image courtesy The Museum of Modern Art, New York. Photo: Martin Parsekian

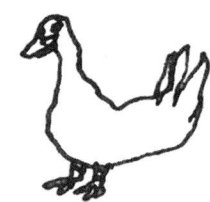